Revolutionary Characters

Also by Gordon S. Wood

The Creation of the American Republic, 1776–1787,
winner of the Bancroft Prize
and the John H. Dunning Prize

The Radicalism of the American Revolution,
winner of the Pulitzer Prize
and the Ralph Waldo Emerson Prize

The American Revolution: A History

The Americanization of Benjamin Franklin,
winner of the Julia Ward Howe Prize

Revolutionary Characters

What Made the Founders Different

Gordon S. Wood

THE PENGUIN PRESS

New York

THE PENGUIN PRESS
Published by the Penguin Group
Penguin Group (USA) Inc., 375 Hudson Street, New York, New York 10014,
U.S.A. • Penguin Group (Canada), 90 Eglinton Avenue East, Suite 700, Toronto,
Ontario, Canada M4P 2Y3 (a division of Pearson Penguin Canada Inc.) • Penguin
Books Ltd, 80 Strand, London WC2R 0RL, England • Penguin Ireland, 25 St.
Stephen's Green, Dublin 2, Ireland (a division of Penguin Books Ltd) • Penguin
Books Australia Ltd, 250 Camberwell Road, Camberwell, Victoria 3124, Australia
(a division of Pearson Australia Group Pty Ltd) • Penguin Books India Pvt Ltd,
11 Community Centre, Panchsheel Park, New Delhi – 110 017, India • Penguin
Group (NZ), Cnr Airborne and Rosedale Roads, Albany, Auckland 1310, New
Zealand (a division of Pearson New Zealand Ltd) • Penguin Books (South Africa)
(Pty) Ltd, 24 Sturdee Avenue, Rosebank, Johannesburg 2196, South Africa

Penguin Books Ltd, Registered Offices:
80 Strand, London WC2R 0RL, England

First published in 2006 by The Penguin Press,
a member of Penguin Group (USA) Inc.

Acknowledgments to the original publishers of these essays
appear in the notes section starting on page 275.
ISBN 1-59420-093-9
Printed in the United States of America

Designed by Marysarah Quinn

To Simon, Nicholas,

Benjamin, Charles,

and Raphael

Preface

ONCE THOMAS JEFFERSON realized in the immediate aftermath of the Revolution that he and his colleagues might become famous, he began to collect portraits and busts of those he came to call "American worthies." Before he left the United States for France in 1784, he commissioned Philadelphia artist Joseph Wright to paint a portrait of George Washington; when he arrived in France he obtained a bust of Benjamin Franklin from Houdon and then acquired another Houdon bust of John Paul Jones. In 1786 during a trip to London he paid a young expatriate Mather Brown to paint a portrait of John Adams, who had become the first U.S. minister of Great Britain. His purpose, he said, was "to add it to those of other principal American characters which I have or shall have." At the same time he comissioned Brown to do a portrait of himself.[1]

This book might be regarded as a written collection of these American worthies. Nearly all of what follows has been previously published, either in articles, reviews, or books, and I am indebted to the original publishers for permission to reprint and use this material. The original sources are cited in the notes. I am especially grateful to two extraordinary editors, Robert Silvers of *The New York Review of Books*, and Leon Wieseltier of *The New Republic;* many of these pieces first appeared in their publications and benefited greatly from their expertise. For this collection, however, all the original publications have been expanded and revised.

I am grateful to the editorial skill of Scott Moyers and Jane Fleming of The Penguin Press. And as always, I am deeply indebted to my wife, Louise, for her support and her keen editorial eye. As to the five young fellows to whom this book is dedicated, they are worthies in their own right. Although they contributed nothing directly to the writing of this book, they certainly helped to make everything worthwhile.

Contents

Revolutionary Characters

Introduction

The Founders and the Enlightenment

A MERICA'S FOUNDING FATHERS, or the founders, as our antipatriarchal climate now prefers, have a special significance for Americans. Celebrating in the way we do this generation that fought the Revolution and created the Constitution is peculiar to us. No other major nation honors its past historical characters, especially characters who existed two centuries ago, in quite the manner we Americans do. We want to know what Thomas Jefferson would think of affirmative action, or George Washington of the invasion of Iraq. The British don't have to check in periodically with, say, either of the two William Pitts the way we seem to have to check in with Jefferson or Washington. We Americans seem to have a special need for these authentic historical figures in the here and now. Why should this be so?

Scholars have a variety of answers. Some suggest that our continual concern with constitutional jurisprudence and original intent accounts for our fascination with the founding and the making of the Constitution. Still others think that we use these eighteenth-century figures in order to recover what was wise and valuable in America's past. They believe that the founders of two hundred years ago have become standards against which we measure our current political leaders. Why don't we have such leaders today? seems to be the implicit question many Americans ask.

Others quite sensibly think that the interest in the revolutionary generation has to do with an American sense of identity. The identities of other nations, say, being French or German, are lost in the mists of time and usually taken for granted (the reason why such nations are having greater problems with immigrants than we are). But Americans became a nation in 1776, and thus, in order to know who we are, we need to know who our founders are. The United States was founded on a set of beliefs and not, as were other nations, on a common ethnicity, language, or religion. Since we are not a nation in any traditional sense of the term, in order to establish our nationhood, we have to reaffirm and reinforce periodically the values of the men who declared independence from Great Britain and framed the Constitution. As long as the Republic endures, in other words, Americans are destined to look back to its founding.

By the time Thomas Jefferson and John Adams died on the same day, July 4, 1826, exactly fifty years following the adoption of the Declaration of Independence, an aura of divinity had come to surround the founding generation. The succeeding generations of Americans were unable to look back at the revolutionary leaders and constitution makers without being overawed by the brilliance of their thought, the creativity of their politics, and the sheer magnitude of their achievement. The founders always seemed larger than life, giants in the earth, "a forest of giant oaks," as Lincoln called them, possessing intellectual and political capacities well beyond those who followed them.

But this view would not hold, unchanging, over time. Lincoln warned that the founders' achievements "must fade upon the memory of the world, and grow more and more dim by the lapse of time."[1] In fact by the

end of the nineteenth century this awe for the founders and their mythical reputation was being questioned, and historians began puncturing
the aura of divinity surrounding them. In 1896 a popular historian of the
period, John Bach McMaster, wrote an essay, entitled "The Political Depravity of the Founding Fathers," in which he contended that "in all the
frauds and tricks that go to make up the worst form of practical politics,
the men who founded our State and national governments were always
our equals, and often our masters." According to McMaster, the founding generation was not above the worst kinds of political shenanigans, including the silencing of newspapers, the manipulation and destruction of
votes, and the creation of partisan gerrymandering.[2]

McMaster's muckraking of the revolutionary leaders was only the beginning of what soon became a full-scale campaign. In 1897 Sydney
George Fisher attempted to refute William Gladstone's view that the
American Constitution was "the most wonderful work ever struck off at
a given time by the brain and purpose of man" with his *Evolution of the
Constitution of the United States, Showing That It Is a Development of Progressive History and Not an Isolated Document Struck Off at a Given Time
or an Imitation of English or Dutch Forms of Government.* Fisher thought
that the reputation of the founders was so inflated with myths and fables
that he devoted his entire career to bringing the events of the American
Revolution and its leaders down to earth. In a paper, *The Legendary and
Myth-Making Process in Histories of the American Revolution*, delivered before the American Philosophical Society in 1912, Fisher called for the
substitution of "truth and actuality for the mawkish sentimentality and
nonsense with which we have been so long nauseated." As his contribution he wrote books with such titles as *The True Benjamin Franklin* (1900)
and *The True History of the American Revolution* (1902).[3]

It was the seemingly divinely inspired and democratic character of the
Constitution, however, that provoked most revisionist scholars. When
Progressive reformers at the beginning of the twentieth century became
increasingly frustrated with the undemocratic character of many of the institutions of the national government, especially a Senate elected by the

state legislatures and a life-tenured Supreme Court, professional academics responded by showing that the Constitution not only was not divinely inspired but was not even a natural expression of American popular democracy. In 1907 J. Allen Smith in his *Spirit of American Government* set forth the emerging view that the Constitution was a reactionary, aristocratic document designed by its checks and balances, difficulty of amendment, and judicial review to thwart the popular will.

With more and more scholars in the Progressive Era stressing the undemocratic nature of the Constitution, the way was prepared for the historiographical explosion that Charles Beard made in 1913 with *An Economic Interpretation of the Constitution of the United States*. Beard's book, which was part of the "revolt against formalism" occurring everywhere in the Western world in those years, became the most influential history book ever written in America. It came to represent and dominate an entire generation's thinking about history and especially about the origins of the Constitution. By absorbing the diffused thinking of Marx and Freud and the assumptions of behaviorist psychology, Beard and others of his generation came to conceive of ideas as rationalizations, as masks obscuring the underlying interests and drives that actually determined social behavior. For too long, it seemed, historians had detached ideas from the material conditions that produced them and had invested them with an independent power that was somehow alone responsible for the determination of events. As Beard pointed out in the introduction to the 1935 edition of his *Economic Interpretation*, previous historians of the Constitution had assumed that ideas were "entities, particularities, or forces, apparently independent of all earthly considerations coming under the head of 'economic.' " Beard, like many of his contemporaries, sought to bring to the fore "those realistic features of economic conflict, stress and strain" that previous historians had ignored.[4]

By suggesting that the framers of the Constitution were motivated by their underlying economic interests, Beard removed the mantle of disinterested virtue that they had traditionally been wrapped in. However crude and mistaken Beard's particular findings have turned out to be, his underlying assumption that people's consciousness and ultimately their behavior were the products of their social and economic circumstances had a lasting effect on American historical scholarship.

After Beard's book, debunking of the myths and legends surrounding the founding generation became increasingly popular. Because George Washington had been especially subject to mythologizing, he was often singled out for deflating. Indeed, in the 1920s the popular writer W. E. Woodward invented the word *debunk* to describe the process of revealing the unattractive qualities of particular characters, and Washington became one of his favorite targets.

Given this century-long tradition of deflating the reputations of the founders, we should not be surprised by any current criticism of the revolutionary generation. Precisely because these founders have become so important to Americans, so central to our sense of who we are, there is a natural tendency to use them as a means of criticizing America and its culture. If one wants to condemn, say, America's treatment of minorities or its imperialistic behavior, there is no better way than to bash one or more of the founders. Indeed, demonizing the founders, especially Jefferson, has become something of a cottage industry over the past forty years or so.

Although criticizing the founding generation has been going on for more than a century, there does seem to be something new and different about the present-day academic vilification. Historians' defaming of these elite white males seems much more widespread than it used to be. Sometimes this criticism has taken the form of historians' purposely ignoring the politics and the achievements of the founders altogether, as if what they did were not all that important. Instead, as has been pointed out, much of the best work on the history of the early Republic during the past several decades has concentrated on recovering the lost voices of ordinary people—a midwife in Maine or a former slave in Connecticut—or on emphasizing the popular cultural matrix of the period that transcends the leadership of the great white males.[5] Of course, historians with no connection to academia or no interest in esoteric academic debates continue to write histories and biographies of the founders that are widely popular. But academic historians over the past forty years have tended to focus on issues of race, class, and gender in the early Republic and to shun issues of politics and political leadership.

When the founders are not ignored but confronted directly, present-day criticism of them is much more devastating than that of the past. Despite his exposing of what he took to be the founders' underlying economic motives, Beard always respected the men who framed the Constitution. "Never in the history of assemblies," he wrote in 1912, "has there been a convention of men richer in political experience and in practical knowledge, or endowed with a profounder insight into the springs of human action and the intimate essence of government."[6]

Recent historians critical of the founders express little of this kind of respect. They are not interested, as earlier critics were, in simply stripping away myths and legends to get at the human beings hidden from view. If anything, some of these critical historians want to dehumanize, not humanize, the founders. Because our present-day culture has lost a great deal of its former respect for absolute values and timeless truths, we have a harder time believing that the eighteenth-century founders have anything important or transcendent to say to us in the twenty-first century. Even in constitutional jurisprudence, which has a natural bias toward discovering the intentions of the framers of the Constitution, the reputation of the founders has lost some of its former appeal, and original intent is no longer taken for granted but has become a matter of contentious debate among scholars and jurists. It appears more evident than ever before that the founders do not share our modern views about important matters, about race, the role of woman, and equality. Hence it is easier now to dismiss them as racists, sexists, and elitists.

Certainly debunking has become much more common for generations of young people raised on reading about J. D. Salinger's Holden Caulfield and his condemnation of adult phoniness. As popular writer Dave Eggers points out, debunking is what he does as a magazine editor. Every day he edits one article after another "in a long line of contrarian articles pointing out the falsity of most things the world believes in, holds dear." Since even "a version of the Bible written for black kids," and "the student loan program," and "the idea of college in general, and work in general, and marriage, and makeup, and the Grateful Dead" are not immune from debunking, it stands to reason that the founders and their achievements would not be either.[7] In fact some historians today do not believe that the revolutionaries got much of anything right. In their scholarly opinion, the Revolution has become pretty much a failure. As one historian has put it, the Revolution "failed to free the slaves, failed to offer full political equality to women, . . . failed to grant citizenship to Indians, [and] failed to create an economic world in which all could compete on equal terms."[8]

Despite all the criticism and debunking of these founders, they still seem to remain for most Americans, if not for most academic historians, an extraordinary elite, their achievements scarcely matched by those of any other generation in American history. Most Americans appear to believe that these revolutionary leaders constituted an incomparable generation of men who had a powerful and permanent impact on America's subsequent history. The founders appear even more marvelous than even those they emulated, the great legislators of classical antiquity, precisely because they are more real. They are not mythical characters but authentic historical figures about whom there exists a remarkable amount of historical evidence. For our knowledge of the founders, unlike that of many of the classical heroes, we do not have to rely on hazy legends or poetic tales. We have not only everything the revolutionary leaders ever published but also an incredible amount of their private correspondence and their most intimate thoughts, made available with a degree of editorial completeness and expertness rarely achieved in the Western world's recovery of its documentary past.

In spite of the extent and meticulousness of this historical recovery, to most Americans the founders still seem larger than life as well as possessing political and intellectual capacities well beyond our own. The awe that most of us feel when we look back at them is thus mingled with an acute sense of loss. Somehow for a brief moment ideas and power, intellectualism and politics, came together—indeed were one with each other—in a way never again duplicated in American history.

There is no doubt that the founders were men of ideas, were, in fact, the leading intellectuals of their day. But they were as well the political leaders of their day, politicians who competed for power, lost and won elections, served in their colonial and state legislatures or in the Congress, became governors, judges, and even presidents. Of course they were neither "intellectuals" nor "politicians," for the modern meaning of these terms suggests the very separation between them that the revolutionaries avoided. They were intellectuals without being alienated and political leaders without being obsessed with votes. They lived mutually in the world of ideas and the world of politics, shared equally in both in a happy combination that fills us with envy and wonder. We know that something happened then in American history that can never happen again.

But there is no point now, more than two centuries later, in continuing to wallow in nostalgia and to aggravate our deep feelings of loss and deficiency. What we need is not more praise of the founders but more understanding of them and their circumstances. We need to find out why the revolutionary generation was able to combine ideas and politics so effectively and why subsequent generations in America could not do so. With the proper historical perspective on the last quarter of the eighteenth century and with a keener sense of the distinctiveness of that period will come a greater appreciation of not only what we have lost by the passing of that revolutionary generation but, more important, what we have gained. For in the end what made subsequent duplication of the remarkable intellectual and political leadership of the revolutionaries impossible in America was the growth of what we have come to value most, our egalitarian culture and our democratic society. One of the prices we had to pay for democracy was a decline in the intellectual quality of American political life and an eventual separation between ideas and power. As the common man rose to power in the decades following the Revolution, the inevitable consequence was the displacement from power of the uncommon man, the aristocratic man of ideas. Yet the revolutionary leaders were not merely victims of new circumstances; they were, in fact, the progenitors of these new circumstances. They helped create the changes that led eventually to their own undoing, to the breakup of the kind of political and intellectual coherence they represented. Without intending to, they willingly destroyed the sources of their own greatness.

GREAT AS THEY WERE, the revolutionary leaders were certainly not demigods or superhuman individuals; they were very much the product of specific circumstances and a specific moment in time. Nor were they immune to the allures of interest that attracted most ordinary human beings. They wanted wealth and position and often speculated heavily in order to realize their aims. Indeed, several of the most prominent founders, such as financier of the Revolution Robert Morris and Associate Justice of the Supreme Court James Wilson, ended up in debtors' prison.

They were not demigods, but they were not democrats either, certainly not democrats in any modern manner. They were never embarrassed by talk of elitism, and they never hid their sense of superiority to ordinary folk. But neither were they contemptuous of common people; in fact they always believed that the people in general were the source of their authority. As historian Charles S. Sydnor pointed out long ago, they were the beneficiaries of a semiaristocratic political system, and their extraordinary leadership was due in large measure to processes that we today would consider undemocratic and detestable.[9]

But even in their own undemocratic time and circumstances they were unusual, if not unique. As political leaders they constituted a peculiar sort of elite, a self-created aristocracy largely based on merit and talent that was unlike the hereditary nobility that ruled eighteenth-century English society. It was not that there were no men of obscure origins who made it in England. Benjamin Franklin's English friend William Strahan, like Franklin, began life as a printer and ended up a member of Parliament.

Edmund Burke, an Irishman of undistinguished origins, rose to become one of the great writers and orators of his age. But there was a difference between Britain and America. Bright Britons of humble origins could have spectacular rises, but they needed patrons and sponsors, those who were often the titled lords and hereditary aristocrats in control of British society. Burke would never have acquired the eminence he did without the patronage of William Hamilton and the marquess of Rockingham. Members of the American revolutionary elite seem much more self-made, no doubt often achieving distinction with the help of patrons, as in Britain, but nonetheless coming to dominate their society in a way that upward-thrusting men like Strahan or Burke never dominated English society.

Eighteenth-century Britain remained under the authority of about four hundred noble families whose fabulous scale of landed wealth, political influence, and aristocratic grandeur was unmatched by anyone in North America. While Charles Carroll of Maryland, one of the wealthiest planters in the American South, was earning what Americans regarded as the huge sum of eighteen hundred pounds a year, the earl of Derby's vast estates were bringing in an annual income of over forty thousand pounds. By English standards, American aristocrats like Washington and Jefferson, even with hundreds of slaves, remained minor gentry at best. Moreover, by the English measure of status, lawyers like Adams and Hamilton were even less distinguished, gentlemen no doubt but nothing like the English nobility. The American revolutionary elite was thus very different from the English aristocracy. By its very difference, however, it was ideally suited to exploit the peculiar character of the eighteenth-century Enlightenment.

THE EIGHTEENTH-CENTURY Anglo-American Enlightenment was preoccupied with politeness, which had a much broader meaning for people then than it does for us today. It implied more than manners and decorum. It meant affability sociability, cultivation; indeed, politeness was considered the source of civility, which was soon replaced by the word *civilization.*

Civilization implied a social process. Societies, it was assumed, moved through successive stages of historical development, beginning in rude simplicity and progressing to refined complexity of civilization. All nations could be located along this spectrum of social development. The various theories of social progress current in the late eighteenth century had many sources, but especially important to the Americans was the four-stage theory worked out by that remarkable group of eighteenth-century Scottish social scientists Adam Smith, John Millar, Adam Ferguson, and Lord Kames. These thinkers posited four stages of evolutionary development based on differing modes of subsistence: hunting, pasturage, agriculture, and commerce. As societies grew in population, so the theory went, people were forced to find new ways of subsisting, and this need accounted for societies' moving from one stage to another. Nearly every thinker saw the aboriginal inhabitants of America as the perfect representatives of the first stage, which Adam Smith called the "lowest and rudest state of society."[10] Indeed, it would be hard to exaggerate the extent to which the European discovery of the Indians in the New World influenced the emergence of the theory of different stages of history. The Indians helped create the notion, as John Locke put it, that "in the beginning all the world was *America.*"[11]

Since civilization was something that could be achieved, everything was enlisted in order to push back barbarism and ignorance and spread civility and refinement. Courtesy books that told Americans how to behave doubled in numbers during the middle decades of the eighteenth century. From such conduct manuals people learned how to act in company, how to clean their bodies, how to refine their tastes. Compilers of dictionaries attempted to find the correct meanings, spellings, and pronunciations of words and freeze them between the covers of their books. In these ways peculiarities of dialect and eccentricities of spelling and pronunciation could be eliminated, and standards of the language could be set. Even dueling, which flourished in the eighteenth century as never before, was justified as a civilizing agent, as a means of refinement; the threat of having to fight a duel compelled gentlemen to control their passions and inhibited them from using "illiberal language" with one another.

All sorts of new organizations and instruments sprang up to spread light and knowledge among people: learned societies, lending libraries, debating clubs, assembly rooms, reading groups, gentlemanly magazines, concerts, galleries, and museums. Eighteenth-century English speakers saw the beginning of culture as a public commodity, as something that was valuable, that gave status, and that could be acquired. The cultural world that we are familiar with today was born in the Age of Enlightenment. And provincial Americans, anxious to display their learning and politeness, were doing all they could to be part of that cultural world.

At the center of this new civilized world was the idea of a gentleman. A gentleman, as the principal teacher of manners in the eighteenth century Lord Chesterfield defined him, was "a man of good behavior, well bred, amiable, high-minded, who knows how to act in any society, in the company of any man."[12] No word in the English language came to denote better the finest qualities of the ideal man than *gentleman*, and it was the enlightened eighteenth century above all that gave it that significance. Defining a proper gentleman was a subject that fascinated the educated public of the eighteenth-century English-speaking world, and writers from Richard Steele to Jane Austen spent their lives struggling with what constituted the proper character of a gentleman; John Adams and Thomas Jefferson were still going at it in their correspondence at the end of their lives.

For many in the eighteenth century, including the American revolutionaries, being a gentleman assumed a moral meaning that was more important than its social significance. Pure monarchists might still define aristocrats exclusively by the pride of their families, the size of their estates, the lavishness of their display, and the arrogance of their bearings, but others increasingly downplayed or ridiculed these characteristics. This enlightened age emphasized new man-made criteria of aristocracy and gentility—politeness, grace, taste, learning, and character—even to the point where titled peers like Lord Chesterfield liked to think their exalted social positions were due to talent and not to inheritance.

To be a gentleman was to think and act like a gentleman, nothing more, an immensely radical belief with implications that few foresaw. It meant being reasonable, tolerant, honest, virtuous, and "candid," an important eighteenth-century characteristic that connoted being unbiased and just as well as frank and sincere. Being a gentleman was the prerequisite to becoming a political leader. It signified being cosmopolitan, standing on elevated ground in order to have a large view of human affairs, and being free of the prejudices, parochialism, and religious enthusiasm of the vulgar and barbaric. It meant, in short, having all those characteristics that we today sum up in the idea of a liberal arts education. Indeed, the eighteenth century created the modern idea of a liberal arts education in the English-speaking world.[13] Of course, as Noah Webster said, having a liberal arts education and thereby becoming a gentleman "disqualifies a man for business."[14]

When John Adams asked himself what a gentleman was, he answered in just these terms of a liberal arts education. "By gentlemen," he said, "are not meant the rich or the poor, the high-born or the low-born, the industrious or the idle: but all those who have received a liberal education, an ordinary degree of erudition in liberal arts and sciences. Whether by birth they be descended from magistrates and officers of government, or from husbandmen, merchants, mechanics, or laborers; or whether they be rich or poor."[15] Whatever their fathers were, however, gentlemen could not themselves be husbandmen, mechanics, or laborers—that is, men who worked for a living with their hands.

This age-old distinction between gentlemen and commoners had a vital meaning for the revolutionary generation that we today have totally lost. It marked a horizontal cleavage that divided the social hierarchy into two unequal parts almost as sharply as the distinction between officers and soldiers divided the army; indeed, the military division was related to the larger social one. Gentlemen, who constituted about 5 to 10 percent of the society, were all those at the top of the social hierarchy who were wealthy enough not to have to work, or at least not to have to work with their hands, and who thus seemed able to act in a disinterested manner in promoting a public good.

Disinterestedness was the most common term the founders used as a synonym for the classical conception of virtue or self-sacrifice; it better conveyed the threats from interests that virtue seemed increasingly to face in the rapidly commercializing eighteenth century. Dr. Johnson had defined *disinterested* as being "superior to regard of private advantage; not influenced by private profit," and that was what the founders meant by the term. We today have lost most of this earlier meaning. Even educated people now use *disinterested* as a synonym for *uninterested*, meaning "indifferent or unconcerned." It is almost as if we cannot quite imagine someone who is capable of rising above a pecuniary interest and being unselfish or impartial where an interest might be present.

In the eighteenth-century Anglo-American world gentlemen believed that only independent individuals, free of interested ties and paid by no masters, could practice such virtue. It was thought that those who had occupations and had to work strenuously for a living lacked the leisure for virtuous public leadership. In the ideal polity, Aristotle had written thousands of years earlier, "the citizens must not live a mechanical or commercial life. Such a life is not noble, and it militates against virtue." For Aristotle not even agricultural workers could be citizens. For men "must have leisure to develop their virtue and for the activities of a citizen."[16] Over several millennia this ancient ideal had lost much of its potency, but some of it lingered even into the eighteenth century. Adam Smith in his *Wealth of Nations* (1776) thought that ordinary people in a modern complicated commercial society were too engaged in their occupations and the making of money to be able to make impartial judgments about the varied interests and occupations of their society. Only "those few, who being attached to no particular occupation themselves," said Smith, "have leisure and inclination to examine the occupations of other people."[17]

These independent gentlemen of leisure who were presumed to be free of occupations and the marketplace were expected to supply the necessary leadership in government. Since well-to-do gentry were "exempted from the lower and less honourable employments," wrote the British philosopher Francis Hutcheson, they were "rather more than others obliged to an active life in some service to mankind. The publick has this claim upon them."[18] All the American founders felt the weight of this claim and often agonized and complained about it. The revolutionary leaders were not modern men. They did not conceive of politics as a profession and of officeholding as a career as politicians do today. Like Jefferson, they believed that "in a virtuous government . . . public offices are what they should be, burthens to those appointed to them, which it would be wrong to decline, though foreseen to bring with them intense labor, and great private loss." Public office was an obligation required of certain gentlemen because of their talents, independence, and social preeminence.[19]

In eighteenth-century America it had never been easy for gentlemen to make this personal sacrifice for the public, and it became especially difficult during the Revolution. Many of the revolutionary leaders, especially those of "small fortunes" who served in the Continental Congress, continually complained of the burdens of office and repeatedly begged to be relieved from those burdens in order to pursue their private interests. Periodic temporary retirement from the cares and turmoil of office to one's country estate for refuge and rest was acceptable classical behavior. But too often America's political leaders, especially in the North, men like Alexander Hamilton and Aaron Burr, had to retire not to relaxation in the solitude and leisure of a rural retreat but to the making of money in the busyness and bustle of a city law practice.[20]

In short, America's would-be gentlemen had a great deal of trouble maintaining the desired classical independence and freedom from the marketplace that philosophers like Adam Smith thought necessary for political leadership. Of course, there were large numbers of southern planter gentry whose leisure was based on the labor of their slaves, and these planters obviously came closest in America to emulating the English landed aristocracy. But some southern planters kept taverns on the side, and many others were not as removed from the day-to-day management of their estates as were their counterparts among the English landed gentry. Their overseers were not comparable to the stewards of the English aristocracy; thus the planters, despite their aristocratic poses, were often very busy, commercially involved men. Despite Jefferson's illusion that the subsistence of these planters was not dependent "on the casualties and caprice of customers," their livelihoods were in fact tied directly to the vicissitudes of international trade, and most of them, if not Jefferson, always had an uneasy sense of being dependent on the market to an extent that the English aristocracy never really felt.[21] Still, the great southern planters of Virginia and South Carolina at least approached the classical image of disinterested gentlemanly leadership, and they knew it and made the most of it throughout the decades following the Revolution.[22]

In northern American society such independent gentlemen standing above the interests of the marketplace were harder to find, but the ideal remained strong. In ancient Rome, wrote James Wilson, magistrates and army officers were always gentleman farmers, always willing to step down "from the elevation of office" and reassume "with contentment and with pleasure, the peaceful labours of a rural and independent life." John Dickinson's pose as a farmer in his popular pamphlet of 1768 is incomprehensible except within this classical tradition. Dickinson, a wealthy Philadelphia lawyer, wanted to assure his readers of his gentlemanly disinterestedness by informing them at the outset that he was a farmer "contented" and "undisturbed by worldly hopes or fears."[23] Prominent merchants dealing in international trade brought wealth into the society and were thus valuable members of the community, but their status as independent gentlemen was always tainted by their concern, as the minister Charles Chauncy of Massachusetts put it, to "serve their own private separate interest."[24]

Wealthy merchants like John Hancock and Henry Laurens knew this, and during the imperial crisis both shed their mercantile businesses and sought to ennoble themselves. Hancock spent lavishly, brought every imaginable luxury, and patronized everyone. He went through the fortune he had inherited from his uncle, but in the process he became the single most popular and powerful figure in Massachusetts politics during the last quarter of the eighteenth century. Laurens knew only too well the contempt in which trading was held in South Carolina, and in the 1760s he began curtailing his merchant activities. During the Revolution he became president of the Continental Congress and was able to sneer at all those merchants like Philadelphia's Robert Morris who were still busy making money. "How hard it is," he had the gall to say in 1779, "for a rich, or covetous man to enter heartily into the kingdom of patriotism."[25]

For mechanics and other middling sorts who worked with their hands, being a disinterested gentleman was generally considered impossible. They were, as one lady poet put it, the "vulgar" caught up "in trade,/ Whose minds by miserly avarice were swayed."[26] Yet many middling people were ambitious and often sought to "pass" as gentlemen, this being the term that was commonly used. Because the aristocracy was so weak and so vulnerable to challenge in America—the perennial problem from the beginning of the first European settlements—it was always difficult to keep upstarts from claiming gentry status. When Washington arrived in Massachusetts in June 1775 to take up leadership of the Continental army, he was stunned to find that many of the New England officers not only had been elected by their men but had been cobblers and common farmers in civilian life. Not having enough gentlemen to staff the officer corps became a continuing problem for Washington and the Continental army. Instead of the status of gentleman entitling a man to be an officer, too many ordinary men tried to use their military rank to prove that they were in fact gentlemen.[27]

Still, revolutionary America was far from an egalitarian society, and most middling sorts, however rich, were not readily accepted as gentlemen. Artisans and tradesmen who had acquired wealth and were politically ambitious, such as Benjamin Franklin of Pennsylvania and Roger Sherman of Connecticut, found that they had to retire from business in order to attain high political office.

As aspiring gentlemen the leaders of the revolutionary generation shared these assumptions about work, politeness, and civilization. They were primed to receive all these new enlightened ideas about civility and gentility. Because America, as the future governor of New Jersey William Livingston declared, was "just emerging from the rude unpolished Condition of an Infant country," it was especially eager to move along the spectrum of social development toward greater refinement and civilization, more so perhaps than England itself.[28] Indeed, all the talk of acquiring the enlightened attributes of a gentleman had a special appeal for all the outlying underdeveloped provinces of the greater British world, Scotland as well as North America.

As historian Franco Venturi once observed, the Enlightenment was created not in the centers of European culture but on its peripheries. It "was born and organized in those places where the contact between a backward world and a modern one was chronologically more abrupt and geographically closer."[29] Both Americans and Scots were provincial peoples living on the edges of the metropolitan English world. Both provincial societies lacked the presence of the great hereditary noble families that were at the ruling center of English political life. In both North America and Scotland, unlike metropolitan England, the uppermost levels of the aristocracy tended to be dominated by minor gentry—professional men or relatively small landowners—who were anxious to have their status determined less by their ancestry or the size of their estates than by their behavior or their learning.

Both the Scots and the North Americans, moreover, were acutely aware of the contrast between civilization and the nearby barbarism of the Highland clans and the North American Indian tribes. Both were keenly aware too of the degrees of civilization and spent much time writing and reading essays on the stages of social progress from rudeness to refinement. They knew that they lived in cruder and more simple societies than the English and that England was well along in the fourth and final stage of social development—commercial society—and had much to offer them in the ways of politeness and refinement. When the twenty-two-year-old Scot James Boswell, the future biographer of Samuel Johnson, first experienced London society, he was very excited and began "to acquire a composed genteel character very different from a rattling uncultivated one which for some time past I have been fond of."[30]

Yet at the same time both the Scots and Americans knew only too well that the polite and sophisticated metropolitan center of the empire was steeped in luxury and corruption. England had sprawling, poverty-ridden cities, overrefined manners, gross inequalities of rank, complex divisions of labor, and widespread manufacturing of luxuries, all symptoms of over-advanced social development and social decay. It was part of the four-stage theory of social development, as Samuel Stanhope Smith of Princeton put it, "that human society can advance only to a certain point before it becomes corrupted, and begins to decline."[31] And to many provincials England in the 1760s and 1770s seemed to be on the verge of dissolution. Those North American colonists who came in direct contact with London were shocked at the notorious ways in which hundreds of thousands of pounds were being spent to buy elections. This "most unbounded licentiousness and utter disregard of virtue," the young law student at the Inns of Court John Dickinson told his parents, could only end, as it always had in history, in the destruction of the British Empire.[32]

At the same time these provincial peoples living on the periphery of the British Empire began to experience an increasing arrogance on the part of the English. Especially with their success over France in the Seven Years' War, the English developed an ever-keener sense of their own Englishness, a sense of nationality distinct from that of the Scots, Irish, and North Americans. The English now began to regard the North American colonists less as fellow Englishmen across the Atlantic than as another set of people to be ruled. Indeed, in 1763 Lord Halifax, former head of the Board of Trade and secretary of state for the Southern Department in charge of the colonies during the Grenville ministry, went so far as to say that "the people of England" considered the Americans, "though H.M.'s subjects, as foreigners."[33]

Hence these provincials in Scotland and North America began to feel an acute ambivalence about being part of the British Empire. Proud of their simple native provinces but keenly aware of the metropolitan center of civilization that was London, both Americans and Scots had the unsettling sense of living in two cultures simultaneously.

Although this experience may have been unsettling, it was at the same time very stimulating and creative.[34] It helps explain why North America and Scotland should have become such remarkable places of enlightenment and intellectual ferment in the English-speaking world during the last part of the eighteenth century. Scots like David Hume, Adam Smith, Adam Ferguson, and John Millar certainly matched, if they did not exceed, the American founders in brilliance and creativity. Benjamin Rush noted as early as 1766 that "useful and pleasing" conversation was coming to characterize both Edinburgh and Philadelphia.[35] Living so close to what they regarded as savagery and barbarism, both the Scottish and North American leaders felt compelled to think freshly about the meaning of being civilized, and in the process they put a heightened emphasis on learned and acquired values at the expense of the traditional inherited values of blood and kinship. Wanting to become precisely the kind of gentlemen that their contemporaries Jane Austen and Edmund Burke idealized, they enthusiastically adopted the new enlightened eighteenth-century ideals of gentility: grace without foppishness, refinement without ostentation, virtue without affectation, independence without arrogance.

All the founders would have heartily endorsed William Livingston's injunctions for becoming truly enlightened gentlemen: "Let us abhor Superstition and Bigotry, which are the Parents of Sloth and Slavery. Let us make War upon Ignorance and Barbarity of Manners. Let us invite the Arts and Sciences to reside amongst us. Let us encourage every thing which tends to exalt and embellish our Characters. And in fine, let the Love of our Country be manifested by that which is the only true Manifestation of it, a patriotic soul and a public Spirit."[36] They struggled to internalize the new liberal man-made standards that had come to define what it meant to be truly civilized—politeness, taste, sociability, learning, compassion, and benevolence—and what it meant to be good political leaders: virtue, disinterestedness, and an aversion to corruption and courtierlike behavior. Once internalized, these enlightened and classically republican ideals, values, and standards came to circumscribe and control their behavior. They talked obsessively about earning a character, which, as Dr. Johnson defined it, was "a representation of any man as to his personal qualities."

Preoccupied with their honor or their reputation, or, in other words, the way they were represented and viewed by others, these revolutionary leaders inevitably became characters, self-fashioned performers in the theater of life. Theirs was not character as we today are apt to understand it, as the inner personality that contains hidden contradictions and flaws. (This present-day view of character is what leads to the current bashing of the founders.) Instead their idea of character was the outer life, the public person trying to show the world that he was living up to the values and duties that the best of the culture imposed on him. The founders were integrally connected to the society and never saw themselves standing apart from the world in critical or scholarly isolation. Unlike intellectuals today, they had no sense of being in an adversarial relationship to the culture. They were individuals undoubtedly, sometimes assuming a classic pose of heroic and noble preeminence, but they were not individualists, men worried about their social identities. They were enmeshed in the society and civic-minded by necessity; thus they hid their personal feelings for the sake of civility and sociability and their public personas. Jefferson and Martha Washington destroyed their correspondence with their spouses because they believed that such letters were exclusively private and had no role to play in telling the world the nature of their public characters. In his infamous "Reynolds Pamphlet," of 1797, in which Hamilton sacrificed his private virtue for the sake of his public virtue, Hamilton argued that the private lives of gentlemen like him should have nothing to do with their public character and their fitness for public office. Benjamin Franklin never thought that his characteristic behavior—his artful posing, his role playing, his many masks, his refusal to reveal his inner self—was anything other than what the cultivated and sociable eighteenth century admired.[37] Today we are instinctively repelled by such calculation, such insincerity, such willingness to adapt and compromise for the sake of society, yet our distaste for such behavior is just another measure of our distance from the pre-Romantic eighteenth century.

The gentility and civility that these revolutionary leaders sought to achieve were public; they made sense only in society. Knowing how to act in company, knowing how to lead and govern men meant being acutely aware of other people and their feelings and reactions. Society needed what Joseph Addison called a "Fraternity of Spectators" who "distinguished themselves from the thoughtless Herd of their ignorant and unattentive Brethren." These "Spectators," consisting of "every one that considers the World as a Theatre, and desires to form a right Judgment of those who are the Actors on it," had the responsibility of creating politeness.[38] A gentleman's behavior was to be judged by how it affected other people and the society.

The culture of gentility and virtuous leadership thus implied audiences, spectators, and characters, a theatrical world of appearances and representations, applause and censure, something that both Washington and John Adams appreciated more than most. Adams always thought he and his colleagues were onstage. At one point he was taken with what he called "The Scenery of the Business" of public life, which he said had "more effect than the characters of the dramatis personae or the ingenuity of the plot." By 1805 he had witnessed enough theater to last a lifetime, and unfortunately he thought he was not one of the stars. "Was there ever a *coup de théâtre*," he asked his friend Benjamin Rush, "that had so great an effect as Jefferson's penmanship of the Declaration of Independence?" And what about Hamilton's demand, "upon pain of a pamphlet," for a command at Yorktown? he asked.[39] Life was theater, and impressions one made on spectators were what counted. Public leaders had to become actors or characters, masters of masquerade.

The revolutionary leaders knew this and committed themselves to be-
having in a certain moral, virtuous, and civilized manner. Indeed, the intense self-conscious seriousness with which they made that commitment
was what ultimately separates them from later generations of American
leaders. But that commitment also sets them sharply apart from the older
world of their fathers and grandfathers. They sought, often unsuccessfully
but always sincerely, to play a part, to be what Jefferson called natural
aristocrats—aristocrats who measured their status not by birth or family
that hereditary aristocrats from time immemorial had valued but by enlightened values and benevolent behavior.

They had good reason for doing so, for they were men of high ambitions yet of relatively modest origins, and this combination made achieved
rather than ascribed values naturally appealing to them. Almost all the revolutionary leaders, even including the second and third ranks of leadership, were first-generation gentlemen. That is to say, almost all were the
first in their families to attend college, to acquire a liberal arts education,
and to display the new eighteenth-century marks of an enlightened gentleman. Of the ninety-nine men who signed the Declaration of Independence or the Constitution, only eight are known to have had fathers
who attended college. (Those revolutionary leaders, such as Benjamin
Franklin, George Washington, and Nathanael Greene, who did not attend
college usually made up for this lack by intensive self-cultivation in liberal enlightened values.) As Benjamin Rush noted in 1790, "Many of the
first men in America are the sons of reputable mechanics or farmers."[40]

Jefferson's father, Peter Jefferson, was a wealthy Virginia planter and
surveyor who married successfully into the prestigious Randolph family.
But he was not a refined and liberally educated gentleman: He did not
read Latin, he did not know French, he did not play the violin, and as far
as we know, he never once questioned the idea of a religious establishment
or the owning of slaves.

His son Thomas was very different. Indeed, all the revolutionaries
knew things that their fathers had not known, and they were eager to
prove themselves by what they believed and valued, by their virtue and dis-

interestedness. But there was one prominent revolutionary leader who did not seek to play the role that the others did. On the face of it, Aaron Burr had all the credentials for being a great founder: He was a Revolutionary War veteran, a Princeton graduate, and a charming and wealthy aristocrat. He eventually became a senator from New York and the vice president of the United States. But something set his character apart from his colleagues. He behaved very differently from the other revolutionary leaders—especially in promoting his own selfish interests at the expense of the public good—and in the end that difference provoked his fellow statesmen into challenging him. Since he became the great exception that proves the rule, recounting his deviant experience helps us better understand the character of the founders.

YET THE VERY high-mindedness of these mainstream founders raises fundamental questions. If it was the intense commitment of this generation of founders to new enlightened values that separates it from other generations, why, it might be asked, and indeed, as it has been asked by recent critical historians, did these so-called enlightened and liberally educated gentlemen not do more to reform their society? Why did they fail to enhance the status of women? Eliminate slavery entirely? Treat the Indians in a more humane manner?

It is true that the founders did not accomplish all that many of them wanted. It turned out that they did not control their society and culture as much as they thought they did. They were also no more able accurately to predict their future than we can ours. In the end many of their enlightened hopes and their kind of elitist leadership were done in by the very democratic and egalitarian forces they had unleashed with their Revolution.

No doubt all the founders assumed instinctively that the western territories would eventually belong to American settlers. But many of them were at the same time scrupulously concerned for the fate of the Indians who occupied those territories; indeed, the statements of Washington's secretary of war Henry Knox in the 1790s about the need for just treatment of the Native Americans a modern anthropologist might even applaud. But purchasing the Indians' rights to the land and assimilating or protecting them in a civilized manner as Knox recommended depended on an orderly and steady pace of settlement. The ordinary white settlers who moved west, flush with confidence that they were indeed the chosen people of God their leaders told them they were, paid no attention to the plans and policies concocted in eastern capitals. They went ahead and rapidly and chaotically scattered westward and thus stirred up warfare with the Indians into which the federal government was inevitably drawn.

Democracy and demography did the same for the other hopes and plans of the founders. All the prominent leaders thought that the liberal principles of the Revolution would eventually destroy the institution of slavery. When even southerners like Jefferson, Patrick Henry, and Henry Laurens publicly deplored the injustice of slavery, from "that moment," declared the New York physician and abolitionist E. H. Smith in 1798, "the slow, but certain, death-wound was inflicted upon it."[41] Of course such predictions could have not been more wrong. Far from being doomed, slavery in the United States in the 1790s was on the verge of its greatest expansion. Indeed, at the end of the revolutionary era there were more slaves in the nation than in 1760.

But such self-deception, such mistaken optimism, by the revolutionary leaders was understandable, for they wanted to believe the best, and initially there was evidence that slavery was dying out. The northern states, where slavery was not inconsequential, were busy trying to eliminate the institution, and by 1804 all had done so. The founders thought the same thing might happen in the southern states. Not only were there more antislave societies created in the South than in the North, but manumissions in the upper South grew rapidly in the years immediately following the end of the War for Independence. Many believed that ending the international slave trade in 1808 would eventually kill off the institution of slavery. The reason the founders so readily took the issue of slavery off the table in the 1790s was this mistaken faith in the future. As

Oliver Ellsworth, the third chief justice of the United States, declared, "As population increases, poor labourers will be so plenty as to render slaves useless. Slavery in time will not be a speck in our country."[42] The leaders simply did not count on the remarkable demographic capacity of the slave states themselves, especially Virginia, to produce slaves for the expanding areas of the Deep South and the Southwest. Also, whatever the revolutionary leaders might have wished for in ending slavery was nullified by the demands of ordinary white planters for more slaves.

If we want to know why we can never again replicate the extraordinary generation of the founders, there is a simple answer: the growth of what we today presumably value most about American society and culture, egalitarian democracy. In the early nineteenth century the voices of ordinary people, at least ordinary white people, began to be heard as never before in history, and they soon overwhelmed the high-minded desires and aims of the revolutionary leaders who had brought them into being. The founders had succeeded only too well in promoting democracy and equality among ordinary people; indeed, they succeeded in preventing any duplication of themselves.

Chapter One

The Greatness of
George Washington

GEORGE WASHINGTON may still be first in war and first in peace, but he no longer seems to be first in the hearts of his countrymen. A recent poll asking who was America's greatest president showed that only 6 percent of those polled named Washington. He was ranked seventh among presidents. Young people in particular did not know much about Washington.

Polls of presidential greatness are probably silly things, but if they are to be taken seriously, then Washington fully deserves the first place he used to hold. He certainly deserved the accolades his contemporaries gave him. And as long as this Republic endures, he ought to be first in the hearts of his countrymen. Washington was truly a great man and the greatest president we ever had.

But he was a great man who is not easy to understand. He became very quickly, as has often been pointed out, more a monument than a man. Even his contemporaries realized that he was not an ordinary accessible human being. Every passing year made him less of a real person. By the early decades of the nineteenth century he had already become statuesque and impenetrable. "Did anyone ever see Washington nude?" Hawthorne asked. "It is inconceivable." Washington "was born with his clothes on, and his hair powdered, and made a stately bow on his first appearance in the world."

Of course, as Emerson once said, "Every hero becomes a bore at last," and Washington was no exception. By the middle of the nineteenth century the eulogies of Washington had become so conventional and so prevalent that a humorist like Artemus Ward could not resist parodying them: "G. Washington was about the best man this world ever set eyes on. . . . He never slopt over! . . . He luved his country dearly. He wasn't after the spiles. He was a human angil in a 3 kornered hat and knee britches."[1]

Despite the continued popularity of Parson Weems's biographical attempt to humanize Washington, the great man remained distant and unapproachable, almost unreal and unhuman. There were periodic efforts to bring him down to earth, to expose his foibles, to debunk his fame, but he remained massively monumental. By our time in the early twenty-first century he seems so far removed from us as to be virtually incomprehensible. He seems to come from another time and another place, from another world.

That's the whole point about him: He did come from another world. And his countrymen knew it almost before he died in 1799. Washington was the only truly classical hero we have ever had. He was admired as a classical hero in his own lifetime. Among his fellow Americans only Franklin rivaled him for international acclaim, and Franklin's reputation was confined to science and philosophy. Washington was much more of a traditional hero. And he knew it. He was well aware of his reputation and his fame earned as the commander in chief of the American revolutionary forces. That awareness of his heroic stature was crucial to Washington. It affected nearly everything he did for the rest of his life.

Washington was a thoroughly eighteenth-century figure. Like Samuel Adams, he was "one of Plutarch's men," and like Adams, he quickly became an anachronism.[2] He belonged to the predemocratic and pre-egalitarian world of the eighteenth century, to a world very different from the one that followed. No wonder he seems to us so remote. He really is. He belonged to a world we have lost, one we were losing even while he lived.

In many respects Washington was a very unlikely hero. To be sure, he had all the physical attributes of a classical hero. He was very tall by contemporary standards, six feet three or so, and was heavily built and a superb athlete. Physically he had what men and women admired. He was both a splendid horseman at a time when that skill really counted and an extraordinarily graceful dancer, and naturally he loved both riding and dancing. He always moved with dignity and looked like a leader.

Yet those who knew him well and talked with him were often disappointed. He never seemed to have very much to say. He was almost certainly not what we today would call an intellectual. We cannot imagine his expressing his views over the uses and abuses of grief in the world in the way Jefferson and John Adams did in their old age. Adams was contemptuous of Washington's intellectual abilities. It was certain, said Adams, that Washington was not a scholar. "That he was too illiterate, unlearned, unread for his station and reputation is equally past dispute." Adams's judgment is surely too harsh. Great men in the eighteenth century did not have to be scholars or intellectuals. But there is no doubt that Washington was not a learned man, especially in comparison with the other founders. He was very ill at ease in abstract discussions. Even Jefferson, who was usually generous in his estimates of his friends, said that Washington's "colloquial talents were not above mediocrity." He had "neither copiousness of ideas nor fluency of words."[3]

Washington, then, was a man of few words and no great thoughts. Obviously he was not a great mind; he was not in the class of Bacon, Locke, Newton, or even Jefferson or Franklin. He was not an intellectual; he was a man of affairs. He knew how to run his plantation and make it pay. He certainly ran Mount Vernon better than Jefferson ran Monticello; indeed, he was one of the most successful of planter businessmen in all of Virginia. Washington's heart was always at Mount Vernon, but also more than his heart: a good part of his mind too. He thought about it all the time. Even when he was president, he devoted a great amount of his energy worrying about the fence posts of his plantation, and his letters dealing with the details of running Mount Vernon were longer than those dealing with the running of the federal government.

But being a man of affairs and running his plantation or even the federal government efficiently were not what made him a world-renowned hero. What was it that lay behind his extraordinary reputation, his greatness?

His military exploits were of course crucial. Still, Washington was not really a traditional military hero. He did not resemble Alexander, Caesar, Cromwell, or Marlborough; his military achievements were nothing compared with those Napoleon would soon have. Washington had no smashing, stunning victories. He was not a military genius, and his tactual and strategic maneuvers were not the sort that awed men. Military glory was not the source of his reputation. Something else was involved. What was it?

Washington's genius, Washington's greatness, lay in his character. He was, as Chateaubriand said, a "hero of an unprecedented kind."[4] There had never been a great man quite like Washington before, and after Napoleon emerged in 1800 as a Caesar-like world-shattering imperialistic hero, it seemed there might never be another like him again. Washington became a great man and was acclaimed as a classical hero because of the way he conducted himself during times of temptation. It was his moral character that set him off from other men.

Washington epitomized everything the revolutionary generation prized in its leaders. He had character and was truly a man of virtue. This virtue was not given to him by nature. He had to work for it, to cultivate it, and everyone sensed that. Washington was a self-made hero, and this impressed an eighteenth-century enlightened world that put great stock in men's controlling both their passions and their destinies. Washington seemed to possess a self-cultivated nobility.

Washington was a child of the Enlightenment. He was very much a man of his age, and he took its moral standards more seriously than did most of his contemporaries. Washington's Enlightenment, however, was never precisely that of, say, Jefferson or Franklin. It did not involve high philosophy or abstract reasoning. To be sure, he was conventionally liberal on matters of religion ("being no bigot myself to any mode of worship"), and though he went to church regularly to keep up decorum, he was not an emotionally religious person. He rarely mentioned Christ in his writings, and he usually referred to God as "the great disposer of human events." But Washington had no dislike of the clergy or of organized Christianity as Jefferson did.[5] He would never have said, as Jefferson did, that "our civil rights have no dependence on our religious opinions, any more than our opinions in physics or geometry."[6] He came to believe devoutly that God or Divine Providence was looking after man's affairs, including his participation in the Revolutionary War. He was also convinced, as he declared in his Farewell Address, that religion was an indispensable prop for both morality and republican government. Although he admired learning, he was not a man of science like Franklin; in fact, like many eighteenth-century gentlemen, he did not believe that "becoming a mere scholar was a desirable education for a gentleman."[7] Washington's Enlightenment was a much more down-to-earth affair, concerned with social behavior and with living in the everyday world of people. His Enlightenment involved civility.

Sometime before his sixteenth birthday Washington copied 110 maxims from a popular seventeenth-century English translation of a 1595 Jesuit etiquette book, *Bienséance de la conversation entre les hommes*, which in turn was borrowed from an Italian volume first published in 1558–59. These *Rules of Civility and Decent Behaviour in Company and Conversa-*

tion, which is the first document we have of Washington's papers, dealt with everything from how to treat one's betters ("In speaking to men of Quality do not lean nor Look them full in the Face . . .") to how to present one's countenance ("Do not Puff up the Cheeks, Loll not out the tongue, rub the Hands, or beard, thrust out the lips, or bite them or keep the Lips too open or too Close") and how to eat with company ("Cleanse not your teeth with the Table Cloth Napkin Fork or Knife . . .").[8]

All the founders were aware of these conventions of civility, and all in varying degrees tried to live up to them. But no one was more serious in following them than Washington. He wanted desperately to know the proper rules of behavior for a liberal gentleman, and when he discovered them, he stuck by them with an earnestness that awed his contemporaries. It is this purposefulness that gave his behavior such a copybook character. He loved Joseph Addison's play *Cato* and saw it over and over and incorporated some of its lines into his correspondence. The play, very much an Enlightenment tract, helped teach him what it meant to be liberal and virtuous, what it meant to be a stoical classical hero.[9]

Washington was obsessed with having things in fashion and was fastidious about his appearance to the world. It was as if he were always onstage, acting a part. Indeed, he always thought of life as "the Stage" on which one was a "Character" making a mark.[10] He was very desirous not to offend, and he shaped his remarks exquisitely to fit the person to whom he was writing, so much so that some historians have accused him of deceit.[11] He worked on his penmanship, spelling, and grammar, and following the Revolutionary War, when he knew he would be a famous man, he went back and corrected what he took to be deficiencies in his earlier writings.[12] "So anxious was he to appear neat and correct in his letters," recalled Benjamin Rush, that he was known to "copy a letter of 2 or [3?] sheets of paper because there were a few erasures on it."[13] His remarkable formality and stiffness in company came from his very self-conscious cultivation of what was considered proper genteel classical behavior.

Precisely because Washington had not attended college and received a liberal arts education, he became punctilious and literal-minded about observing and adopting what he had formally missed. Colleges like William and Mary were always an "Object of Veneration" to him, and he repeatedly expressed his "consciousness of a defective education."[14] He was forever embarrassed that he had never learned any foreign languages. In the 1780s he refused invitations to visit France in part because he felt it would be humiliating for someone of his standing to have to converse through an interpreter. He said that it was his lack of a formal education that kept him from setting down on paper his recollections of the Revolution. It was even widely rumored that his aides composed his best letters as commander in chief. His lack of a college education, however, did not keep him from expressing his hard-earned gentility in other ways. He loved attending tea tables; during the months of deliberations over the new constitution in 1787 his diary entries note little more than his continual attendance at tea.[15]

He was apt to remain quiet in the presence of sharp and sparkling minds. Some called his diffidence shyness, but whatever the source, this reticence was certainly not the usual characteristic of a great man. "His modesty is astonishing to a Frenchman," noted Jacques Pierre Brissot de Warville. "He speaks of the American War, and of his victories, as of things in which he had no direction." This modesty only added to his gravity and severity. "Most people say and do too much," one friend recalled. "Washington . . . never fell into this common error." Washington may not always have been a great dinner party companion, but he certainly had what John Adams ruefully lacked: the "gift of silence."[16]

Washington sometimes may have moved diffidently in the social world, but in the political world he knew how to make a dramatic move. One of his most impressive acts was his freeing of his slaves in his will. Of all the well-known founders who were major slaveholders, including Jefferson, Madison, and Patrick Henry, Washington was the only one who actually ended up freeing his slaves. He was of course no fiery abolitionist, and in his lifetime he never spoke out publicly against the institution of slavery. Instead he arrived at his conclusion that slavery was immoral and inconsistent with the ideals of the Revolution gradually, privately, and with difficulty.

Prior to the Revolution Washington, like most eighteenth-century Americans, especially Virginians, took slavery very much for granted. Eighteenth-century society was composed of many degrees of inequality and unfreedom, and slavery seemed to be merely the most base and degraded status in a hierarchy of dependencies. Although we today can scarcely imagine one person's owning another, that was certainly not the case in early-eighteenth-century America. After all, slavery had existed for thousands of years without any substantial criticism, and this was still true in early-eighteenth-century America.

On the eve of the Revolution all the colonies were implicated in African slavery in one way or another. Of the total American population of 1.5 million in 1760, at least one-fifth—over 300,000 men, women, and children—was enslaved. Washington's Virginia, the largest and richest colony, had the most slaves, more than 140,000, or 40 percent of its population. During the first half of the eighteenth century Virginian planters, even educated and sensitive ones like William Byrd, showed no guilt or defensiveness over their holding hundreds of slaves on their plantations. It was a cruel and brutal age, and the life of the lowly everywhere seemed cheap.

The American Revolution changed all this. The revolutionaries did not need Dr. Johnson ("How is it that we hear the loudest yelps for liberty among the drivers of negroes?") to tell them about the glaring inconsistency between their appeals to liberty and their owning of slaves. In the new republican society of equal citizens dedicated to liberty, slavery suddenly became an anomaly, a "peculiar institution" that, if it were to continue, now needed defending and justifying. It was no accident that the first antislave society in the world was organized in Philadelphia in 1775. All the revolutionary leaders became aware of the excruciating contradiction between their revolution on behalf of liberty and American slavery. Washington was no exception.

But Washington's awakening to the evils of slavery did not come suddenly or easily. It was no simple matter for him to come to question what he had unquestioningly accepted or to challenge what was after all the very basis of his and Virginia's way of life. As a civic-minded southern planter deeply immersed in his society and its culture, he held views on slavery before the Revolution that were indistinguishable from those of his fellow Virginia planters. As he sought to increase the wealth and productivity of Mount Vernon, he bought more and more slaves, selling some only on rare occasions. By 1774 he had over a hundred slaves on his plantation. Although he was a good master, constantly concerned with the health and welfare of his slaves, he did not agonize over his holding human beings in bondage. When he criticized the institution, as he did on several occasions prior to the Revolution, he did so because he believed that slavery made his workers inefficient and lazy, not that it was immoral or inhumane. In 1774 he endorsed the Fairfax Resolves, which included a recommendation that no more slaves should be imported into the British colonies. Many Virginians wanted to end the slave trade because they had more slaves than they knew what to do with. Washington, however, was at the time purchasing additional slaves from the West Indies.

When Washington became commander in chief of the Continental army, he was forced by military circumstances to change his original view that blacks not become soldiers. Finding African Americans among the New England troops in 1775 was an eye-opening experience for him, and he began advocating the recruitment of free blacks into the Continental army. In 1778 he allowed Rhode Islanders to raise an all-black regiment of soldiers, and in 1779 he cautiously approved a plan to grant slaves their freedom in return for military service. Since he understood only too well the deeply rooted fears and prejudices of his fellow southerners, he was not surprised when the plan failed. Still, through the years of the war Washington had led a racially integrated army composed of as many as five thousand African American soldiers. Although as commander in chief he did not speak out publicly against slavery, he was slowly and privately rethinking the issue of black bondage.

By the time he returned to Mount Vernon at the end of the war, he had concluded that slavery needed to be abolished, not simply because it was an inefficient labor system but, more important, because it violated everything the Revolution was about. Reluctant as he was to confront the society and culture in which he had to live, he said nothing publicly against slavery. But privately he vowed in 1786 not to purchase any more slaves; at the time he had over two hundred, nearly half of whom were too young or too old to work. As he told a fellow Virginian, he had come to hope against hope that some plan could be adopted by which slavery could be eliminated "by slow, sure, & imperceptible degrees."[17] He knew only too well that any other plan would be politically impossible.

By 1794, as he contemplated retirement from the presidency, he was seriously considering freeing what he called "a certain species of property which I possess, very repugnant to my own feelings."[18] But there were problems. Not only did the difficulty of translating his immense landholdings into ready cash stymie his efforts to liberate his slaves, but the fact that a majority of his slaves, who now numbered close to three hundred, did not belong to him but were dower slaves who belonged to Martha and her heirs complicated matters. In the summer of 1799, six months before his death, he decided to deal with the problem as best he could from beyond the grave. He drew up a new will, composed secretly in his own hand, probably because what he wanted to do with his slaves was opposed by his neighbors, his family, and perhaps even Martha. This will is one of the most important documents he ever wrote. Because his and Martha's slaves had so intermarried, he stated that only upon the death of his wife would all his slaves be freed. But he did not just throw his slaves out into the world. Not only did he forbid any of the freed slaves from being transported out of Virginia "under any pretense whatsoever," but he directed that all the freed slaves who were too young or too old to be independent should be supported for as long as necessary. Not only were the young to be cared for until age twenty-five, but they were to be taught to read and write and prepared for "some useful occupation." Knowing the feelings of his family, not to mention the larger Virginia world, he loaded his will with imperatives, "most pointedly and most solemnly" enjoining his executors "religiously" to fulfill his commands "without evasion, neglect, or delay."[19]

Washington's will was almost immediately printed in pamphlet form and circulated throughout the country. However the country, or at least the southern portion of it, was not yet ready for the message it contained. His legacy regarding emancipation died aborning.

That was not true of another bequest that Washington had earlier left to the nation. In 1783 Washington, consummate actor that he was, made his most theatrical gesture, his most moral mark, and the results were monumental. The greatest act of his life, the one that made him internationally famous, was his resignation as commander in chief of the American forces. This act, together with his circular letter to the states in which he promised his retirement, was what he called his legacy to his countrymen. No American leader has ever left a more important legacy.

Following the signing of the peace treaty and British recognition of American independence, Washington stunned the world when he surrendered his sword to the Congress on December 23, 1783, and retired to his farm at Mount Vernon. As Garry Wills has shown, this was a highly symbolic act, a very self-conscious and unconditional withdrawal from the world of politics.[20] In order to enhance the disinterestedness of the political advice he offered in the circular letter to the states he wrote six months before his actual retirement, he promised not to take "any share in public business hereafter." He even resigned from his local vestry in order to make his separation from the political world complete.

His retirement from power had a profound effect everywhere in the Western world. It was extraordinary; a victorious general's surrendering his arms and returning to his farm was unprecedented in modern times. Cromwell, William of Orange, Marlborough—all had sought political rewards commensurate with their military achievements. Though it was widely believed that Washington could have become king or dictator, he wanted nothing of the kind. He was sincere in his desire for all his soldiers "to return to our Private Stations in the bosom of a free, peaceful and happy Country," and everyone recognized his sincerity. It filled them with awe. Washington's retirement, said the painter John Trumbull, writing from London in 1784, "excites the astonishment and admiration of this part of the world. Tis a Conduct so novel, so unconceivable to People, who, far from giving up powers they possess, are willing to convulse the empire to acquire more." King George III supposedly predicted that if Washington retired from public life and returned to his farm, "he will be the greatest man in the world."[21] Jefferson was not exaggerating when he declared in 1784 that "the moderation and virtue of a single character . . . probably prevented this revolution from being closed, as most others have been, by a subversion of that liberty it was intended to establish."[22]

Washington was not naive. He was well aware of the effect his resignation would have. He was trying to live up to the age's image of a classical disinterested patriot who devotes his life to his country, and he knew at once that he had acquired instant fame as a modern Cincinnatus. His reputation in the 1780s as a great classical hero was international, and it was virtually unrivaled. Franklin was his only competitor, but Franklin's greatness still lay in his being a scientist, not a man of public affairs. Washington was a living embodiment of all the classical republican virtue the age was eagerly striving to recover.

Despite his outward modesty, Washington realized he was an extraordinary man, and he was not ashamed of it. He lived in an era when distinctions of social rank were still accepted. He took for granted the differences between him and more ordinary men. When he could not take those differences for granted, he cultivated them. He used his natural reticence to reinforce the image of a stern and forbidding classical hero. His aloofness was notorious, and he worked at it. When Gilbert Stuart had uncharacteristic difficulty in putting Washington at ease during a sitting for a portrait, the artist in exasperation finally pleaded, "Now, sir, you must let me forget that you are General Washington and that I am Stuart, the painter." Washington's reply chilled the air: "Mr. Stuart need never feel the need of forgetting who he is, or who General Washington is." No wonder the portraits look stiff.[23]

Washington had earned his reputation, his "character," as a moral hero, and he did not want to dissipate it. He spent the rest of his life guarding and protecting his reputation and worrying about it. He believed Franklin made a mistake going back into public life in Pennsylvania in the 1780s. Such involvement in politics, he thought, could only endanger Franklin's already achieved international standing. In modern eyes Washington's concern for his reputation is embarrassing; it seems obsessive and egotistical. But his contemporaries understood. All gentlemen tried scrupulously to guard their reputations, which is what they meant by their honor. Honor was the esteem in which they were held, and they prized it. To have honor across space and time was to have fame, and fame was what the founders were after, Washington above all.[24] And he got it, sooner and in greater degree than any other of his contemporaries. Naturally, having achieved what all his fellow revolutionaries still anxiously sought, he was reluctant to risk it.

Many of his actions after 1783 can be understood only in terms of this deep concern for his reputation as a virtuous leader. He was constantly on guard and very sensitive to any criticism. Jefferson said no one was more sensitive. Washington judged all his actions by what people might think of them. This sometimes makes him seem silly to modern minds, but not to those of the eighteenth century. In that very suspicious age in which people were acutely "jealous" of what great men were up to, Washington thought it important that people understand his motives. The reality was not enough; he had to appear virtuous. He was obsessed that he not seem base, mean, avaricious, or unduly ambitious. No one, said Jefferson, worked harder than Washington in keeping "motives of interest or consanguinity, of friendship or hatred" from influencing him. He had a lifelong preoccupation with his reputation for "disinterestedness."[25]

This preoccupation explains the seemingly odd fastidiousness and caution of his behavior in the 1780s. In 1783 he welcomed the formation of the Order of the Cincinnati and agreed to be its first president. Nothing was dearer to him than this fraternity of retired revolutionary army officers, until a great popular outcry was raised against it. Washington was bewildered and shaken, and he appealed to his friends for advice. Jefferson got Washington to put pressure on the order to reform itself and eliminate its hereditary character by appealing to the one argument that Washington could not resist: that his leadership of this aristocratic society would tarnish his reputation for classical virtue.

In the winter of 1784–85 Washington was led into temptation once again, and it was agony. The Virginia Assembly presented him with 150 shares in the James River and Potomac canal companies in recognition of his services to the state and the cause of canal building. What should he do? He did not believe he could accept the shares. Acceptance might be "considered in the same light as a pension" and might compromise his reputation for virtue. Yet he believed passionately in what the canal companies were doing and had long dreamed of making a fortune from such canals. Moreover, he did not want to show "disrespect" to the assembly or to appear "ostentatiously disinterested" by refusing this gift.[26]

Few decisions in Washington's career caused more distress than this one. He wrote to everyone he knew—to Jefferson, to Governor Patrick Henry, to William Grayson, to Benjamin Harrison, to George William Fairfax, to Nathanael Greene, even to Lafayette in France—seeking "the best information and advice" on the disposition of the shares. "How would this matter be viewed then by the eyes of the world?" he asked. Would not his reputation for virtue be harmed? Would not accepting the shares "deprive me of the principal thing which is laudable in my conduct?"—that is, his disinterestedness.

The story would be comic if Washington had not been so deadly earnest. He certainly understated the situation when he told his correspondents that his mind was "not a little agitated" by the problem.[27] In letter after letter he expressed real anguish. This was no ordinary display of scruples such as government officials today show over a conflict of interest; in 1784 and 1785 Washington was not even holding public office.

Once again Jefferson found the key to Washington's anxieties and told him that declining to accept the shares would only add to his reputation for disinterestedness. So Washington gave them away to the college that eventually became Washington and Lee.

Washington suffered even more anguish over the decision to attend the Philadelphia Convention in 1787. Many believed that his presence was absolutely necessary for the effectiveness of the convention, but the situation was tricky. He implored friends to tell him "confidentially what the public expectation is on this head, that is, whether I will or ought to be there?" How would his presence be seen? How would his motives be viewed? If he attended, would he be thought to have violated his pledge to withdraw from public life? But if he did not attend, would his staying away be thought to be a "derilection to Republicanism"? Should he squander his reputation on something that might not work?[28]

What if the convention should fail? The delegates would have to return home "chagrined at their ill success and disappointment. This would be a disagreeable circumstance for any one of them to be in; but more particularly so for a person in my situation." Even Madison had second thoughts about the possibility of misusing such a precious asset as Washington's reputation. What finally convinced Washington to attend the convention was the fear that people might think he wanted the federal government to fail so that he could then manage a military takeover. He decided, as Madison put it, "to forsake the honorable retreat to which he had retired and risk the reputation he had so deservedly acquired." No action could be more virtuous. "Secure as he was in his fame," wrote Henry Knox with some awe, "he has again committed it to the mercy of events. Nothing but the critical situation of his country would have induced him to so hazardous a conduct."[29]

When the convention met, Washington was at once elected its president. Although the convention usually turned itself into a committee of the whole, meaning that Washington did not have to preside over the debates, he apparently said very little during its deliberations. Perhaps he recognized that anything he said or proposed would stymie debate since no one would dare contest him. Only at the very end of the convention did he speak out in favor of reducing the minimum number of people for a representative from forty to thirty thousand. It was an exceedingly minor point, and with Washington's backing, it was agreed to unanimously. It was his way of saying to his colleagues that he favored the Constitution.

No doubt Washington's presence and his leadership gave the convention and the proposed Constitution a prestige that they otherwise could not have had. His backing of the Constitution was certainly essential to its eventual ratification. "Be assured," James Monroe told Jefferson, "his influence carried this government."[30] Washington, once committed to the Constitution, worked hard for its acceptance. He wrote letters to friends and let his enthusiasm for the new federal government be known. Once he had identified himself publicly with the new Constitution he became very anxious to have it accepted. Its ratification was a kind of ratification of himself.

After the Constitution was established, Washington still believed he could retire to the domestic tranquillity of Mount Vernon. But everyone else assumed that he would become president of the new national government. Once again this widespread expectation aroused all his old anxieties about his reputation. He had promised the country that he would permanently retire from public life. How could he now assume the presidency without being "changeable with levity and inconsistency; if not with rashness and ambition?" His protests were sincere. He had so much to lose and so little to gain. But he did not want to appear "too solicitous for reputation." He was certain, he told his friend Henry Lee, "whensoever I shall be convinced the good of my country requires my reputation to put at risque; regard for my own fame will not come in competition with an object of so much magnitude."[31]

But Washington could not continue to pose the issue starkly in this way as one between duty and reputation. For the more he thought about it, the more that both accepting and not accepting the presidency became matters of reputation, especially after Hamilton suggested to him that there might be "greater hazard to that fame, which must be and ought to be dear to you, in refusing your future aid to the system than in affording it." It was not easy to make decisions when a concern for one's virtue was viewed as unvirtuous. Nothing could make him abandon his retirement, Washington told Benjamin Lincoln, "unless it be a *conviction* that the partiality of my Countrymen had made my services absolutely necessary, joined to a *fear* that my refusal might induce a belief that I preferred the conservation of my own reputation & private ease, to the good of my Country."[32]

Washington's apparent egotism and his excessive coyness, his extreme reluctance to get involved in public affairs and endanger his reputation have not usually been well received by historians. Douglas Southall Freeman, his great biographer, thought that Washington in the late 1780s was "too zealously attentive to his prestige, his reputation and his popularity—too much the self-conscious national hero and too little the daring patriot."[33] Historians might not understand his behavior, but his contemporaries certainly did. They rarely doubted that Washington was trying always to act in a disinterested way. His anxious queries about how would this or that look to the world, his hesitations about serving or not serving, his expressions of scruples and qualms—all were part of his strenuous effort to live up to the classical idea of a virtuous leader. He had never accepted a salary as commander in chief of the Continental army, and although the Congress made him accept a salary as president, he wanted it understood that he had tried to refuse it. He seemed to epitomize public virtue. Even if John Adams was not all that impressed with George Washington, Adams's wife, Abigail, was certainly taken with him. She admired his restraint and trusted him. "If he was not really one of the best-intentioned men in the world," she wrote, "he might be a very dangerous one." As historian Garry Wills has so nicely put it, Washington "gained power from his readiness to give it up."[34]

THE PRESSURE on Washington to serve as president was immense, and he gave way; naturally, he was elected with every possible electoral vote, the only president in American history so honored. As the first president he faced circumstances that no other president has ever faced, and he was the only person in the country who could have dealt with them. The American people had been reared in monarchy and had never known a distant chief executive who had not been a king. Somehow Washington had to satisfy their deeply rooted yearnings for patriarchal leadership while creating a new elective republican president. Since the United States had never had an elected chief executive like the one created by the Constitution of 1787, Washington had virtually no precedents to follow. Not only did he have to justify and to flesh out the new office of the presidency, but he also had to put together the new nation and prove to a skeptical world that America's grand experiment in self-government was possible. That he did all this in the midst of a revolutionary world at war and did it without sacrificing the republican character of the country is an astonishing achievement, one that the achievements of no other president, however great, can begin to match.

There is no doubt that many American leaders in 1789 thought that there had been too much democracy in the states in the 1780s and that this excessive democracy needed to be curbed without doing violence to republican principles. That had been one of the reasons behind the making of the new Constitution. All the Federalists, as the supporters of the new Constitution called themselves, knew that if democracy were to be curbed, then what was needed in the new government was more power. And power in eighteenth-century Anglo-American political theory essentially meant monarchy. According to the conventional conception of an eighteenth-century balanced or mixed constitution, too much democracy required the counterbalancing of some more monarchy.

But by 1789 the Federalists knew only too well that they could not speak openly about the need for more monarchy in the government. Nevertheless, many of them privately shared the opinion of Benjamin Rush that the new government was one "which unites with the vigor of monarchy and the stability of aristocracy all the freedom of a simple republic."[35] Even Madison, as devoted to republicanism as any of the founders, expected the new federal government to play the same superpolitical neutral role that the British king had been supposed to play in the empire.[36]

Other Federalists like Alexander Hamilton were even more disillusioned with the democratic consequences of the Revolution and wanted even stronger doses of monarchy injected into the body politic. In fact Hamilton and other high-toned Federalists, who in the 1790s clung to the name of the supporters of the Constitution, wanted to create a centralized fiscal-military state that would eventually rival the great monarchical powers of Europe on their own terms. Yet they knew that whatever aspects of monarchy they hoped to bring back into America would have to be placed within a republican framework. Perhaps, as has been suggested, the Federalists really intended to create another Augustan age, but they never openly declared this to be their aim.[37] Augustus after all had sought to incorporate elements of monarchy into the Roman Empire while all the time paying lip service to republicanism.

If some monarchical power were to be instilled in the new system, the energetic center of that power would be the presidency. For that reason it was the office of the president that made many Americans most suspicious of the new government. The executive or chief magistracy was after all the traditional source of tyranny and, as Benjamin Franklin pointed out, the source in America from which monarchy would naturally emerge.

Although Americans were used to congresses, an independent presidency was a new office for them. A single strong national executive was bound to remind them of the king they had just cast off. When James Wilson in the Philadelphia Convention moved that the executive "consist of a single person," a long uneasy silence had followed. The delegates knew only too well what such an office implied. John Rutledge complained that "the people will think we are leaning too much towards Monarchy." The creation of the presidency, warned Edmund Randolph, "made a bold stroke for monarchy."[38] But the convention had resisted these warnings and had gone on to make the new chief executive so strong, so kinglike, precisely because the delegates expected George Washington to be the first president.

Indeed, Washington was the only American in 1789 who possessed the dignity, patience, restraint, and reputation for republican virtue that the untried but potentially powerful office of the presidency needed at the outset. Many people, including Jefferson, expected that Washington might be president for life, that he would be a kind of elective monarch.[39] Indeed, we shall never understand events of the 1790s until we take seriously, as contemporaries did, the possibility of some sort of monarchy's developing in America. Republicanism was new and untried. Monarchy still prevailed almost everywhere; it was what much of the world was used to, and history showed that sooner or later most republics had tended to develop into kingly governments.

As the theory of four stages of social development showed (and the story of what had happened to ancient Rome was a prime example), the natural evolution of societies and states seemed to be from simple agrarian republican youth to complex commercial monarchical maturity. William Short, viewing the new Constitution from France, was not immediately frightened by the power of the executive. But he thought that "the President of the eighteenth century" would "form a stock on which will be grafted a King in the nineteenth." Others, like George Mason of Virginia, believed that the new government was destined to become "an elective monarchy," and still others, like Rawlins Lowndes of South Carolina, assumed that the government so closely resembled the British form that everyone naturally expected "our changing from a republic to monarchy."[40] To add to the confusion, Vice President John Adams, honest to the core and with little sense of political correctness, was already speaking publicly of America's being a monarchical republic or a republican monarchy.

From the outset Washington's behavior often savored of monarchy. His journey from Mount Vernon to the capital in New York in the spring of 1789, for example, took on the air of a royal procession. He was saluted by cannons and celebrated in elaborate ceremonies along the way. Everywhere he was greeted by triumphal rejoicing and acclamations of "Long live George Washington!" With Yale students debating the advantages of an elective over a hereditary king, suggestions of monarchy were very much in the air. "You are now a King, under a different name," James

McHenry told Washington in March 1789 and wished that the president "may reign long and happy over us."[41] It was not surprising therefore that some people referred to Washington's inauguration as a "coronation."[42]

So prevalent was the thinking that Washington resembled an elected monarch that some even expressed relief that he had no heirs.[43] Washington was sensitive to these popular anxieties about monarchy, and for a while he had thought of holding the presidency for only a year or so and then resigning and turning the office over to Vice President Adams. In the initial draft of his inaugural address he pointed out that "the Divine Providence hath not seen fit, that my blood should be transmitted or my name perpetuated by the endearing though sometimes seducing channel of immediate offspring." He had, he said, "no child for whom I could wish to make a provision—no family to build in greatness upon my country's ruins." Madison talked him out of this draft, but Washington's desire to show the public that he harbored no monarchical ambitions remained strong.[44] His protests testified to the widespread sense that monarchy was a distinct possibility for America.

Sensitive to charges that he had royal ambitions, Washington was often uncertain about the role he ought to play as president. He realized that the new government was fragile and needed dignity, but how far in a monarchical European direction ought he to go to achieve that dignity? Aware that whatever he did would become a precedent for the future, Washington sought the advice of those close to him, including the vice president and the man he soon made his secretary of the treasury, Alexander Hamilton. How often should he meet with the public? How accessible should he be? Should he dine with members of Congress? Should he host state dinners? Could he ever have private dinners with friends? Should he make a tour of the United States? The only state ceremonies that late-eighteenth-century Americans were familiar with were those of the European monarchies. Were they applicable to the young Republic?

Hamilton thought that most people were "prepared for a pretty high tone in the demeanour of the Executive," but probably not as high a tone as was desirable. "Notions of equality," he said, were as "yet . . . too general and too strong" for the president to be properly distanced from the other branches of the government. In the meantime, suggested Hamilton, the president ought to follow the practice of "European Courts" as closely as he could. Only department heads, high-ranking diplomats, and senators should have access to the him. "Your Excellency," as Hamilton referred to Washington, might hold a half hour levee no more than once a week and then only for invited guests. He could give up to four formal entertainments a year but must never accept any invitations or call on anyone. Vice President Adams for his part urged Washington to make a show of "Splendor and Majesty" for his office. The president needed an entourage of chamberlains, aides-de-camp, and masters of ceremonies to conduct the formalities of his office.[45]

Washington realized that he had to maintain more distance from the public than the presidents of the Confederation Congress had. They had reduced their office, he said, to "perfect contempt," having been "considered in no better light than as a maître d'hôtel . . . for their table was considered as a public one and every person who could get introduced conceived that he had a right to be invited to it." He knew that too much familiarity was no way "to preserve the dignity and respect that was due to the first magistrate."[46]

As uncomfortable as he often was with ceremony, Washington knew that he had to make the presidency "respectable," and when he became president, he spared few expenses in doing so. Although he was compelled to accept his twenty-five-thousand-dollar presidential salary—an enormous sum for the age—he spent nearly two thousand dollars of it on liquor and wine for entertaining. In his public appearances he rode in a elaborately ornamented coach drawn by four and sometimes six horses, attended with four servants in livery, followed by his official family in other coaches. "When he travels," declared a British observer, "it is in a very kingly style."[47] In Washington's public pronouncements he referred to himself like a king in the third person, and he sat for dozens of state portraits, all modeled on those of European monarchs. Indeed, much of the iconography of the new nation, including its civic processions, was copied from monarchical symbolism.[48]

Washington may have been a simple republican, at heart just a country gentleman who was in bed every night by nine-thirty, but there is no doubt that he was concerned with what he called "the style proper for the Chief Magistrate." He conceded that a certain monarchical tone had to be made part of the government, and he was willing up to a point to play the part of a republican king. Although he may not in fact have been a king, he certainly managed to look like one. Throughout his life people repeatedly remarked upon his natural "dignity" and his "gallant bearing and commanding figure." He was, as John Adams later caustically remarked, "the best actor of presidency we have ever had."[49]

Obsessed with the new government's weakness, other Federalists were even more eager than Washington to bolster its dignity and respectability. Most believed that this could be best done by adopting some of the ceremony and majesty of monarchy—by making, for example, Washington's birthday celebrations rival those of the Fourth of July. Like the king of England speaking to Parliament from the throne, the president delivered his inaugural address personally to the Congress, and like the two houses of Parliament, both houses of Congress formally responded and then waited upon the president at his residence. The English monarchy was the model for the new republican government in other respects as well. The Senate, the body in the American government that most closely resembled the House of Lords, voted that writs of the federal government ought to run in the name of the president, just as writs in England ran in the name of the king. Although the House refused to go along, the Supreme Court did use the Senate's form for its writs. The Senate also tried to have all American coins bear the head of the president, as was the case with the European monarchs.

Although the high-toned Federalists eventually lost this proposal to put the president's impression on the coins, they made many such attempts to surround the new government with some of the trappings of monarchy. They drew up elaborate monarch-like rules of etiquette at what soon came to be denounced as the "American Court."[50] They established excruciatingly formal levees for the president that resembled those held by kings in Europe. In these levees, critics charged, Washington was to be "seen in public on Stated times like an Eastern Lama."[51]

If the president was to resemble a European monarch, what should his title be? Led by Vice President Adams, the Senate debated for a month in 1789 the proper title for the president. He could not be called simply His Excellency, for governors of the states were called that. "A royal or at least a princely title," said Adams, "will be found indispensably necessary to maintain the reputation, authority, and dignity of the President." Only something like "His Highness, or, if you will, His Most Benign Highness" would do.[52] Eventually, under Adams's prodding a Senate committee reported the title "His Highness the President of the United States of America, and Protector of their Liberties." When Jefferson learned of Adams's obsession with titles and the Senate's action, he could only shake his head and recall Benjamin Franklin's now-famous characterization of Adams as someone who means well for his country, is always an honest man, often a wise one, and sometimes and in some things is absolutely out of his senses.[53]

Perhaps in this respect not really out of his senses, for apparently Washington himself had initially favored for a title "His High Mightiness, the President of the United States and Protector of Their Liberties."[54] But when the president heard the criticism that such titles smacked of monarchy, he immediately changed his mind and was relieved when the House of Representatives under Madison's leadership succeeded in fixing the simple title of Mr. President.

Still, the talk of royalizing the new Republic continued and heightened the fears of many Americans. Monarchy after all implied much more than simply the presence of a single ruler. It meant a large bureaucracy, a standing army, authority exercised from the top down, and numerous devices for extracting men and money from the society in order to wage war. The financial program of Secretary of the Treasury Hamilton, with its funded debt and Bank of the United States, was modeled on that of the British monarchy. Indeed, like the British ministers of His Majesty George III's government, Hamilton sought to use patronage and every other source of influence to win support for his and Washington's programs. To many other Americans, however, it looked as if British monarchical corruption had spread to America.

Because of these very real apprehensions of monarchy and monarchical corruption, the first decade or so under the new American Constitution could never be a time of ordinary politics. In fact the entire period was wracked by a series of crises that threatened to destroy the national government that had been so recently and painstakingly created. The new expanded Republic of the United States was an unprecedented political experiment, and everyone knew that. No similar national republic in modern times had ever extended over such a large extent of territory. Since all theory and all history were against the success of this republican experiment, the political leaders worried about every unanticipated development. With even Washington's having suggested at the conclusion of the Constitutional Convention that the new federal government might not last twenty years, most political leaders in the 1790s had no great faith that the Union would survive.[55] In such uneasy and fearful circumstances politics could never be what we today regard as normal.

The parties that emerged in the 1790s, the Federalists and the Republicans, were not modern parties, and competition between them was anything but what some scholars used to call the first party system. No one thought that the emergence of parties was a good thing; indeed, far from building a party system in the 1790s, the nation's leaders struggled to prevent one from developing. The Federalists under the leadership of Washington, Adams, and Hamilton never saw themselves as a party but as the beleaguered legitimate government beset by people allied with revolutionary France out to destroy the Union. Although the Republicans under the leadership of Jefferson and Madison did reluctantly describe themselves as a party, they believed they were only a temporary one, designed to prevent the United States from becoming a Federalist-led

British-backed monarchy. Since neither the Federalists nor the Republicans accepted the legitimacy of the other, partisan feelings ran very high, making the bitter clash between Hamilton and Jefferson, for example, more than just personal. The 1790s became one of the most passionate and divisive decades in American history, and we came as close to civil war as we would come until the actual Civil War in 1861.

More than any other person Washington held this divided country together. With the leaders of these two hostile parties, Hamilton and Jefferson, in the cabinet, Washington was able to use his immense prestige and good judgment to restrain fears, limit intrigues, and stymie opposition that otherwise might have escalated into serious violence. In 1794 he delicately combined coercion and conciliation and avoided bloodshed in putting down the Whiskey Rebellion, an uprising of hundreds of farmers in western Pennsylvania. Despite the intense partisan feelings that existed throughout the country, he never entirely lost the respect of all the party leaders, and this respect allowed him to reconcile, resolve, and balance the clashing interests.

It was the people's trust in Washington that enabled the new government to survive. And it was Washington acting as a republican monarch who was most responsible for making the presidency the powerful national office it became. Even an unsympathetic British observer was forced to admit that Washington possessed "the two great requisites of a statesman, the faculty of concealing his own sentiments, and of discovering those of other men."[56] He always understood the exercise of authority; he had led an army and indeed had more people working for him at Mount Vernon than he initially did in the new federal government. He was a systematic and energetic administrator. He kept careful records and communicated regularly with his department heads, to whom he delegated considerable authority. Yet he always made it clear that they were merely his assistants and responsible to him alone. Although he surrounded himself with brilliant advisers, including Hamilton as secretary of the treasury and Jefferson as secretary of state, he was always his own man and determined that the government speak with a single voice. Lacking the genius and the intellectual confidence of his advisers, he consulted them often and moved slowly and cautiously to judgment, but when ready to act, he acted decisively, and in the case of controversial decisions, such as his acceptance of Hamilton's Bank of the United States or his Proclamation of Neutrality in 1793, he did not second-guess himself. By filling out the executive and making it efficient and responsible, he made the presidency the dominant branch of the new government.

Washington knew that whatever he did would set precedents for the future. "We are a young Nation," he said, "and have a character to establish. It behooves us therefore to set out right for first impressions will be lasting."[57] He was particularly concerned with the relations between the president and the Senate. He envisioned the Senate's role in advising and consenting to appointments and treaties as that of a council, similar to what he had been used to as commander in chief, and thus he assumed that much of the Senate's advice and consent, if not with appointments, at least with treaty making, would be done orally.

In August 1789 the president went to the Senate to get its advice and consent to a treaty he was negotiating with the Creek Indians. Instead of offering their advice and consent in the way Washington's senior officers had during the Revolutionary War, the senators began debating each section of the treaty, with the president impatiently glaring at them. When one senator finally moved that the treaty be submitted to a committee for study, Washington jumped to his feet in exasperation and cried, "This defeats every purpose of my coming here." He calmed down, but when he finally left the Senate chamber, he was overheard to say he would "be damned if he ever went there again."[58] He did return two days later, but neither he nor the Senate enjoyed this personal confrontation. The advice part of the Senate's role in treaty making was more or less permanently forgotten. When the president issued his Proclamation of Neutrality in 1793, he did not even bother to ask for the consent of the Senate, and thus he further established the executive as the nearly sole authority in the conduct of foreign affairs.

In dealing with the world, Washington was an utter realist. He always sought, as he put it in 1775, at the outset of the war against Britain, to "make the best of mankind as they are, since we cannot have them as we wish."[59] In the great struggle over acceptance of the treaty with Great Britain negotiated by John Jay in 1794 and ratified by the Senate in 1795, Washington made a series of courageous decisions. With the United States and Britain on the verge of war because of British seizures of neutral American ships, sending Jay to England in the first place was one, and signing the treaty amid an outcry of popular opposition was another. Standing up to the attempt by the House of Representatives in March 1796 to scuttle the ratified treaty by refusing to vote funds to implement it was still another. Washington refused to recognize a role for the House in the treaty-making process. To do so, he said, not only "would be to establish a dangerous precedent" but also would violate the Constitution, which allowed only the president and Senate to make treaties.[60]

If any single person was responsible for establishing the young Republic on a firm footing, it was Washington. He was nearly as much of an aristocrat as the United States ever produced, in his acceptance of social hierarchy and in his belief that some were born to command and most to obey. Although he trusted the good sense of the people in the long run, he believed that they could easily be misled by demagogues. He was a realist who had no illusions about human nature. "The motives which predominate most human affairs," he said, "are self-love and self-interest." The common people, like the common soldiers in his army, could not be expected to be "influenced by any other principles than those of interest."[61]

With these assumptions he realized only too keenly the fragility of the new nation. As president he devised a number of schemes for creating a stronger sense of nationhood. He understood the power of symbols; the reason he was willing to sit for long hours to have his portrait painted was to encourage respect for the new national government. In the absence of long-existing feelings of nationalism in the 1790s, popular celebrations of Washington became a substitute for patriotism; commemorations of his birthday did in fact come to rival those of the Fourth of July. It is not too much to say that for many Americans he stood for the Union.

As president he was always acutely sensitive to the varying interests of the country and fervent in his efforts to prevent the nation from fragmenting and falling apart. After he became president, he exchanged salutations with twenty-two leading religious groups and made a practice of attending the church services of a variety of denominations, including that of Roman Catholicism, and in a remarkable display of liberality for the age he assured the Jews of Newport, Rhode Island, that America was an enlightened place where "everyone shall sit in safety under his own vine and fig tree, and there shall be none to make him afraid." He undertook his two long royallike tours of the country in 1789 and 1791 in order to bring the government to the farthest reaches of the land and reinforce the loyalty of people who had never seen him.[62] He promoted roads and canals and the post office—anything and everything that bound the different states and sections together. He spent so much time considering appointments to offices because he wanted not only to get the best men available but also to build local support throughout the country for the new federal government. He thought constantly about the future of the nation and those he called the "unborn Millions."[63] More than any other person he was responsible for backing Pierre L'Enfant in designing the magnificent federal city that was to bear his name. Since he hoped that the United States would eventually become a great nation rivaling, if not surpassing, the powerful states of Europe, he wanted a capital that would suit this potentially great nation. If Jefferson had had his way the national capital would have been the size of a college campus, fifteen hundred acres.

Washington never took the unity of the country for granted. He knew that if the Union broke apart, it would be between the northern and southern sections. In fact he told his secretary of state Edmund Randolph in 1795 that if the United States dissolved, he had made up his mind to join the North—understandable given his evolving attitude toward slavery.[64] But he wanted nothing more than for the United States to stay together, and he remained preoccupied throughout his presidency with creating the sinews of nationhood. Even in the social life of the "republican court" at the capital in New York and then after 1790 in Philadelphia, he and his wife, Martha, acted as matchmakers in bringing together couples from different parts of the United States. With their own marriage and those of other Virginia families as examples, the Washingtons tended to think of marriage in dynastic terms, as a means of building alliances and consolidating a ruling aristocracy for the sprawling extent of America. He and Martha arranged sixteen marriages, including that between James Madison and Dolley Payne.[65] More than anyone in the country, Washington promoted the sense of Union that Lincoln and others later upheld.

As in the case of his career as commander in chief, Washington's most important act as president was his giving up of the office. The significance of his retirement from the presidency is easy for us to overlook, but his contemporaries knew what it meant. Most people assumed that Washington might be president as long as he lived. Hence his persistent efforts to retire from the presidency enhanced his moral authority and helped fix the republican character of the Constitution. He very much wanted to retire in 1792, but his advisers and friends thought otherwise. Madison admitted that when he first urged Washington to accept the presidency, he had told him that he could protect himself from accusations of overweening ambition by "a voluntary return to public life as soon as the state of the Government would permit," but the state of the government, said Madison, was not yet secure. Washington sought to discover what others thought, and everywhere the answer was the same: He must stay on. Hamilton even tried the ultimate argument: that retirement when he was needed would be "critically hazardous to your own reputation." But it was left to a female friend, Eliza Powel, to develop this point and hammer it home. If Washington followed his inclinations and retired from the presidency, she wrote, his enemies would attack his reputation. They would say "that Ambition had been the moving spring of all your Actions" and that now when the going was tough and his fame could not be enhanced, he "would run no further Risque" for the public.[66] How to preserve one's reputation without at the same time allowing concern for that reputation to overcome one's duty was a peculiar dilemma of the eighteenth century. Washington stayed on for another term.

However, in 1796 he was so determined to retire that no one could dissuade him, and his voluntary leaving of the office set a precedent that was not broken until FDR secured a third term in 1940. But so strong was the sentiment for a two-term limit that the tradition was written into the Constitution in the Twenty-second Amendment in 1951. Washington's action in 1796 was of great significance. That the chief executive of a state should willingly relinquish his office was an object lesson in republicanism at a time when the republican experiment throughout the Atlantic world was very much in doubt.

WASHINGTON'S FINAL YEARS in retirement were not happy ones. The American political world was changing, and he struggled to comprehend it. During his final years in office he and his administration had been subjected to vicious partisan criticism, and he felt the criticism deeply; indeed, Jefferson thought that Washington took such public attacks to heart "more than any person I ever yet met with."[67] Washington watched with dismay what he believed was the growing interference of the French government in American politics. For him the Republican party had become "the French Party." It was, he said, "the curse of this country," threatening the stability and independence of the United States.[68] He saw plots and enemies everywhere and became as much of a high-toned Federalist as Hamilton.

His fear was real; his sense of crisis was deep. He and other Federalists thought that the French might invade the country and together with the Republican party, "the French Party," overthrow the government. "Having Struggled for eight or nine years against the Invasion of our Rights by one Power, & to establish an Independence of it," he wrote in

1798, "I could not remain an unconcerned Spectator of the attempts of another Power to accomplish the same object, though in a different way, with less pretensions—indeed without any at all."[69] He thus listened attentively to all the urgent Federalist calls that he come out of retirement and head the army that the Congress had created to meet the French invasion.

Though he again expressed reluctance and asked whether becoming commander in chief would not be considered "a restless Act, evincive of my discontent in retirement," he was far more eager in 1798 to step back into the breach and do his duty than he ever had been before. It was a measure of his despair with this "Age of Wonders!"[70]

Before he could actually commit himself, President John Adams acted and appointed him commander of all the military forces of the United States. Washington accepted but scarcely comprehended how it had come about. The next thing he knew he was on his way to Philadelphia to organize the army. Events were outrunning his ability to control them or even to understand them, and he more and more saw himself caught up in "the designs of Providence."[71] His command was a disaster. He wrangled over the appointments of the second-in-command, intrigued against Adams, and interfered with his cabinet. When neither the French invasion nor the American army materialized, Washington crept back to Mount Vernon thoroughly disillusioned with the ways of American politics.

In June 1799 Governor Jonathan Trumbull, Jr., of Connecticut with the backing of many Federalists urged Washington once again to stand for the presidency in 1800. Only Washington, Trumbull said, could unite the Federalists and save the country from "a French President." Finally Washington had had enough. In his reply he no longer bothered with references to his reputation for disinterestedness and his desire to play the role of Cincinnatus. Instead he talked about the new political conditions that made his candidacy irrelevant. In this new democratic era of party politics, he said, "personal influence," distinctions of character, no longer mattered. If the members of the Jeffersonian Republican party "set up a broomstick" as candidate and called it "a true son of Liberty" or "a Democrat" or "any other epithet that will suit their purpose," it still would "command their votes in toto!" But even worse, the same was true of the Federalists. Party spirit now ruled all, and people voted only for their party candidate. Even if he were the Federalist candidate, Washington was "thoroughly convinced I should not draw a *single* vote from the Anti-federal side." Therefore his standing for election made no sense; he would "stand upon no stronger ground than any other Federal character well supported."[72]

Washington wrote all this in anger and despair, but though he exaggerated, he was essentially right. The political world was changing, becoming democratic, and parties, not great men, soon became the objects of contention. To be sure, the American people continued to long for great heroes as leaders, and right up through Eisenhower they have periodically elected military leaders, Washingtons manqué, to the presidency. But democracy made such great heroes no longer essential to the workings of American government. Although Washington had aristocratic predilections and never meant to popularize politics, he nonetheless was crucial in making this democracy feasible. He was an extraordinary man who made it possible for ordinary men to rule. There has been no president quite like him, and we can be sure that we shall not see his like again.

Chapter Two

The Invention of
Benjamin Franklin

WASHINGTON WAS CERTAINLY a superb actor who knew how to play the role of a military and political leader as no one else could. But of the founders, the real master of masquerade has to be Benjamin Franklin. No one in eighteenth-century America assumed more personas and played more roles than he. Indeed, except for his contributions to the science of electricity, which were truly fundamental, it is not easy to figure out who he really is and why we should celebrate him as a great founder. Of all the great revolutionary leaders, he seems the most puzzling and the most difficult to understand.

Franklin is a bundle of contradictions. At one and the same time he is both the most American and the least American of the revolutionary leaders. His is the classic American success story—rising from very obscure origins to preeminence—a self-made man, an artisan from an insignificant family who became what today would be a multimillionaire. Despite his spectacular rise, however, he never seems to have shed his lowly origins. He remains a symbol of rustic democracy—more so than any of the other founders.

He seems the most folksy, to have the greatest common touch. Ordinary people can identify with him in ways they cannot with the other founding fathers such as Washington and Jefferson. "George Washington was but a noble British officer, made a Republican by circumstances," declared the *New York Times* in 1856. "Franklin was a Republican by birth, by labor, by instinct, and by thought."[1] By the twentieth century Americans had begun calling him Ben.[2]

Yet this folksy prototypical American was at the same time the most European, the most cosmopolitan, the most worldly of the founders. He was an internationally renowned scientist. He hobnobbed with lords and aristocrats in Britain and Europe. He conversed with kings and even dined with them. Certainly no other American leader lived more years abroad than Franklin. In fact he spent the bulk of the last thirty-three years of his life living outside America, in Britain and France. At several points it was doubtful that he would ever return to America, or wanted to, or even cared much about America. Far from being a natural and thoroughgoing American, Franklin was not sure where he rightly belonged. Was he English? Or British? Or did he really belong in France? We should not take his Americanness for granted. Nor should we take his participation in the Revolution for granted.

AT THE BEGINNING of the imperial crisis in the early 1760s, the crisis that ended with the breakup of the British Empire and the independence of the United States, no one could have identified Franklin with a radical cause. Certainly no one could have predicted that he would become one of the leaders of the American Revolution. In 1760 there were few

Englishmen who were as dedicated to the greatness of the British Empire as he.

It is hard to see any difference at all in 1760 between Franklin and the man who eventually came to symbolize for Americans the arch-Tory and the foremost enemy of American liberty and American independence, Thomas Hutchinson, the last civilian governor of the colony of Massachusetts. Both Franklin and Hutchinson were good Enlightenment figures, literate, reasonable men, with a deep dislike of religious enthusiasm. Both were imperial officials, dedicated to the British Empire. They had in fact cooperated in forming in 1754 the Albany Plan of Union which presented a farsighted proposal for intercolonial cooperation and imperial defense. Both Franklin and Hutchinson were getting-along men, believers in prudence, calculation, affability, and the playing of parts, and they made their way in that monarchical society by getting along and playing parts. Both were believers in the power of a few reasonable men, men like themselves, to run affairs. Both regarded the common people with a certain patronizing amusement, unless of course they rioted; then they were filled with disgust.

It is certainly not easy from the vantage point of the early 1760s to predict that the two men's paths would eventually diverge so radically. In many respects Franklin seems the least likely of revolutionaries. Certainly his participation in the Revolution was not natural or inevitable; indeed, Franklin came very close to remaining, as his son did, a loyal member of the British Empire. On its face, it is not a simple matter to understand why Franklin took up the revolutionary cause at all.

First of all, Franklin, unlike the other founders, was not a young man. He was born in 1706 and was thus seventy years old in 1776, not an age that one associates with passionate revolutionaries. He was by far the oldest of the revolutionary leaders—twenty-six years older than Washington, twenty-nine years older than John Adams, thirty-seven years older than Jefferson, and nearly a half century older than Madison and Hamilton. Because he came from an entirely different generation from the rest of the founders and had lived longer under British rule, he was more deeply committed to the British Empire than they were.

More important, unlike these other revolutionary leaders, Franklin already had an established reputation; prior to the Revolution he was already world-famous. He had everything to lose and seemingly little to gain by participating in a revolution. The other American revolutionary leaders were young men, virtually unknown outside their remote provinces. We can generally understand why they might have become revolutionaries. They were men of modest origins with high ambitions who saw in the Revolution opportunities to achieve that fame that Hamilton called "the ruling passion of the noblest minds."[3] But Franklin was different. He alone already had the position and the fame that the others only yearned for. Because of his scientific discoveries concerning electricity, which were real contributions to basic science, he had become a celebrity throughout the Atlantic world. He had been made a member of the Royal Society and had received honorary degrees from universities in America and Britain, including St. Andrews and Oxford. Philosophers and scientists from all over Europe consulted him on everything from how to build a fireplace to why the oceans were salty. Well before the Revolution he was one of the most renowned men in the world and certainly the most famous American.

Since he scarcely could have foreseen how much the Revolution would enhance his reputation and turn him into one of America's greatest folk heroes, why at his age would he have risked so much?

We do not usually ask the question of why Franklin became a revolutionary. Somehow we take his participation in the Revolution for granted. Because he is so identified with the Revolution and with America, we can scarcely think of him as anything but a thoroughgoing American. But this is a problem of what historians generally call whiggism, the anachronistic foreshortening that tends to see the past and persons in the past as anticipations of the future. Franklin has become such a symbol of America that we have a hard time thinking of him as anything but an American folk hero or as the spokesman for American capitalism. We have over two hundred years of images imposed on Franklin that have to be peeled away before we can recover the man who existed before the Revolution. Franklin in the late 1760s and early 1770s was not fated to abandon the British Empire and join the American cause. How he became estranged from that empire and became, almost overnight, a fiery revolutionary is a story that was not at all foreordained.

FRANKLIN IS NOT an easy man to get to know. Although he wrote more pieces about more things than any of the other founders, he was never very revealing of himself. He always seems to be holding back something of himself; he is reticent, detached, not wholly committed. We sense in Franklin the presence of calculated restraint, a restraint perhaps bred by his stunning rise and the kind of hierarchical and patronage-ridden world he had to operate in.[4] Certainly there were people in Philadelphia who never let him forget "his original obscurity" and that he had sprung from "the meanest Circumstances."[5] Despite his complaining that he was never able to order things in his life, we sense that he was always in control of his character and was showing us just what he wanted us to see. Only at moments in the early 1770s and at the end of his life do we sense a world that was spinning out of his grasp.

Beyond the restrained and reserved character of his personal writings is the remarkable character of his public writings, especially his *Autobiography*—"this most famous of American texts," one scholar calls it.[6] Literary scholars have continually interpreted and reinterpreted the *Autobiography* but still cannot agree on what Franklin was trying to do in writing it. Among the founders, Jefferson and Adams also wrote autobiographies, but theirs are nothing like Franklin's. His *Autobiography* resembles a work of fiction in which we cannot be sure that the leading character is the same as the author. Indeed, much of the reader's enjoyment of the *Autobiography* comes from the contrast between Franklin's descriptions of the "awkward ridiculous Appearance" the teenage printer made upon his arrival in Philadelphia and "the Figure I have since made there."[7] It is hard to interpret the *Autobiography* since, as scholars have pointed out, Franklin moves between several personas, especially between the innocence of youth and the irony of a mature man.[8]

In all of Franklin's writings his wit and humor, his constant self-awareness, his assuming of different personas and roles make it difficult to know how to read him. He was a man of many voices and masks who continually mocked himself.[9] Sometimes he was a woman, like "Silence Dogood," "Alice Addertongue," "Cecilia Shortface," and "Polly Baker," saucy and racy and hilarious. At other times he was the "Busy Body," or "Obadiah Plainman," or "Anthony Afterwit," or "Richard Saunders," also known as "Poor Richard," the almanac maker. Sometimes he wrote in the London newspapers as "An American" or "A New England-Man." Other times he wrote as "A Briton" or "A London Manufacturer" and shaped what he wrote accordingly. During his London years he wrote some ninety pseudonymous items for the press, using forty-two different signatures.[10] For each of the many pieces he wrote both in Philadelphia and in London he had a remarkable ability to create the appropriate persona. Indeed, all his many personas contribute nicely to the particular purpose of his various works, whether they are essays, skits, poems, or satires. And his personas and voices were many. "Just as no other eighteenth-century writer has so many moods and tones or so wide a range of correspondents," declares the dean of present-day Franklin scholars, "so no other eighteenth-century writer has so any different personae or so many different voices as Franklin." No wonder we have difficulty figuring out who this remarkable man is.[11]

Of all the founders, he may have had the fullest and deepest understanding of human nature. At one moment he could describe human beings as vain and self-centered and at the next moment emphasize their benevolence and concern for others. Just as he had a remarkable capacity to see all sides of human nature, so too could he appreciate other points of view. He loved turning conventional wisdom on its head, as, for example, when he argued for the virtue and usefulness of censure and backbiting.[12] But then again are we sure that he is not putting us on? Is he serious? Or is he being ironic? Is he sincere, or is he using his usual trickery to make his point? We cannot be certain.

Certainly no one of the founders was more conscious of the difference between appearances and reality. Not only did he continually comment on that difference, but he was never averse to maintaining the discrepancy between appearance and reality. If one could not actually be industrious and humble, at least, he said, one could appear to be so.

Although he wrote against disguise and dissimulation and asked, "Who was ever cunning enough to conceal his being so?" we know that he was the master of camouflage and concealment. "We shall resolve to be what we would seem," he declared, yet at the same time he seems to have delighted in hiding his innermost thoughts and motives. "Let all Men know thee," Poor Richard said, "but no man know thee thoroughly: Men freely ford that see the shallows."[13]

While sometimes bowing to the emerging romantic cult of sincerity, he remained firmly rooted in the traditional eighteenth-century world of restraining one's inner desires and feelings in order to be civil and get along. He never thought that his characteristic behavior—his artful posing, his role playing, his many masks, his refusal to reveal his inner self—was anything other than what the cultivated and sociable eighteenth century admired. He was a thoroughly social being, enmeshed in society and civic-minded by necessity. Not for him the disastrous assertions of antisocial autonomy and the outspoken sincerity of Molière's character Alceste in *Le Misanthrope*. Like many in the eighteenth century, Franklin preferred the sensible and prudent behavior of Alceste's friend Philinte, who knew that the path of good sense was to adapt to the pressures and contradictions of society.[14] Unlike, say, John Adams, Franklin never wore his heart on his sleeve; he kept most of his intentions and feelings to himself. He was a master at keeping his own counsel. As Poor Richard said, "Three may keep a Secret, if two of them are dead."[15] Behind all the masks and voices we really do not know who Franklin is. He is many-sided, everything to everyone, it seems.

Few of the founders have taken on such symbolic and imaginative significance. Franklin has come to stand for America in all its many-sidedness. He seems to represent everything that is both good and bad about America. Thus for imaginative writers and spiritual seekers he has represented America's bourgeois complacency, its get-ahead materialism, its utilitarian obsession with success, the unimaginative superficiality and vulgarity of American culture that kill the soul. He is Babbittry and Main Street rolled into one.

D. H. Lawrence's vicious attack in the 1920s is only the most famous criticism of Franklin as the embodiment of bourgeois values, the kind of values that intellectuals and especially imaginative writers and artists do not like. Nineteenth-century American writers such as Edgar Allan Poe, Henry David Thoreau, Herman Melville, and Mark Twain had said much the same thing.

Yet Franklin has also stood for American values that even imaginative writers sometimes esteem. He has represented America's social mobility, the capacity of ordinary people to make it to the top, the American dream. He has stood for American levelheadedness, pragmatism, inventiveness, and concern for the happiness and prosperity of common people in the here and now.

In short, he is one of the most massively symbolic figures in American history.

To understand the man and the symbol, we need to disentangle the eighteenth-century Franklin from the image, explain a little of what he was like and why he might have joined the Revolution, and then suggest some the ways he began to become a symbol during the Revolution and in the decades following his death in 1790. We shall see that the Franklin Americans have known through most of their national history is essentially an invention of the nineteenth century.

THERE IS NO DOUBT that Franklin was a man of extraordinary talent, and the trajectory of his career was extraordinary too. It was a rags to riches story. But it would be a mistake to overemphasize this aspect of his life, as if his career were unique and he were somehow prefiguring the Horatio Alger success stories of the next century. Rising from obscure origins to success and eminence was not unheard of in the eighteenth century or earlier, and Franklin's rise, however spectacular, was not unique in English history.

In the eighteenth century in both America and Britain many young men moved up the social ladder. As was mentioned in the Introduction, William Strahan, Franklin's lifelong British friend and associate, began as a journeyman printer like Franklin and eventually became very rich, richer perhaps than Franklin; he even acquired a seat in Parliament. In America there was a brilliant young merchants' clerk, seventeen years old, named Alexander Hamilton, who was rescued from his "groveling" obscurity in St. Croix by perceptive patrons and sent to the mainland for an education.[16] In that very different monarchical world patrons were often on the lookout for bright young lads to bring along. Patronizing inferiors and creating obligations, after all, were important marks of an aristocrat in that rank-conscious age.

Patronage was the basic means of social mobility in the eighteenth century, and Franklin's rise was due to it, as a careful reading of his *Autobiography* shows. He could never have made it in the way he did in that hierarchical society if he had not been helped by men of influence and supported at crucial points. When his brother-in-law, a ship captain who sailed a commercial sloop between Massachusetts and the Delaware region, learned that Franklin was in Philadelphia, working in a printshop, he wrote to persuade the young runaway to return to Boston. The brother-in-law happened to show Franklin's reply to William Keith, governor of Pennsylvania, who could not believe that a seventeen-year-old could have written such a letter. "He said," Franklin recalled, "I appear'd a young Man of promising Parts, and therefore should be encouraged."[17] The governor invited Franklin out for a drink in a local tavern and offered to help establish him as an independent printer if his father would supply the capital.

Keith was not the only colonial governor to notice Franklin. In the following year, 1724, en route back from Boston, where Franklin had failed to get money from his father, he stopped off in New York with a trunkful of his books that he retrieved from Boston. An eighteen-year-old with a trunk of books was a rare enough occurrence in colonial New York that the governor of that colony, William Burnet, asked to meet with the young man to converse about authors and books.

When prominent Pennsylvanians grasped Franklin's genius, they were quick to patronize him. Thomas Denham, William Allen, Andrew Hamilton, and others supported him in a variety of ways, lending money, inviting him to their homes, introducing him to others, becoming his "friends," which was the common euphemism of the day for patron-client relations. All "these Friends were . . . of great Use to me," Franklin recalled, "as I occasionally was to some of them."[18] No doubt his own conspicuous talent was the main source of his rise, but once he had caught people's attention, "the leading Men . . . thought it convenient to oblige and encourage me."[19] So it went. In the end Franklin was never quite as self-made as he sometimes implied or as the nineteenth century made him out to be.

Yet he did succeed, in an extraordinary way. He became not just a wealthy printer but an entrepreneur. He had partnerships and shares in a number of printing businesses in other colonies. He established at least eighteen paper mills at one time or another; in fact he may have been the largest paper dealer in the English-speaking world.[20] He owned a good deal of rental property in Philadelphia and in many of the coastal towns.[21] He was a substantial creditor, practically a banker, with a great amount of money out on loan, some loans as small as two shillings and others as large as two hundred pounds.[22] Moreover, throughout much of his life he was deeply involved in land speculation.

In 1748, at the age of forty-two, Franklin believed he had acquired sufficient wealth and gentility to retire from active business. This retirement had far more significance in the mid-eighteenth century than it would today. It meant that Franklin could at last become a gentleman, a man of leisure who no longer would have to work for a living.

Franklin's retirement was a major event for him, and he took it very seriously. He had a coming-out portrait painted by Robert Feke. He acquired several slaves and moved to a new and more spacious house in "a more quiet Part of the Town," renting a house on the northwest corner of Sassafras (Race) and Second streets. He left his printing office and shop in the old quarters on Market Street, where his new partner, David Hall, moved in to run the firm. Since most artisans worked where they lived, separating his home from his business in this way was a graphic indication that Franklin had left his occupation as a tradesman behind.

Once he became a gentleman and a "master of my own time," Franklin thought he would do what other gentlemen did: write and engage in "Philosophical Studies and Amusements." As he told the New York official and scientist Cadwallader Colden, he now had "leisure to read, study, make experiments, and converse at large with such ingenious and worthy Men as are pleas'd to honour me with their Friendship or Acquaintance on such Points as may produce something for the common benefit of Mankind, uninterrupted by the little Cares and Fatigues of Business."[23] But, as he says in his *Autobiography*, "the Publick, now considering me as a Man of Leisure, laid hold of me for their Purposes." Indeed, he said, "Every Part of our Civil Government, and almost at the same time, impos[ed] some Duty on me."[24] As a gentleman—that is, as a man of leisure—he was brought into government. He became a member of the Philadelphia City Council in 1748, he was appointed a justice of the peace in 1749, and in 1751 he became a city alderman and was elected from Philadelphia to be one of the twenty-six members of the very clubby eastern- and Quaker-dominated Pennsylvania Assembly.

He was not unhappy with all these public offices. He saw himself becoming an eighteenth-century "great man," by which he meant in political terms. He saw public service as the prime obligation of a gentleman. By the mid-1750s he had his eye on the higher reaches of the British Empire. In 1753 he became deputy postmaster of North America, a royal of-ficeholder, but he wanted more. "Life," he wrote in 1756, was "like a dra-matic Piece" and thus "should finish handsomely. Being now in the last Act, I begin to cast about for something fit to end with."[25] He scarcely could have foreseen how handsomely it would end.

Already he felt constrained by the provincial arena of America. In 1749 in his pamphlet *Proposals Relating to the Education of Youth in Pennsylvania*, he had written that encouragement of learning and advancement for young men were greater in Europe than in America. In Europe a poor man's son, if he studied hard, could rise in either the law or church to high offices and "to an extraordinary pitch of grandeur." In America perhaps one could become a militia colonel, but in Europe one might be able "to have a voice in Parliament, a Seat among the Peers," maybe become "first minister to govern Nations, and even mix his blood with Princes."[26]

Franklin was very ambitious. He wanted a share in what was the most important phenomenon of the eighteenth-century, the extraordinary ex-pansion of the British Empire. Britain, that little island on the north-western periphery of Europe, with a population only a third that of France, was bidding fair to dominate the world, and Franklin wanted to play a central role in its expansion. He was sure that if only reasonable right-thinking men, men like himself or Thomas Hutchinson, could in-troduce "less partial, more generous and sounder Politics," they could make the empire a dominion of unprecedented greatness. He expressed great confidence in the integrity of the British Empire and the beneficence of royal officials at Whitehall.

From his correspondence of the 1750s and early 1760s we would never know what an American folk and revolutionary hero Franklin later be-came. He was exasperated by the petty disputes between the colonial as-semblies and the colonial governors. He wanted something like the Albany Plan of Union of 1754 enacted independently by the ministry and Parliament and simply imposed on the colonies. "I doubt not but they will make a good one," he said.[27]

In 1757 he went "home to England" as the agent of the Pennsylvania

Assembly in order to persuade the Crown to oust the Penn family as proprietors of Pennsylvania and make Pennsylvania a royal province.[28] It was rumored that he hoped to become the first royal governor of Pennsylvania.

Although in his mission he was ostensibly the agent of the Pennsylvania Assembly, he was in reality the king's man. No one could have been more loyal. His confidence in the virtue and good sense of politicians at the highest levels of the British government was so great that it bewildered and amazed even some of his English friends. He even prominently displayed in his Philadelphia home a picture of George III's "dearest friend" and chief minister in 1762, Lord Bute, and bragged of his acquaintance with him.

Franklin was the complete Anglophile in these years of the late 1750s and early 1760s. Other colonial Americans visiting London, such as Charles Carroll and John Dickinson, often contrasted the luxury and corruption they perceived in English life with the virtue and simplicity of America. But not Franklin. He had none of the provincial need to denigrate the metropolitan center. In fact, by the early 1760s he had begun filling his letters with disparaging comments about the provinciality and vulgarity of America in contrast with the sophistication and worthiness of England. Britain, "that little Island," he wrote in 1763, enjoyed, "in almost every Neighbourhood, more sensible, virtuous and elegant Minds, than we can collect in ranging 100 Leagues of our vast Forests."[29] No one brought up in England, he said, could ever be happy in America. He claimed it was not England but America that was corrupt and luxury-loving, and the great danger was that the English nation, if it did not draw off some of its wealth, "would, like ours, have a Plethora in its Veins, productive of the same Sloth, and the same feverish Extravagance."[30] Everywhere in the Old World he saw contrasts with provincial America that mortified him. The Sunday gaiety of the people of Flanders, together with their ordered prosperity, for example, only reminded him, by contrast, of how narrow and straitlaced and how silly was Puritan New England.[31]

Franklin had totally succumbed to the sophistication of English life.

He talked endlessly of staying in England. When he knew he had to return to Pennsylvania in 1762 to look after his post office business, he said his heart belonged in England, and he vowed he would soon return.

In the early 1760s Franklin was very much the loyalist and royal supporter. He had no inkling of the impending imperial crisis and no sense as yet of any disparity of interests between Britain and its colonies. Some of his closest allies were imperial officials and royal supporters. In 1762, in no small part because of his influence with Lord Bute, his son William was appointed royal governor of New Jersey at age thirty-two. Franklin seems to have had his own sights on an imperial office.

He was very much an elitist, his "political Faith" being generally "that what our superiors think best for us, is really best." He expressed little confidence in the common people and abhorred popular disorder and mob violence of any sort. John Wilkes, the Paxton Boys, the Sons of Liberty, and "weak Government" all were distasteful to him.[32]

By December 1764 he was back in England, where his involvement in the Stamp Act the next year revealed his misunderstanding of popular government and the weakness of his elitist approach to politics. Like the other colonial agents, he naturally opposed the act, which was to tax a variety of colonial items, including newspapers, licenses, indentures, and playing cards. But when Franklin saw that passage of the tax was inevitable, he accepted it. After all, he said, empires cost money. In making the best of the situation, he procured for his friend John Hughes the stamp agency in Philadelphia. He almost ruined his position in American public life and almost cost Hughes his life.

Franklin was shocked by the mobs that effectively prevented enforcement of the Stamp Act everywhere in the North American continent. Not only was he totally out of touch with colonial feelings, but comments he made to Hughes reveal how much of a devoted royalist he was. He told Hughes to remain cool in the face of the mobbings. "A firm Loyalty to the Crown and faithful Adherence to the Government of this Nation . . ." he said, "will always be the wisest Course for you and I to take, whatever may be the Madness of the Populace or their blind Leaders."[33]

Only his four-hour testimony before Parliament denouncing the act in 1766 saved his reputation in America. The American reaction to the Stamp Act shook Franklin, and his earlier confidence in the wisdom of British officials became increasingly punctuated by doubts and resentments. He now bristled at the "insolence, contempt, and abuse" that English officials heaped upon the colonists, and he began to feel his "Americanness" as never before.

During the next four or five years Franklin was very ambivalent and felt himself caught in a widening gulf that he tried to bridge. As he said, the English thought him too American, while the Americans thought him too English. He sought to calm the passions on both sides and belittled the plots and conspiracies that both British officials and the colonists saw.

He had not, however, given up his ambition to make it within the imperial hierarchy. Suddenly in the summer of 1768 the possibility of a subministerial position in the Grafton government was dangled before him. Several appointments with the duke of Grafton were broken by Grafton, but Franklin did get to meet with Grafton's close colleague Lord North, who told Franklin that if he could be persuaded to stay in England, the government hoped to "find some way of making it worth your while." Franklin replied that he would "stay with pleasure if I could any ways be useful to government." He told his son that he would be "either promoted or discarded."[34]

But Lord Hillsborough, who was opposed to Franklin's land schemes for settling the trans-Appalachian West of North America, was the head of the new American Department, created in 1768, and blocked any appointment. Still, Franklin did not give up hope. Elections occur, ministers change, and Hillsborough might be ousted from the ministry.

It is in this context that we can best understand Franklin's remarkable interview with Hillsborough in January 1771, an interview that Franklin regarded as so significant that he immediately transcribed it in dramatic form. When Hillsborough coldly refused to accept Franklin's credentials as the agent for the Massachusetts Assembly, Franklin was stunned. He realized that Hillsborough would never have taken such a step if he had not had the backing of the ministry in general. He found himself, as his friend William Strahan explained to Franklin's son, "not only on bad Terms with Lord Hillsborough, but with the *Ministry in general.*"[35] All the flattering expectations that he had had over the previous three years of his becoming an important player in imperial affairs were suddenly shattered.

It was in the aftermath of this failure in 1771 that Franklin began thinking about his life. For the next six months he was confused and dispirited. He seemed to lose all his zest and ambition and thought himself useless. He went on a series of journeys around the British Isles, and on one of these visits to a country house of a friend he began writing his *Autobiography.*

The first part of his life, up to age twenty-five—the best part, most critics have agreed—was thus written in a mood of frustration, nostalgia, and defiance. Look, he suggested, he was not really a dependent courtier seeking office at some superior's pleasure. He was his own independent man who against overwhelming odds had made it. No British lord could take that away from him. This first part of his *Autobiography* thus became a salve for his wounds and a justification for his apparent failure in British politics. It was also an admonition to his high-living son, to whom it was addressed and who was continually badgering his father for money, to cut his expenses and do as his father had done.

But then the signals from the British government shifted: Hillsborough changed his tone toward him and invited him to his Irish estates. Even better, Hillsborough was ousted from the ministry, and Lord Dartmouth was appointed in his place. Since Dartmouth was a friend of Franklin's and was sympathetic to America and western expansion, Franklin once again became optimistic that he might play a role in imperial politics.

With no further emotional need for it, Franklin dropped the writing of his *Autobiography*, which he did not resume until 1784 in France following the successful negotiation of the treaty establishing American independence. With imperial possibilities opening up once more, he became involved in the affair of the Hutchinson letters, which ultimately destroyed his position in England.

In the late 1760s Thomas Hutchinson, then lieutenant governor of Massachusetts, had written some letters to a friend in England urging that stern measures, including the abridging of English liberties in America, were needed to maintain the colonies' dependency on Great Britain. Somehow Franklin got his hands on these letters and late in 1772 sent them to Massachusetts in order, as he said, to convince the American people that blame for the imperial crisis lay solely with a few mischievous colonial officials like Hutchinson. Thus the ministry in London would be cleared of responsibility for the crisis, and the way would be opened for rational settlement of the differences between the mother country and the colonies. This would give Dartmouth, with Franklin's help, a chance to straighten things out.

This was a gross miscalculation, for the letters he sent to Massachusetts only further inflamed the imperial crisis. Contrary to much conventional wisdom, Franklin was not at all a shrewd politician or a discerning judge of popular passions, certainly not of the prerevolutionary passions of these years. To be sure, he was free of the wild suspicions and conspiratorial notions that beguiled many on both sides of the imperial conflict. But he suffered from a naive confidence in the power of reason and a few good men to arrange complex matters. As late as 1775 he was still persuaded that the issues separating Britain and the colonies were "a mere Matter of Punctilio, which Two or three reasonable People might settle in half an Hour." He had little or no comprehension of the structural forces and the popular passions that limited individual action. In the end he was convinced that the glorious empire to which he had devoted so much of his life was broken by "the mangling hands of a few blundering ministers."[36]

The British ministry now held Franklin responsible for the crisis. On January 29, 1774, he was viciously and publicly attacked before the Privy Council and other observers by Alexander Wedderburn, the solicitor general, for being a thief and something less than a gentleman. This was virtually the last straw. He was supposed to have whispered to Wedderburn upon leaving the cockpit, "I will make your master a LITTLE KING for this."[37]

Two days later Franklin was fired as deputy postmaster. Although for a few more months he continued vainly to try and save the empire, advising even Lord Chatham in a last-ditch peace proposal, he finally came to realize that the empire and his role in it were over.

IN MARCH 1775 he sailed for America and became a passionate patriot, more passionate than most. The Revolution in fact became a very personal matter for Franklin, more personal perhaps than for any of the other revolutionary leaders. Even John Adams, who was no slouch when it came to hating, was startled by the degree of Franklin's revolutionary fervor and his loathing of the king.

Part of this passion was no doubt calculated. Franklin had to overcome suspicions that many of his countrymen had of him. Some thought his position in the 1760s and 1770s had been sufficiently ambiguous that he might not be a true patriot after all. Some even thought that he might be a British spy. Franklin's need to overcome this suspicion explains the extraordinary letter he wrote in July 1775 to his lifelong English friend William Strahan: "You are a Member of Parliament and one of that Majority which doomed my Country to Destruction. You have begun to burn our Towns, and murder our People. Look upon your Hands! They are stained with the Blood of your Relations! You and I were long Friends: You are now my Enemy, and I am, Yours, B. Franklin."[38]

Since he was trying to convince his fellow Americans of his patriotism, he let people in Philadelphia see this outrageous letter, but of course he never sent it. Within days he was writing his usual affectionate letters to Strahan.

Some of his anger and passion were calculated, but not all by any means. Franklin had had his deepest aspirations thwarted by the officials of the British government, and he had been personally humiliated by them as none of the other revolutionaries had been. His participation in the Revolution was a profoundly emotional affair. He was deeply hurt and very bitter over his treatment by the British. To the surprise of his colleagues like John Adams, he had no sympathy whatsoever for the loyalists during the peace talks. He never forgave his son William for remaining loyal to the British Crown and went out of his way to disown and wound him.

In 1776 he was prepared for a new role on behalf of America. Even before the Revolution Franklin was aware that he was valued abroad in Europe more than in England. As his frustration with Britain mounted in the early 1770s, his awareness of his Continental reputation had grown. "Learned and ingenious foreigners that come to England almost all make a point of visiting me," he bragged to his son in 1772, "for my reputation is still higher abroad than here." Several of the foreign ambassadors have "assiduously cultivated my acquaintance, treating me as one of their own."[39]

He was beginning to see the English stage as limited and that his reputation abroad "in foreign courts" as a kind of ambassador for America more than compensated for his loss of influence in England. Thus by the time he was sent to Paris by the new United States government in 1776 as its diplomatic agent, he was emotionally prepared to play the role of the representative American.

France furthered the process of Franklin's Americanization. The eight years he spent there helped mold his image as the symbolic American. In this sense Franklin belonged to France before he belonged to America.

The French first created the modern image of Franklin that we are familiar with: the bourgeois Poor Richard moralist, the symbol of rustic democracy, the simple backwoods philosopher. It was Franklin's genius to understand how the French saw him and to exploit that image for the American cause.

Franklin's mission seemed impossible from the start. France was initially unwilling to recognize the new country and was anxious not to get into a premature war with Britain. The United States had virtually nothing to offer the French monarchy, except the unlikely prospect of breaking up the British Empire. Franklin was an old man, seventy years of age in 1776, and suffering from a variety of ailments. He was bitterly disliked by his fellow commissioners and viewed with suspicion by many Americans back home. After all, he had spent nearly all of the previous two decades living in London, and his son William, the former royal governor of New Jersey, was a notorious Loyalist, under arrest in America. No wonder some Americans thought that Franklin might be a spy working for the British.

Despite these difficulties, he succeeded admirably. He was the greatest diplomat America has ever had. Not only did he bring the monarchy of Louis XVI into the war on behalf of the new Republic, but during the course of that long war he extracted loan after loan from an increasingly impoverished French government. No other American could have done what he did.

He brought to France an established reputation as a great scientist and philosopher, the native genius who had come out of the wild woods of America to astonish the world. To many of the French aristocracy Franklin embodied America, and many of them were in love with the idea of America, with its primitiveness, its innocence, and its liberty. Caught up in radical chic, they used their image of America and Franklin to criticize the luxury and corruption of their own society. They sang songs in praise of liberty, republicanism, and equality. They flocked to see Beaumarchais's *Barber of Seville* and to listen to Mozart's *Marriage of Figaro*, even though those pieces deliver a very antiaristocratic message. Many of the French aristocrats, like La Rochefoucauld, were passionate advocates of abolishing the very privileges to which they owed their positions and fortunes. They had no idea where it all would lead. La Rochefoucauld was later stoned to death by a frenzied revolutionary mob.

Franklin was part of this radical chic. He was lionized by the nobility. His face appeared everywhere, on medallions, on snuffboxes, on candy boxes, in rings, in statues, in prints; women did their hair à la Franklin.

Franklin told his daughter that all these images have made "your father's face as well known as that of the moon."[40] The king, Louis XVI, became so jealous of the adoration paid Franklin by a member of his court that he presented that courtier with a chamber pot displaying Franklin's face on the inside.

It was Franklin's genius to know what the French wanted from him and to play his part to perfection. He dressed in a simple brown and white linen suit and wore a fur cap, no wig, and no sword at Versailles, the most elaborate and protocol-ridden court in all of Europe. And the court and the French nobility loved it. Assuming that everyone from Pennsylvania was a simple Quaker, many Frenchmen thought Franklin had to be one too. He could do no wrong. Franklin remained quiet in large gatherings—his spoken French was so bad—but the French were impressed by his republican reticence.

His Poor Richard maxims about the making of money were described as sublime philosophy worthy of Voltaire and Montaigne. With the French philosophe Condorcet we have a perfect example of Gallic logic. Poor Richard, said Condorcet, was a "unique work in which one cannot help recognizing the superior man without it being possible to cite a single passage where he allows his superiority to be perceived." Anticipating later French theories of deconstruction, Condorcet admitted that there was nothing in the thought or style of Franklin's work that showed anything above "the least developed intelligence." But "a philosophic mind," said Condorcet, could discover the "noble aims and profound intentions" behind the maxims and proverbs.[41]

Despite the popularity of his Poor Richard maxims, Franklin was anything but the bourgeois businessman in France. He understood the French aristocratic love of honor and liberality and tried to tell the American foreign secretary Robert Livingston how the French should be approached. "This is really a generous nation, fond of glory and particularly that of protecting the oppressed." The French nobility is not really interested in trade, said Franklin. To tell them that it will be in their interest to help us "seems as much to say, help us, and we shall not be obliged to you."

Franklin knew better. Vergennes, the French foreign minister, noted that all the Americans had "a terrible mania for commerce." But not Franklin. "I believe his hands and heart are equally pure."[42]

In an important sense the French invented something of the Ben Franklin that we now know. They had a need of him before his fellow Americans did. Franklin was able to parlay this need into French support for the American cause. No wonder the eight years in France became the happiest of his life. He was doing what he most yearned to do: shape events on a world stage. In these circumstances in 1784 he resumed writing his *Autobiography* and wrote the second part of it, which presumes man's control over his life.

AFTER THE PEACE TREATY was signed, Franklin reluctantly had to come to America to die, even though all his friends were in France. He now knew that his destiny was linked to America. When he arrived in 1785, his fellow Americans did not know what to make of him. They knew he was an international hero, along with Washington the most celebrated American in the world, but they were not quite sure why. He had not led the revolutionary movement like John Adams. He had not written a great revolutionary document like Jefferson. He had not led armies like Washington.

When he died in 1790, there was only one public eulogy, and that was given by William Smith, his inveterate enemy, simply because Smith, as vice president of the American Philosophical Society, was assigned the task. Even someone like former Governor James Bowdoin of Massachusetts was honored with a dozen or so funeral orations. Washington's published eulogies numbered in the hundreds. The French outdid themselves honoring Franklin. The most famous eulogy was that of Mirabeau, delivered in the French National Assembly; the Assembly published it and proclaimed three days of mourning, the first gesture of this kind it had ever made. By contrast the United States Senate refused to join the House in endorsing a resolution honoring Franklin.

To make matters worse, Smith's eulogy before the APS was a half-hearted affair. Since the gentlemen who were members of the APS were embarrassed by Franklin's lowly origins, Smith had to apologize for his humble beginnings and dismiss his youth as unimportant.

Americans still saw Franklin as a patriot and scientist, not as the homespun Poor Richard bourgeois moralist of later years. Only in the years following his death in 1790 and the publication of his *Autobiography* in 1794 did Franklin's image change. Over the next thirty years numerous editions and abridgments of the *Autobiography* flooded the country. After 1798 editors began adding the Poor Richard essays to editions of the *Autobiography*.

The rise of artisans and businessmen in the nineteenth century accounts mostly for this new materialistic image of Franklin. They discovered in Franklin a symbol for their cause, just as the French had. They founded Franklin Institutes and mechanics' associations and used Franklin to justify the challenge they were making to gentlemen who, like aristocrats for millennia, had scorned those who worked for a living in trade. Franklin's life became an object lesson for young men, as someone who had made it, as the 1810 edition of his life put it, "without fortune and without patronage." He was a self-made man, a shaper of his own destiny.

Franklin was identified in the early nineteenth century less as an eighteenth-century gentleman and philosopher than as the poor printer who worked hard and became rich. Unlike Smith's eulogy, these accounts stressed Franklin's humble origins and his youth.

One of the best was an 1817 biography by Parson Weems: "O you time-wasting, brain-starving young men, who can never be at ease unless you have a cigar or a plug of tobacco in your mouths, go on with your puffing and champing—go on with your filthy smoking, and your still more filthy spitting, keeping the cleanly housewives in constant terror for their nicely waxed floors, and their shining carpets—go on I say; but remember, it was not in this way that our little Ben became the GREAT DR. FRANKLIN."[43]

The identification of Franklin with hard work and bourgeois materialism was a product of early-nineteenth-century developments that took place after Franklin's death. This was the bourgeois image that imaginative writers like Poe, Thoreau, Melville, and Lawrence attacked. It is this image of the hardworking self-made businessman that seems to have most endured. However great a founder Franklin was—and his crucial diplomacy in the Revolution makes him second only to Washington in importance—as long as the principal business of America remains business, it is the symbolic Franklin of the bumptious capitalism of the early Republic that is likely to continue to dominate American culture.

Chapter Three

The Trials and Tribulations
of Thomas Jefferson

FRANKLIN MAY HAVE BECOME a symbol for the American dream of getting on and making it, especially making lots of money, but no one has embodied America's democratic ideals and democratic hopes more than Thomas Jefferson. "All honor to Jefferson," Abraham Lincoln declared on the eve of the Civil War. By setting forth the explosive idea that "all men are created equal," said Lincoln, Jefferson had created "a rebuke and a stumbling block" to the appearance of all future tyranny and oppression. "The principles of Jefferson," said Lincoln, "are the definitions and axioms of free society."[1]

Almost from the beginning Jefferson has been a symbol, a touchstone, of what we as a people are supposed to be; he has become someone invented, manipulated, turned into something we Americans like or dislike, fear or yearn for within ourselves—whether it is populism or elitism, agrarianism or racism, atheism or liberalism. We are continually asking ourselves whether Jefferson still survives or what is yet living in the thought of Jefferson, and we quote him on every side of every major question in our history. Most Americans think of Jefferson much as our first professional biographer, James Parton, did. "If Jefferson was wrong," wrote Parton in 1874, "America is wrong. If America is right, Jefferson was right."[2]

As Merrill Peterson showed us in his superb book *The Jeffersonion Image in the American Mind*, published nearly a half century ago, the image of Jefferson in American culture has always been "a sensitive reflector . . . of America's troubled search for the image of itself."[3] And the symbolizing, the image mongering, the identifying of Jefferson with America have not changed a bit in the decades since Peterson's book was published, even though the level of professional historical scholarship has never been higher. If anything, during these turbulent times the association of Jefferson with America has become more complete. Over the past four decades or so many people, including some historians, have concluded that something is seriously wrong with America. And if something is wrong with America, then something has to be wrong with Jefferson.

PROBABLY THE opening blast in this modern criticism of Jefferson was Leonard Levy's *Jefferson and Civil Liberties: The Darker Side* (1963).[4] This was no subtle satire, no gentle mocking of the ironies of Jefferson's inconsistencies and hypocrisies; Levy's book was a prosecutor's indictment. Levy ripped off Jefferson's mantle of libertarianism to expose his "darker side": his passion for partisan persecution, his lack of concern for basic civil liberties, and his self-righteousness that became at times out-and-out ruthlessness. Far from being the skeptical enlightened intellectual, allowing all ideas their free play, Jefferson was portrayed by Levy and other historians as something of an ideologue, a doctrinaire thinker eager to fill the young with his political orthodoxy while censoring all those books he did not like. He did not have an open or questioning mind after all.

Not only did Jefferson not have an original or skeptical mind, but he could in fact be downright doctrinaire, an early version of a knee-jerk liberal. His reaction to European society and culture, says historian Bernard Bailyn, was "an eighteenth-century stereotype—a boldly liberal, high-minded, enlightened stereotype, but a stereotype nonetheless—a configuration of liberal attitudes and ideas which he accepted uncritically, embellishing them with his beautifully wrought prose but questioning little and adding little."[5] In this respect he was very different from his more skeptical and inquisitive friend James Madison. Jefferson could, for example, understand the opening struggles of the French Revolution only in terms of a traditional liberal antagonism to an arrogant and overgrown monarchy.[6] He supported the addition of a bill of rights to the federal Constitution not because he had thought through the issue the way Madison had, but largely because a bill of rights was what good governments were supposed to have. All his liberal aristocratic French friends said so; indeed, as he told his fellow Americans, "the enlightened part of Europe have given us the greatest credit for inventing this instrument of security for the rights of the people, and have been not a little surprised to see us so soon give it up."[7] One almost has the feeling that Jefferson advocated a bill of rights in 1787 and 1788 out of embarrassment over what his liberal French associates would think. One sometimes has the same feeling about his antislavery statements, many of which seem to have been shaped to the expectations of enlightened foreigners.

It is in fact his views on black Americans and slavery that have made Jefferson most vulnerable to modern censure. If America has turned out to be wrong in its race relations, then Jefferson had to be wrong too. Who could not find the contrast between Jefferson's great declarations of liberty and equality and his lifelong ownership of slaves glaringly embarrassing? Jefferson undoubtedly hated slavery and believed that the self-evident truths he had set forth in 1776 ought eventually to doom the institution in the United States. Early in his career he tried unsuccessfully to facilitate the manumission of slaves in Virginia, and in the 1780s he worked hard to have slavery abolished in the new western territories. But unlike Washington, he himself was never able to free all his slaves. More than that, as recent historians have emphasized, he bought, bred, and flogged his slaves and hunted down fugitives in much the same way his fellow Virginia planters did—all the while declaring that American slavery was not as bad as that of the ancient Romans.[8]

Some recent historians have even claimed that Jefferson's attitudes and actions toward blacks are so repugnant at present that identifying the Sage of Monticello with antislavery actually discredits the reform movement. Jefferson could never really imagine freed blacks living in a white man's America, and throughout his life he insisted that the emancipation of the slaves had to be accompanied by their expulsion from the country. He wanted all blacks sent to the West Indies, or Africa, or anywhere out of the United States. In the end, it has been said, Jefferson loaded such conditions on the abolition of slavery that the antislavery movement could scarcely get off the ground. In response to the pleas of younger men that he speak out against slavery he offered only excuses for delay.[9]

His remedy of expulsion was based on racial fear and antipathy. While he had no apprehensions about mingling the blood of the white man with that of the Indian, he never ceased expressing his "great aversion" to miscegenation between blacks and whites. When the Roman slave was freed, he "might mix with, without staining the blood of his master." When the black slave was freed, however, he had "to be removed beyond the reach of mixture." Although Jefferson believed that the Indians were uncivilized, he always admired them and made all sorts of environmental explanations for their differences from whites. Yet he was never able to do the same for the African American. Instead he continually suspected that the black man was inherently inferior to the white in both body and mind.[10]

It has been suggested that Jefferson's obsession with black sensuality shared by so many other Americans was largely a projection of his own repressed—and apparently in the case of his attractive mulatto slave Sally Hemings not-so-repressed—libidinal desires. The charge that Jefferson maintained Hemings as his mistress for decades and fathered several children by her was first made by an unscrupulous newspaperman, James Callender, in 1802. Since the publication in 1998 of the DNA test results showing that someone in the male Jefferson line fathered the children of Sally Hemings, most historians have concluded that Jefferson was indeed intimate with his household slave and fathered at least some of the Hemings children. In this respect his behavior was no different from that of other southern planters.[11]

Because some historians have continued to deny that Jefferson was the father of the Hemings children, the debate lingers but seems less and less relevant. Whether the Hemings relationship actually existed or not, there is no denying that Jefferson presided over a household in which miscegenation that he believed was morally repugnant was taking place.[12] Thus any attempt to make Jefferson's Monticello a model patriarchal plantation is fatally compromised at the outset.

Everyone, it seems, sees America in Jefferson. So the shame and guilt that Jefferson must have suffered from his involvement in slavery and racial mixing best represent the shame and guilt that white Americans feel in their tortured relations with blacks. Where Jefferson for Vernon Louis Parrington and his generation of the 1920s, 1930s, and 1940s was the solution to America's difficulties, Jefferson for this present generation has become the problem. The Jefferson that emerges out of much recent scholarship therefore resembles the America many critics have visualized in the past four decades: self-righteous, guilt-ridden, racist, doctrinaire, and filled with liberal pieties that under stress are easily sacrificed.

Wherever we Americans have a struggle over what kind of people we are, there we will find Jefferson. Jefferson stood for the rights of individuals, and these rights have been carried to extremes in recent years. So Jefferson and his Declaration of Independence are at fault.[13] Actually Jefferson's Federalist critics in the eighteenth century were even more harsh on his obsession with rights. He talked endlessly of rights, said one typical Federalist satirist, and loved them so much that he promoted the rights of weeds to flourish. And why not? Doesn't each plant have "an equal right to live. . . . And why should wheat and barley thrive/ Despotic tyrants of the field?"[14]

Others have raised the possibility that America was not always a liberal, capitalistic society devoted to individual rights. If so, then our image of Jefferson as the representative American would have to change. Thus in the historiographical upheaval of the 1970s and 1980s, involving the recovery in revolutionary America of a classical republican culture that emphasized virtue, corruption, and the public good rather than private rights and profit making, Jefferson necessarily became a central bone of contention. In light of this classical republican tradition, he lost his reputation for being a simple follower of Locke concerned only with individual rights. Instead he became a stoical classicist frightened by cities, money-making, and corruption and obsessed with inculcating the proper social and moral conditions to sustain an agrarian republic of independent yeomen farmers who were free of the marketplace.

Some historians—particularly J. G. A Pocock—in their excitement over this discovery of a tradition of classical republicanism in early America, got carried away and declared that the American Revolution, far from being a progressive event moving America into a new liberal, capitalistic world, was in fact "the last great act of the Renaissance." Since America had been born in a "dread of modernity," its spokesman, Jefferson, had to be backward-looking and opposed to the great economic changes sweeping through the Atlantic world.[15]

This was too much for other historians, who were eager to recover what was still living and progressive in the thought of Thomas Jefferson. When Garry Wills in *Inventing America* (1978) argued that Jefferson's Declaration of Independence owed less to the possessive individualism of John Locke than to the communitarian sentiments of the Scottish moralist Francis Hutcheson, scholars were quick to reassert Locke's influence.[16] After all, the character of America was at stake. One critic even accused Wills's emphasizing Jefferson's communitarianism of aiming "to supply the history of the Republic with as pink a dawn as possible."[17] Several historians—especially Joyce Appleby—set about restoring some needed balance to our understanding of the Revolution and of course Thomas Jefferson. Others of the founders may have been elitist, backward-looking, and pessimistic about the loss of virtue, but, said Appleby, certainly not

Jefferson. Jefferson may have been a student of the classics, but he never accepted the antique notion that men achieve fulfillment only in the public arena. And he may have been an agrarian, but he was a modern one who accepted commerce. "More than any other figure in his generation," said Appleby, "Jefferson integrated a program of economic development and a policy for nation-building into a radical moral theory." He was "not the heroic loser in a battle against modernity" but the liberal, progressive winner, confident of the future and eager to promote the individual's right to pursue happiness and further the commercial prosperity of America free from the deadening hand of government. The American people, argued Appleby, were less concerned with virtue, corruption, and community than with equality, private rights, and the selling of their produce all over the Atlantic world, and in the 1790s they saw in Jefferson and his Democratic-Republican party the proper agency for their optimistic hopes and dreams. "Jefferson," wrote Appleby, "rallied his countrymen with a vision of the future that joined their materialism to a new morality" built on his sublime faith in the self-governing capacities of free individuals.[18]

So Jefferson was back leading Americans into their democratic, commercial future, a symbol once again of liberal America. But if this means that Jefferson becomes too much a supporter of capitalism, then we have the work of Richard K. Matthews as an antidote. Matthews has discovered "a different, alternative Jefferson" for a different, alternative America, "a Jefferson who not only presents a radical critique of American market society but also provides an image for—if not a road map to—a consciously made, legitimately democratic American future." Matthews's Jefferson believed in permanent revolution, a kind of communitarian anarchism, and widespread political participation by the people. He was, concludes Matthews, an authentic American democratic radical.[19]

So it has gone for much of our history, Jefferson standing for America and carrying the moral character of the country on his back. No historical figure can bear this kind of symbolic burden and still remain a real person. Beneath all the images, beneath all the allegorical Jeffersons, there once was a human being with every human frailty and foible. Certainly Jefferson's words and ideas transcended his time, but he himself did not.

The human Jefferson was essentially a man of the eighteenth century, a very intelligent and bookish slaveholding southern planter, enlightened and progressive, no doubt, but, like all human beings, possessing as many weaknesses as strengths, as much folly as wisdom, as much blindness as foresight.

Jefferson was tall—six feet two—and gangling, with a reddish freckled complexion, bright hazel eyes, and copper-colored hair, which he tended to wear unpowdered in a queue. Unlike his fellow revolutionary John Adams, whom he both fought and befriended for fifty years, he was reserved, self-possessed, and incurably optimistic. He disliked personal controversy and was always charming in face-to-face relations with both friends and enemies. But at a distance he could hate, and thus many of his opponents concluded that he was two-faced and duplicitous.

He was undoubtedly complicated. He mingled the most lofty visions of the spread of liberty and democracy everywhere with astute backroom politicking. He spared himself nothing and was a compulsive shopper, yet he extolled the simple yeoman farmer who was free from the lures of the marketplace. He hated the obsessive moneymaking, the proliferating banks, and the liberal capitalistic world that emerged in the northern states in the early nineteenth century, but no one in America did more to bring that world about. Although he kept the most tidy and meticulous accounts of his daily transactions, he never added up his profits and losses. He thought public debts were the curse of a healthy state, yet his private debts kept mounting as he borrowed and borrowed again to meet his rising expenditures. He was a sophisticated man of the world who loved no place better than his beloved and remote mountaintop home in Virginia.

It is true that much of Jefferson's thinking was conventional, though, as has been pointed out, he did have "an extraordinary gift of lending grace to conventionalities."[20] He had to be conventional, or he could never have had the impact he had on his contemporaries. His writing of the Declaration of Independence, he later correctly recalled, was "not to find out new principles, or new arguments, never before thought of . . . ; but to place before mankind the common sense of the subject, in terms so plain and firm as to command their assent, and to justify ourselves in the independent stand we are compelled to take."[21]

Jefferson's extraordinary impressionability, learning, and virtuosity were the sources of his conventionality. He was very well read, extremely sensitive to the avant-garde intellectual currents of his day, and eager to discover just what was the best, most politically correct, and most enlightened in the world of the eighteenth century. It was his insatiable hunger for knowledge and the remarkable receptivity of his antennae for all that was new and progressive that put him at the head of the American Enlightenment.

The eighteenth-century Enlightenment represented the pushing back of the boundaries of darkness and what was called Gothic barbarism and the spreading of light and knowledge. This struggle occurred on many fronts. Some saw the central battle taking place in natural science and in the increasing understanding of nature. Some saw it occurring mostly in religion with the tempering of enthusiasm and the elimination of superstition. Others saw it taking place mainly in politics, in the driving back of the forces of tyranny and in the creating of new free governments. Still others saw it in the spread of civility and refinement and in the increase in the small, seemingly insignificant ways that life was being made easier, more polite, more comfortable, more enjoyable for more and more people. In one way or another all these Enlightenment activities involved the imposition of order and reason on the world. To contemplate aesthetically an ordered universe and to know the best that was thought and said in the world—that was enlightenment.

Jefferson participated fully in all these aspects of the eighteenth-century Enlightenment. He was probably the American revolutionary leader most taken with the age's liberal prescriptions for enlightenment, gentility, and refinement. He was born in 1743 the son of a wealthy but uneducated and ungenteel planter from western Virginia. He attended the College of

William and Mary, the first of his father's family to attend college. Like many of the revolutionary leaders who were also the first of their families to acquire liberal arts educations in college, he wanted a society led by an aristocracy of talent and taste. For too long men had been judged by who their fathers were or whom they married. In a new enlightened republican society they would be judged by merit and virtue and taste alone.

Jefferson was not one to let his feelings show, but even today we can sense beneath the placid surface of his autobiography, written in 1821 at the age of seventy-seven, some of his anger at all those Virginians who prided themselves on their genealogies and judged men by their family backgrounds. In the opening pages Jefferson tells us that the lineage of his Welsh father was lost in obscurity; he was able to find in Wales only two references to his father's family. His mother, on the other hand, was a Randolph, one of the most distinguished families of Virginia. The Randolphs, Jefferson said with about as much derision as he ever allowed himself, "trace their pedigree far back in England & Scotland, to which let every one ascribe the faith & merit he chooses."[22] He went on to describe his efforts in 1776 in Virginia to bring down that "distinct set of families" that had used several legal devices to confine the inheritance of property to the eldest son (primogeniture) and to special lines of heirs (entail) to form themselves "into a Patrician order, distinguished by the splendor and luxury of their establishments." Historians have often thought Jefferson exaggerated the power of primogeniture and entail and this "Patrician order." Not only was the docking of entails very common in Virginia, but the "Patrician order" does not appear all that different from its challengers. However, Jefferson clearly saw a difference, and it rankled him. The privileges of this "aristocracy of wealth," he wrote, needed to be destroyed in order "to make an opening for the aristocracy of virtue and talent," of which he considered himself a prime example. Such natural aristocrats, he said were "the most precious gift of nature, for the instruction, the trusts, and government of society."[23]

To become a natural aristocrat, one had to acquire the attributes of a natural aristocrat: enlightenment, gentility, and taste. We shall never un-

derstand the young Jefferson until we appreciate the intensity and earnestness of his desire to become the most cosmopolitan, the most liberal, the
most genteel, and the most enlightened gentleman in all America. From
the outset he was the sensitive provincial quick to condemn the back-
wardness of his fellow colonials. At college and later while studying law
at Williamsburg he played the violin, learned French, and acquired the
tastes and refinements of the larger world. At frequent dinners with Governor Francis Fauquier and his teachers William Small and George
Wythe, Jefferson said he "heard more good sense, more rational and philosophical conversations than in all my life besides." Looking back, he called
Williamsburg "the finest school of manners and morals that ever existed
in America."[24] Although as a young man he had seen very few works of
art, he knew from reading and conversation what was considered good,
and in 1771 he wrote a list, ranging from the *Apollo Belvedere* to a Raphael
cartoon, of the celebrated paintings, drawings, and sculptures that he
hoped to acquire in copies. By 1782, "without having quitted his own
country," this earnest autodidact with a voracious appetite for learning had
become, as the French visitor the chevalier de Chastellux noted, "an American who . . . is a Musician, Draftsman, Surveyor, Astronomer, Natural
Philosopher, Jurist, and Statesman."[25]

In time Jefferson became quite proud of his gentility, his taste, and his
liberal brand of manners. He came to see himself as a kind of impresario
for America, rescuing his countrymen from their "deplorable barbarism"
by introducing them to the finest and most enlightened aspects of European culture.[26] When Americans in the 1780s realized that a statue of
Washington was needed, "there could be no question raised," he wrote
from Paris, "as to the Sculptor who should be employed, the reputation
of Monsr. Houdon of this city being unrivalled in Europe." No American could stand up to his knowledge. When Washington timidly expressed misgivings about Houdon's doing the statue in Roman style, he
quickly backed down in the face of Jefferson's frown, unwilling, as he said,
"to oppose my judgment to the taste of Connoisseurs."[27]

Jefferson's excitement over the sixteenth-century Italian Andrea Palladio, whose *Four Books of Architecture* was virtually unknown in America, was that of the provincial discovering the cosmopolitan and discriminating taste of the larger world. He became contemptuous and even ashamed of the "Gothic" Georgian architecture of his native Virginia, and he sought in Monticello to build a house that would do justice to those models that harked back to Roman antiquity. In the 1780s he badgered his Virginia colleagues into erecting as the new state capitol in Richmond a magnificent copy of the Maison Carrée, a Roman temple from the first century A.D. at Nîmes because he wanted an American public building that would be a model for the people's "study and imitation" and "an object and proof of national good taste." It was a building, he said, that "has pleased universally for near 2000 years." Almost single-handedly he became responsible for making America's public buildings resemble Roman temples.[28]

No American knew more about wine than Jefferson. On his trips around Europe in 1787 and 1788 he spent a great deal of time investigating French, Italian, and German vineyards and wineries and making arrangements for the delivery of wine to the United States. Everyone in America acknowledged his expertise in wine, and three presidents sought his advice about what wines to serve at presidential dinners. In everything, from gardening and food to music, painting, and poetry, Jefferson wanted the latest and most enlightened in English or European fashion.

It is easy to make fun of Jefferson and his parvenu attitudes and behavior. But it would be a mistake to dismiss his obsession with art and good taste merely as a trivial affectation or as the simple posturing and putting on of airs of an American provincial who would be the perfect gentleman. Jefferson may have been more earnest and enthusiastic about such matters than the other revolutionary leaders, but he was by no means unique in his concern for refining the sensibilities of himself and those of the American people. This was a moral and political imperative of all of the founders. To refine popular taste was in fact a moral and political imperative of all the enlightened of the eighteenth century.

The fine arts, good taste, and even good manners had political implications. As the English philosopher Lord Shaftesbury had preached, morality and good taste were allied: "the science of virtuosi and that of virtue itself become, in a manner, one and the same."[29] Connoisseurship, politeness, and genteel refinement were connected with public morality and political leadership. Those who had good taste were enlightened, and those who were enlightened were virtuous.

But virtuous in a modern, not an ancient, manner. Such a new modern virtue was associated with affability and sociability, with love and benevolence. This affability and sociability were connected with good taste and with politeness, which the Pennsylvanian James Wilson and his friend William White defined in 1768 as "*the natural and graceful expression of the social virtues.*" Politeness and refinement tamed and domesticated the severe classical conception of virtue. Promoting social affection was in fact the object of the civilizing process. "What does the idea of politeness and refinement of a people suppose?" asked a writer in the *New York Magazine* of 1792. "Is it not this, that they cultivate intimate friendships; that they mutually sympathize with the misfortunes of each other, and that a passionate show of affections is promoted."[30] This new social virtue was less Spartan and more Addisonian, less the harsh self-sacrifice of antiquity and more the willingness to get along with others for the sake of peace and prosperity. Virtue became identified with politeness, good taste, and one's instinctive sense of morality.[31] As the eighteenth-century Scottish philosopher Lord Kames said, "a taste in the fine arts goes hand in hand with the moral sense, to which indeed it is nearly allied."[32]

To understand this new social virtue, this new mingling of politeness and morality, Jefferson did not have to read the works of Lord Kames, Francis Hutcheson, or any other of the Scottish moral sense school; the Englishmen Shaftesbury and Bishop Butler were no less important in spreading these ideas that politeness and refinement were natural social adhesives. And it was not just these great minds; there was hardly an educated person in all of eighteenth-century America who did not at one time or another try to describe people's moral sense and the natural forces of love and benevolence holding society together. Jefferson's emphasis on the moral sense was scarcely peculiar to him.

This modern virtue that Jefferson and others extolled was very different from that of the ancient republican tradition. Classical virtue had flowed from the citizen's participation in politics; government had been the source of his civic consciousness and public-spiritedness. But modern virtue flowed from the citizen's participation in society, not in government, which the liberal-minded increasingly saw as the source of the evils of the world. Society—the affairs of private social life—bred sympathy and the new domesticated virtue. Mingling in drawing rooms, clubs, and coffeehouses, partaking of the innumerable interchanges of the daily comings and goings of modern life, created affection and fellow feeling, which Jefferson and other liberals thought were all the adhesives really necessary to hold an enlightened people together. Some even argued that commerce, that traditional enemy of classical virtue, was in fact a source of modern virtue. Because it encouraged intercourse and confidence among people and nations, commerce, it was said, actually contributed to benevolence and fellow feeling.

Jefferson celebrated this superiority of society over government. Indeed, the conventional liberal division between society and government was the premise of his political thinking: his faith in the natural ordering of society, his belief in the common moral sense of ordinary people, his idea of minimal government. "Man," he said, "was destined for society. His morality, therefore, was to be formed to this object. He was endowed with a sense of right and wrong, merely relative to this. . . . The moral sense, or conscience, is as much a part of a man as his leg or arm. . . . This sense is submitted, indeed, in some degree, to the guidance of reason; but it is a small stock which is required for this." All human beings had "implanted in our breasts" this "love of others," this "moral instinct"; these "social dispositions" were what made democracy possible.[33]

The importance of this domesticated modern virtue to Jefferson's and other Americans' thinking can scarcely be exaggerated. Unlike classical virtue, it was not nostalgic or backward-looking but progressive and indeed radical. It laid the basis for all reform movements of the nineteenth century as well as for all subsequent modern liberal thinking. We still yearn for a world in which we all will love one another.[34]

Probably no American leader took this belief in the natural sociability of people more seriously than Jefferson. His scissors-and-paste redoing of the New Testament in the early years of the nineteenth century, his Jefferson Bible, grew out of his desire to reconcile Christianity with the Enlightenment and at the same time to answer all those critics who said that he was an enemy of all religion. Jefferson discovered that Jesus, with his prescription for each of us to love our neighbors as ourselves, actually spoke directly to the modern enlightened age. Jefferson's version of the New Testament offered a much-needed morality of social harmony for a new republican society.

Jefferson's faith in the natural sociability of people also lay behind his belief in minimal government. In fact Jefferson would have fully understood the Western world's recent interest in devolution and localist democracy. He believed in nationhood but not in the modern idea of the state. He hated all bureaucracy and all the coercive instruments of government; he sometimes gave the impression that government was only a device by which the few attempted to rob, cheat, and oppress the many. He certainly never accepted the modern idea of the state as an entity possessing a life of its own, distinct from both rulers and ruled. For Jefferson there could be no power independent of the people, in whom he had an absolute faith.

ALTHOUGH HE WAS NOT a modern democrat, assuming as he did that a natural aristocracy would lead the country, he had a confidence in the capacity and the virtue of the people to elect that aristocracy that was unmatched by any of the other founders. Jefferson, like the other founders, had doubts about all officials in government, even the popularly elected representatives in the lower houses of the legislatures ("173 despots would surely be as oppressive as one," he said of the Virginia House of Delegates

in 1785), but he always thought that the people, if undisturbed by demagogues or Federalist monarchists, would eventually set matters right. He
saw little potential conflict between what we today call positive and negative liberty, between the people and individual rights. He was one of
those who paid no attention to what his friend Madison called that "essential distinction, too little heeded, between assumptions of power by the
General Government, in opposition to the will of the constituent body,
and assumptions by the constituent body through the Government as the
organ of its will."[35] It was never the people but only their elected agents
that were at fault. The many were always being set upon and abused by
the few, and those few included all the officials of government, even those
elected by the people.

Not only did Jefferson thus refuse to recognize the structure and institutions of a modern state, but he scarcely accepted the basic premise of
a state—that is, its presumed monopoly of legitimate control over a pre-
scribed territory. For him, during his first presidential administration, the
United States was really just a loosely bound confederation, not all that
different from the government of the former Articles of Confederation.
Hence his vision of an expanding empire of liberty over a huge continent
posed no problems for his relaxed idea of a state. "Who can limit the extent to which the federative principle may operate effectively?" he asked
in his second inaugural address. In fact Jefferson always conceived of his
"empire of liberty" as one of like principles, not of like boundaries. As long
as Americans believed certain things, they remained Americans, regardless of the boundaries of the government they happened to be in. At times
he was remarkably indifferent to the possibility that a western confederacy might break away from the eastern United States. What did it matter? he asked in 1804. "Those of the western confederacy will be as much
our children & descendents as those of the eastern."[36]

Jefferson and his fellow Republicans saw all the western land as the
means of escaping from the fate of the European nations. With land
available for farmers far into the future, America's social development
could be retarded, and the country would not be compelled to enter the

final commercial stage of manufacturing, luxury, and urban decadence that was afflicting the European states. Believing that no one in his right mind would abandon farming to work in urban industry, Jefferson and his followers believed that America's expansion across space would save them from the ravages of time. With so much land to farm, a surplus landless population would not develop, as it had in Europe, and Americans would not have to migrate to cities in search of work in manufacturing luxuries. This agrarian vision of America's future was fundamental to the separation between the Jeffersonian Republicans and the Federalists.[37]

It was not the only thing separating them. Jefferson's contempt for the modern state and his extraordinary faith in the natural sociability of people as a substitute for the traditional force of government were equally important. When the Jeffersonians extended their faith in the natural sociability of people to the international sphere, the Federalists and especially Alexander Hamilton could only dismiss them as hopeless pie-in-the-sky dreamers. Jefferson and other enlightened leaders came to believe that commerce among nations in international affairs was the equivalent to affection among people in domestic affairs; both were natural expressions of relationships that needed to be freed of monarchical obstructions and interventions. Hence, in 1776 and the years following, Jefferson and other revolutionary idealists hoped to do for the world what they were doing for the society of the United States: change the way people related to one another. They looked forward to a rational world in which corrupt monarchical diplomacy and secret alliances, balances of power, and dynastic rivalries would be replaced by the natural ties of commerce. If the people of the various nations were left alone to exchange goods freely among themselves, then international politics would become republicanized and pacified, and indeed war itself would be eliminated. Jefferson's and the Republican party's "candid and liberal" experiments in "peaceable coercion"—the various efforts of the United States to use nonimportation and ultimately Jefferson's disastrous Embargo of 1807–09 to change international behavior—were the inevitable consequences of this sort of idealistic republican confidence in the power of commerce.[38]

Although Jefferson's thinking may often have been conventional, it was usually an enlightened conventional radicalism that he espoused. So eager was he to possess the latest and most liberal of eighteenth century ideas that he could easily get carried away. He, like "others of great genius," had "a habit," as Madison gently put it in 1823, "of expressing in strong and round terms impressions of the moment." So Jefferson alone of the founding fathers was unperturbed by Shays's Rebellion. "I like a little rebellion now and then," he said. "It is like a storm in the Atmosphere." It was too bad that some people were killed, but "the tree of liberty must be refreshed from time to time with the blood of patriots and tyrants. It is its natural manure." Similar rhetorical exaggeration accompanied his response to the bloody excesses of the French Revolution. Because "the liberty of the whole earth" depended on the success of the French Revolution, he wrote in 1793, lives would have to be lost. "Rather than it should have failed, I would have seen half the earth desolated. Were there but an Adam & an Eve left in every country, & left free, it would be better than as it now is."[39] Unlike Coleridge and Wordsworth and other disillusioned European liberals, Jefferson remained a champion of the French Revolution to the end.

He saw it after all as a movement on behalf of the rights of man that had originated in the American Revolution. And to the American Revolution and the rights of man he remained dedicated until his death. In the last letter he wrote he expressed his lifelong belief that the American Revolution would be "the signal of arousing men to burst the chains under which monkish ignorance and superstition had persuaded them to bind themselves, and to assume the blessings and security of self-government." He foresaw that eventually the whole world "(to some parts sooner, to others later, but finally to all)" would follow the American lead. Sentiments like these became the source of America's messianic sense of obligation to promote the spread of freedom and democracy throughout the world.[40]

YET DURING Jefferson's final years in retirement these expressions of confidence in the future progress of the Enlightenment came fewer and farther between. The period between Jefferson's retirement from the presidency in 1809 and his death in 1826 was a tumultuous one in American history, marked by war with the British and Indians, a severe commercial panic, the rapid growth of democracy and evangelical religion, and the Missouri crisis over the spread of slavery. It was not a happy time for Jefferson. To be sure, there was the Sage of Monticello relaxing among his family and friends and holding court on top of his mountain for scores of visiting admirers. There was his reconciliation with John Adams and the wonderful correspondence between the two old revolutionaries that followed. There was his hard-fought establishment of the University of Virginia. But there was not much else to comfort him.

The world around him, the world he had helped create, was rapidly changing, in ways that Jefferson found bewildering and sometimes even terrifying. The American Revolution was unfolding in radical and unexpected ways. American society was becoming more democratic and more capitalistic, and Jefferson was not prepared for either development. By the end of his life Jefferson had moments of apprehension that the American Revolution, to which he had devoted his life, was in danger of failing. In response he spoke and acted in ways that are not in accord with what we now like to think of as Jeffersonian principles. He turned inward and began conjuring thoughts, stirring up demons, and spouting dogmas in a manner that many subsequent historians and biographers have found embarrassing and puzzling.

After Jefferson retired from public life in 1809, he became more narrow-minded and localist than he had ever been before. He had always prided himself on his cosmopolitanism, yet upon his retirement from the presidency he returned to Virginia and never left it. In fact, he almost never again lost sight of his beloved Blue Ridge. He cut himself off from many of the current sources of knowledge of the outside world and became, as one of his visitors, George Ticknor, noted, "singularly ignorant & insensible on the subjects of passing politics." He took only one newspaper, the *Richmond Enquirer*, and seemed to have no strong interest in receiving mail. In all this he differed remarkably from his friend and neighbor James Madison. Madison, said Ticknor, "receives multitudes of newspapers, keeps a servant always in waiting for the arrival of the Post—and takes anxious note of all passing events."[41]

Jefferson's turning inward was matched by a relative decline in the place of Virginia in the Union. In 1776 Virginia was the richest and most populous state in the country and rightly regarded itself as the heart and soul of the nation. By the 1820s, however, the state was rapidly becoming a besieged and bewildered backwater whose principal business was the selling of slaves. Decay was everywhere, and Jefferson felt it at Monticello. Despite his lifelong aversion to public debts, his private debts kept mounting, and he kept borrowing, taking out new loans to meet old ones. He tried to sell his land, and when he could not, he sold his slaves instead. He feared that he might lose Monticello and complained constantly of his debts, but he refused to cut back on his lavish hospitality and expensive wine purchases.

Unable to comprehend the economic forces that were transforming the country and destroying the upper South, Jefferson blamed the banks and the speculative spirit of the day for both his and Virginia's miseries. It is true that he accepted the existence of commerce and, after the War of 1812, even some limited manufacturing for the United States. But the commerce he accepted was tame and traditional stuff compared with the aggressive commerce that was taking over northern America in the early nineteenth century. Jefferson's idea of commerce essentially involved the sale abroad of agricultural staples—wheat, tobacco, and cotton. His commerce was not the incessant trucking and trading, the endless buying and selling with each other that came to characterize the emerging Yankee world. That kind of dynamic domestic commerce and all the capitalistic accoutrements that went with it—banks, stock markets, liquid capital, paper money—Jefferson feared and despised.

He did want comforts and prosperity for his American farmers, but like some modern liberals, he had little or no appreciation of the economic forces that made such prosperity and comforts possible. He had no comprehension of banks and thought that the paper money they issued was

designed "to enrich swindlers at the expense of the honest and industrious part of the nation." He could not understand how "legerdemain tricks
upon paper can produce as solid wealth or hard labor in the earth. It is
vain for common sense to urge that *nothing* can produce *nothing*."[42] As far
as he was concerned, the buying and selling of stocks and the raising of
capital were simply licentious speculation and wild gambling, all symptoms of "commercial avarice and corruption."[43]

The ultimate culprit in the degeneration of America, he thought, was
the corrupt and tyrannical course of the national government. The Missouri crisis of 1819–20, provoked by northern efforts to limit the spread of
slavery in the West, was to Jefferson "a fire bell in the night," a threat to
the Union and to the revolutionary experiment in republicanism. He believed that the federal government's proposed restriction on the right of
the people of Missouri to own slaves violated the Constitution and men-
aced self-government. Congress, he said, had no right "to regulate the conditions of the different descriptions of men composing a state." Only each
state had the "exclusive right" to regulate slavery.[44] If the federal government arrogated to itself that right, then it would next declare all slaves in
the country free, "in which case all the whites within the United States
south of the Potomac and Ohio must evacuate their States, and most fortunate those who can do it first."[45]

Jefferson despaired of stopping the spread of federal consolidation and
commercial values and bemoaned "the degeneracy of public opinion from
our original and free principles." He became a bitter critic of the usurpations of the Supreme Court and a more strident defender of states' rights
than he had been even in 1798, when he wrote the Kentucky Resolution, justifying the right of a state to nullify federal laws. While Madison remained
a nationalist and upheld the right of the Supreme Court to interpret the
Constitution, Jefferson lent his wholehearted support to the most dog-
matic, impassioned, and sectional-minded elements in Virginia, including
the arch state rightists Spencer Roane and John Randolph. He became
parochial and alarmist, and his zeal for states' rights, as even his sympathetic biographer Dumas Malone admitted, "bordered on fanaticism."[46]

He was more frightened and fanatical than he had to be, and he went further backward to the principles of 1798 than he had to go, further certainly than his friend and fellow Virginian James Madison ever went. For someone as optimistic and sanguine in temperament as Jefferson usually was, he had a lot of gloomy and terrifying moments in the years between 1809 and 1826. What happened? What accounts for these moments of gloom and these expressions of fanaticism? How can we explain Jefferson's uncharacteristic but increasingly frequent doubts about the future?

Certainly his personal troubles—his rising debts, the threat of bankruptcy, the fear of losing Monticello—were part of it, but they are not the whole explanation. Something more is involved in accounting for the incongruous nature of his years of retirement than these outside forces, and that something seems to lie within Jefferson himself, in his principles and outlook, in his deep and long-held faith in popular democracy and the future.

No one of the revolutionary leaders believed more strongly in progress and in the capacity of the American people for self-government than did Jefferson. No one was more convinced that the Enlightenment was on the march against the forces of medieval barbarism and darkness and religious superstition and enthusiasm. In fact so sure was he of the future progress of American society that he was intellectually and emotionally unprepared for what happened in the years following his retirement from public office. He was unprepared for the emergence of ordinary obscure people into dominance, unprepared for the very popular revolution that he and his Democratic-Republican party had inspired. In the end Jefferson was victimized by his overweening confidence in the people and by his naive hopefulness in the future. The Enlightenment, the democratic revolution he had contributed so much to bring about, and his own liberal and rosy temperament finally did him in.

None of the other major founding fathers was as optimistic and confident of the people as Jefferson was. All the problems of the present, he believed, would eventually be taken care of by the people. This sublime faith in the people and the future is the source of the symbolic power he has had for succeeding generations of Americans. He was never more American than when he told John Adams in 1816 that he liked "the dreams of the future better than the history of the past."[47]

He was always optimistic; indeed, he was a virtual Pollyanna about everything. His expectations always outran reality, whether it was French aristocrats who turned out to be less liberal than his friend Lafayette, or garden vegetables that never came up, or misbehaving students at the University of Virginia who violated their honor code, or an American Revolution that actually allowed people to pursue their pecuniary happiness. He was the pure American innocent. He had little understanding of man's capacity for evil and had no tragic sense whatsoever.

Through his long public career while others were wringing their hands, Jefferson remained calm and hopeful. He knew slavery was a great evil, but he believed his generation could do little about it. Instead he counseled patience and a reliance on the young who would follow. When one of those younger men, Edward Coles, actually called on Jefferson in 1814 to lend his voice in the struggle against slavery, he could only offer his confidence in the future. "The hour of emancipation is advancing, in the march of time. It will come. . . ."[48]

It was the same with every difficulty. In one way or another he expected things to work out. In 1814 he saw his financial troubles coming at him and his household like "an approaching wave in a storm; still I think we shall live as long, eat as much, and drink as much, as if the wave had already glided under the ship. Somehow or other these things find their way out as they come in, and so I suppose they will now."[49] Was not progress on the march and were not science and enlightenment everywhere pushing back the forces of ignorance, superstition, and darkness? The future, he believed, was on his side and on the side of the people. A liberal, democratic society would be capable of solving every problem, if not in his lifetime, surely in the coming years.

But Jefferson lived too long, and the future and the coming generation were not what he had expected. His correspondence in the last decades of his life was punctuated with laments over "the rising generation, of which I once had sanguine hopes."[50] Although he continued in his public letters, especially to foreigners, to affirm that progress and civilization were still on the march, in private he became more and more apprehensive of the future. He sensed that American society, including Virginia, might not be getting better after all but actually going backward. The people were not becoming more refined, more polite, and more sociable; if anything, they were more barbaric and more factional than they had been. Jefferson was frightened by the divisions in the country and by the popularity of Andrew Jackson, whom he regarded as a man of violent passions and unfit for the presidency. He felt overwhelmed by the new paper money business culture sweeping the country, and he never appreciated how much his democratic and egalitarian principles had contributed to its rise.

Ordinary people, in whom he placed so much confidence, more certainly than his friend Madison, were not becoming more enlightened. Superstition and bigotry, which Jefferson identified with organized religion, were actually reviving, released by the democratic revolution he had led. He was temperamentally incapable of understanding the deep popular strength of the evangelical Christian forces that were seizing control of American culture in these early decades of the nineteenth century. He became what we might call a confused secular humanist in the midst of real moral majorities. While Jefferson in 1822 was still predicting that there was not a young man now alive who would not die a Unitarian, Methodists and Baptists and other evangelicals were gaining adherents by the tens of thousands in the Second Great Awakening and transforming American society. In response all Jefferson could do was blame the defunct New England Federalists and an equally bewildered New England clergy for spreading both evangelical Christianity and capitalism throughout the country.

Jefferson's solution to this perceived threat from New England and its "pious young monks from Harvard and Yale" was to hunker down in Virginia and build a university that would perpetuate true republican principles.[51] "It is in our seminary," he told Madison, "that that vestal flame is to be kept alive."[52] Yet even building the university brought sorrow and shock. The Virginia legislature was not as eager to spend money for higher education as he expected. His support of the university became more of a political liability than an asset in the legislature.

The people actually seemed more sectarian and less rational than they had been at the time of the Revolution. They did not appear to know who he was, what he had done. Was this the new generation on which he rested all his hopes? During the last year of his life, at a moment, says his biographer Malone, of "uneasiness that he had never known before," Jefferson was pathetically reduced to listing his contributions during sixty-one years of public service in order to justify a legislative favor.[53] No wonder he sometimes felt cast off. "All, all dead!" he wrote to an old friend in 1825, "and ourselves left alone midst a new generation whom we know not, and who know not us."[54]

These were only small cracks in his optimism, only tinges of doubt in his democratic faith, but for an innocent like him they were enough. Jefferson went further in states' rights principles and in his fears of federal consolidation than Madison did because he had such higher expectations of the Revolution and the people. He had always invested so much more of himself intellectually and emotionally in the future and in popular democracy than Madison had. Jefferson was inspired by a vision of how things cold and should be. Madison tended much more to accept things as they were. Madison never lost his dark foreboding about the America yet to come, and he never shed his skepticism about the people and popular majorities. But Jefferson had nothing but the people and the future to fall back on; they were really all he ever believed in. That is why we remember Jefferson and not Madison.

Chapter Four

Alexander Hamilton and the Making of a Fiscal-Military State

A	LTHOUGH ALEXANDER HAMILTON, America's first
	secretary of the treasury, has never acquired for Americans
	the symbolic importance of Jefferson or Franklin, he has
developed some symbolic significance. During the latter part of the nineteenth century Hamilton emerged as the founder of big state financial
capitalism. In the 1890s the presidential campaign manager Mark Hanna
and the Republican party, along with many other Americans, came to li-
onize Hamilton as they did no other founder. Not only did they believe
that Hamilton had single-handedly created modern American capitalism,
but as John D. Morse, the editor of the American Statesman Series, declared in 1898, "he was the real maker of the government of the United
States."[1] When a Hall of Fame honoring distinguished Americans was established at New York University in 1900, Hamilton was the first person

selected. Theodore Roosevelt especially admired him. Even the Progressive reformer and first editor of the *New Republic* Herbert Croly called him "a sound thinker, the constructive statesman" who sponsored a "vigorous, positive, constructive national policy . . . that implied a faith in the powers of an efficient government to advance the national interest."[2]

Hamilton was undoubtedly a big government man, but because he also seemed to favor big business, conservative Republicans during the first part of the twentieth century continued to praise him. One of his early-twentieth-century biographers called him the first American businessman. "For as a man," wrote Robert Warshow in 1931, "he was not noble; as a politician, he was not an eminent success; as a statesman, apart from financial measures, he was not superior. But as a business man, not in all this period was any man to match him, nor in all the years of American history can any figure dwarf him in this, his natural field."[3]

With Republicans embracing Hamilton the businessman (it was the Coolidge administration that put him on the ten-dollar bill), the Democrats were naturally drawn to Thomas Jefferson, Hamilton's lifelong enemy. Indeed, the earlier conflict in the 1790s between these two founders seemed to many Democrats to presage the continuing struggle of American history between the forces of aristocracy and the forces of democracy. If Hamilton spoke for the business interests, then, said the Democrats, Jefferson spoke for the mass of the people.

In such a conflict the spokesman for the few could scarcely stand against the spokesman for the many. FDR knew the significance of symbols, and against all the logic of the New Deal, he made Jefferson, the great minimal government president, a Democratic party icon. When the Republicans relegated Jefferson to the little-used two-dollar bill, Roosevelt retaliated by placing him on the popular nickel and on the first-class three-cent stamp. With the New Deal's championing of Jefferson, climaxing with the building of the Jefferson Memorial in Washington in 1943 (which contains nary a Jeffersonian word about the beauties of small government), Hamilton's reputation went into decline, not to be revived until the decades following World War II. In the 1950s and early 1960s

Hamilton was celebrated for his nationalism, for his administrative genius, for his financial expertise, and for his hardheaded realism in foreign affairs. But someone as skeptical of the people as Hamilton could scarcely replace Jefferson as a symbol of America's democratic heritage.

The severe criticism of Jefferson's slaveholding and racial attitudes over the past several decades has offered an opportunity for some positive reappraisals of Hamilton. He was after all opposed to slavery and worked to end it in his home state of New York. Also, in a land of immigrants he was the only one of the leading founders not born in what became the United States. In a major exhibition in 2004–05 at the New-York Historical Society, Hamilton was once again celebrated as "the man who made modern America."

Despite periodic biographies and occasional op-ed tributes in the *Wall Street Journal*, it seems unlikely that Hamilton can ever acquire a warm place in the hearts of most Americans. Wall Street might erect a statue in his honor, but it is doubtful that an elaborate Hamilton Memorial will ever arise in the District of Columbia. Tens of thousands flock to Washington's Mount Vernon, Jefferson's Monticello, and now even Madison's Montpelier, but very few bother to visit Hamilton's home, the Grange, hidden on a back street in northern Manhattan. Many present-day liberal Democrats might find Hamilton's vision of a positive Leviathan state very appealing, but they would surely be turned off by his realpolitik view of the world, his desire to maintain a large standing army and build a strong military state, and his doubts about democracy. ("Democracy," Hamilton said in 1804, was "our real Disease," one that was poisoning the American "Empire.") Most present-day Republicans, for all their enthusiasm for Hamilton's vision of a powerful military machine, do not want a Leviathan state that manages the economy and taxes people. So for the foreseeable future Hamilton seems to have few friends among those who would use the founders to further their particular causes. Perhaps he was right when he lamented a few years before his death at the hands of Aaron Burr "that this American world was not made for me."[4]

Instead of trying to enlist Hamilton on behalf of one present-day cause or another, as we are wont to do with the founders, we might seek to understand this eighteenth-century statesman on his own terms and in his own time.

Hamilton was born in Nevis in the British West Indies in 1755 (though Hamilton thought he had been born in 1757). Because his father, James Hamilton, the younger son of a Scottish laird who had come to the Caribbean to make his fortune as a merchant, and his mother, Rachel Lavien, were not legally married, Hamilton's birth was illegitimate, a blemish that his later enemies never let him forget. John Adams's sneering comment that Hamilton was "the bastard brat of a Scotch pedlar" was only one of the more colorful reminders of his disreputable origins. After his father abandoned the family in 1765 and his mother died in 1768, the fourteen-year-old Hamilton ended up keeping the books for a merchant in St. Croix, yearning all the while for a war in order to escape from what he called his "groveling condition of a clerk . . . to which my fortune, etc., condemns me." This passion for war, jarring as it may be to us in the twenty-first century, is an important clue to Hamilton's temperament and to the aristocratic world in which he lived.

It was not a war, however, but the support of patrons that rescued him from the West Indies. Like many of the founders, he first attracted attention by something he had written, in his case a colorful description of a hurricane published in a local newspaper in 1772. A Presbyterian clergyman and other West Indian friends decided to send the promising young man to New York for an education. By the next year Hamilton was on his way to America. He never looked back.

Although he preferred Princeton to King's College (later Columbia) because it was "more republican," President John Witherspoon of Princeton would not let him take the accelerated program that he wanted, so Hamilton entered King's College as a special student in the fall of 1773. Still a teenager, he began contributing pieces on the patriot side of the deepening crisis with Great Britain, including in 1774 and 1775 two long, impressive pamphlets. With the outbreak of hostilities between Britain and the colonies in 1775 Hamilton at last had the war that he had longed for. By early 1776 he had become a captain of a New York artillery company.

After serving with distinction as an artillery officer with the Continental army and impressing his superiors, he was promoted in March 1777 at the age of twenty-two to lieutenant colonel and appointed to the staff of the commander in chief, General George Washington, as an aide-de-camp. Washington took to the young man at once and developed a fatherly affection toward him. Yet the relationship had to have had its moments of tension, for Hamilton was much too touchy about his honor for it to remain harmonious. Early in 1781 Washington expressed some anger at Hamilton's ten-minute delay in presenting himself, saying, "I must tell you Sir that you treat me with disrespect." Hamilton declared that he was not conscious of any disrespect, but exhibiting his hair-trigger temper, he resigned on the spot as Washington's aide. An hour later a remorseful Washington tried to patch things up, but the proud twenty-six-year-old Hamilton would have none of it.

Hamilton stayed on Washington's staff until a replacement aide could be found, all the while pleading with the commander in chief to give him a field command. When he threatened to resign his commission, Washington finally relented and at the end of July 1781 gave Hamilton the command of a New York light infantry battalion—just in time for the young commander to participate in the siege of Yorktown. So eager was Hamilton to show his scorn for death and earn military honor at Yorktown that he openly paraded his battalion in front of the enemy lines, leading one of his subordinate officers later to complain that Hamilton was an officer who "wantonly exposed the lives of his men."[5] Finally, after more pleading, he had his opportunity for glory, and on October 14, 1781, Hamilton led a successful bayonet night attack on a British redoubt; naturally he was first over the enemy parapet, shouting for his men to follow.

Because he was raised in the West Indies and came to the North American continent as a teenager, Hamilton had little of the emotional attachment to a particular colony or state that the other founders had (when Jefferson talked about "my country," he meant Virginia). Hamil-

ton was primed to think nationally, and from the outset of the Revolution he focused his attention on the government of the United States. As
early as 1779, even before the war was over, Hamilton was writing long,
thoughtful letters to prominent Americans about the defects of the Confederation and the ways for reforming it. Not only, he said, did the
Congress need the power to tax, but the government required "a proper
executive." Congress itself could never exert "energy," a word that he and
Washington both came to value. "It is impossible such a body, numerous
as it is, constantly fluctuating, can ever act with sufficient decision or with
system. Two thirds of the members, one half the time, cannot know what
has gone before." These calls for a stronger central government were soon
expanded and published in a series of impressive essays entitled "The
Continentalist" in a New York newspaper.[6]

In 1782 the New York Assembly elected Hamilton, at age twenty-
seven, one of its representatives to the Confederation Congress. There he
met James Madison of Virginia, and a fruitful collaboration for the
strengthening of the national government was born. This partnership led
from the stymied efforts to add to the powers of the Confederation in the
early 1780s to the Annapolis Convention in 1786, then to the Philadelphia
Convention in 1787, and finally to the production of *The Federalist*, the
eighty-five essays written in New York in 1787 and 1788 in support of the
Constitution that have become a classic of American political thought. It
was Hamilton who conceived of *The Federalist* and talked Madison and
John Jay into helping him. Because of illness, Jay wrote only five papers.
Of the remainder, Madison wrote twenty-nine, Hamilton fifty-one.

Although the hand of each author can often be uncovered under the
pseudonym Publius, it is remarkable how much the essays assume a consistent tone. The authors were not political theorists but working politicians. They were trying to express not what they truly believed about the
Constitution but what would best counter the Anti-Federalist arguments
against it. During the Philadelphia Convention Hamilton had proposed
a president and a senate elected for life and had declared that the British
government was "the best in the world" and that "he doubted much

whether any thing short of it would do in America."[7] But in the ratification debates in 1787 and 1788 he hid whatever doubts he had about the proposed Constitution and made the strongest case he could for it. In this respect he was no different from his collaborator Madison, the so-called father of the Constitution, who believed at the end of the convention that the final document differed so much from his original plan that it would inevitably fail.

By 1789, at age thirty-four, Hamilton was on the verge of his greatest accomplishments. He had risen fast and married well, to Elizabeth Schuyler, daughter of one of the most important families of New York. He impressed everyone he met. Although he was short—about five feet seven—and slight in build, his excitable nature commanded attention, and men and women were readily attracted to him. To Catherine Schuyler, the youngest of the Schuyler sisters, he "exhibited a natural, yet unassuming superiority." With a "high expansive forehead, a nose of the Grecian mold, a dark bright eye, and the lines of a mouth expressing decision and courage," he had "a face never to be forgotten."[8] But it was his ready grasp of statecraft that really impressed. The worldly French politician and diplomat Talleyrand, who knew kings and emperors and spent some time in the United States in the mid-1790s as a refugee from the French Revolution, actually ranked Hamilton over Napoleon and William Pitt as the greatest statesman of the age.

In September 1789 President Washington appointed Hamilton secretary of the treasury. It was almost a preordained choice. Washington's confidants like Robert Morris, the financier of the Revolution, knew that Hamilton was the best man for the job, but it was Washington who most wanted him as secretary of the treasury. Like many revolutionary army officers, Washington and Hamilton had experienced the war from the center and had developed a continental perspective and a passion for the Union that neither ever lost. Although the two men had similar realistic assumptions about human nature and shared a common outlook on the future of the United States, it was actually Washington's sensitive appreciation of his surrogate son's brilliance together with his careful handling of Hamilton's extremely high-strung and arrogant nature that ultimately made their very successful collaboration possible.

As secretary of the treasury Hamilton was the most important minister in the new administration. In emulation of Britain's first lord of the treasury, Hamilton saw himself as a kind of prime minister to Washington's monarchlike presidency. He sometimes even talked about "my administration." Because he believed that "most of the important measures of every government are connected with the treasury," he felt justified in meddling in the affairs of the other departments and in taking the lead in organizing and administering the government.[9]

Unlike Jefferson as head of the State Department and Henry Knox as head of the War Department, Hamilton as secretary of the treasury had an extraordinary degree of authority and independence. President Washington treated Jefferson and Knox as only advisers and often immediately involved himself in the conduct of foreign affairs and military matters. He treated Hamilton very differently party because he knew little about public finance but also because he believed the Treasury Department was constitutionally different from the other departments. When Congress created the departments of State and War in 1789, it simply declared that the secretaries were to perform such duties as the president required. When it created the Treasury Department, however, it made no mention of the president and instead required the secretary to report directly to the Congress. Unwilling to encroach on the authority of Congress, Washington thus gave Hamilton a much freer hand in running the Treasury than he gave the other secretaries.[10]

Emboldened in this way, Hamilton began interfering in the legislative business of Congress. Indeed, one of the reasons the House of Representatives in the early Congresses dispensed with standing committees was that it soon came to rely on the heads of the executive departments, in particular, the secretary of the treasury, to draft most of its bills. At the end of July 1789 the House of Representatives set up a Committee of Ways and Means to advise it on financial matters, but on September 2, 1789, the Treasury Department was created. On September 11 Alexander Hamilton was appointed secretary of the treasury, and six days later the House discharged its Committee of Ways and Means, stating that it would rely on Hamilton instead for its financial knowledge. Not until 1795, after Hamilton's resignation from the Treasury Department, did the House reestablish its Ways and Means Committee.

Hamilton set out to do for America what early-eighteenth-century English governments had done in establishing Great Britain as the greatest power in the world. Hamilton greatly admired the English constitution, the English constitution as it was—unreformed. Jefferson recalled a dinner party in 1791 in which he, Hamilton, and John Adams were present. In the course of the conversation someone mentioned the English constitution, at which Adams observed, "Purge that constitution of it's corruption, and give to it's popular branch equality of representation, and it would be the most perfect government ever devised by the wit of man." At that point, said Jefferson, "Hamilton paused and said, 'purge it of it's corruption, and give to it's popular branch equality of representation, & it would become an impracticable government: as it stands at present, with all it's supposed defects, it is the most perfect government which ever existed."[11] With such a startling statement, surely designed to provoke both Adams and Jefferson, Hamilton was only echoing the realistic observations of David Hume. For Hume the Crown's ministers' use of money and patronage to influence members of Parliament, whether or not called "by the invidious appellations of *corruption* or *dependence*," was simply a necessity if the Crown were to carry out its responsibility for governing the realm.[12]

Hamilton was nothing if not a hardheaded realist, and in the 1790s he set out to do what the successful eighteenth-century British ministers had done, in effect, to "corrupt" the society for the sake of stable government. He sought to use monarchicallike governmental influence both to tie the leading commercial interests to the government and to create new hierarchies of interest and dependency that would substitute for what he believed was the lack of virtue in America.

Hamilton knew there were many men in America—merchants, speculators, stockjobbers, and others—who were eager only to make money off the government. Even though these moneyed men may have been selfish schemers, the new government, he believed, needed their support, indeed needed the support of all the influential people at the top of the society, whatever their character or level of virtue and disinterestedness. In traditional eighteenth-century fashion, Hamilton saw these few at the top extending their influence and patronage down through the various levels and degrees of the society. Hamilton, like most Federalists, assumed that politics was largely a matter of securing the support of these influential gentry patrons at the top. Capture these few, he thought, and a statesman inevitably captures the whole society.

The way to do so was to appeal to the interests of these few influentials. Interest—there was no better or firmer tie between people He had known that from his earliest years at King's College and had repeated it ever since. "Men will pursue their interest," he said in 1788. "It is as easy to change human nature, as to oppose the strong current of the selfish passions. A wise legislator will gently divert the channel, and direct it, if possible, to the public good." This realistic view of human nature was one of the ties he had with Washington. Although Hamilton assumed that nearly everyone else was self-interested (Washington was an exception), he himself always remained extraordinarily scrupulous in maintaining his personal disinterestedness and freedom from corruption. Let others, including congressmen, become "speculators" and "peculators," he said, but not he; he would be, as he put it in one of his mocking moods, one of those "public fools who sacrifice private to public interest at the certainty of ingratitude and obloquy." He would stand above all the interested men and harness and use them. Although he later and rather defensively denied that he had ever made interest "the weightiest motive" behind his various programs, there is no doubt that he meant to strengthen central authority and the Union "by increasing the number of ligaments between the Government and the interests of Individuals."[13] Hamilton's financial program, like all his measures, was designed not to make money for any particular group but to create a great and powerful nation-state. Like all the great European state builders before him, he aimed to use the powerful tool of patronage.[14]

He and the other Federalists sought to form throughout the country rings of local interests loyal to the government. In communities up and down the continent Hamilton and the other Federalist leaders used patronage of various sorts to create hierarchies of support for the new government. Unlike the practice of the states, where thousands of state, town, and county public functionaries were elected, all executive and judicial offices in the federal government, except for the president and vice president, were appointed, not elected. As early as 1782 Hamilton had foreseen the importance of the federal government's having this immense power to appoint all its own officers. The goal of such appointments, said Hamilton, was "to create in the interior of each State, a mass of influence in favor of the Federal Government." Force alone could not support the government, and besides, its use was disagreeable and unpredictable. "It will be wise to obviate the necessity of it," he wrote. Building support for the government could best be done "by interesting such a number of individuals in each State, in support of the Federal Government, as will be counterpoised to the ambition of others, and will make it difficult to unite the people in opposition to the first and necessary measures of the Union."[15]

When he became head of the Treasury, Hamilton had hundreds of officials to appoint and was thus in a prime position to carry out his aim. Since these customs officials, revenue agents, and postmasters were located in every large town and section of the United States and touched every aspect of economic life in America, they were important for building support for the new government, even among former opponents of the Constitution.

Although Hamilton denied being a monarchist, Gouverneur Morris later recalled that he was "on Principle opposed to republican and attached to monarchical Government."[16] With his illegitimate background, Hamilton had no vested interest in the monarchical claims of blood. But he did reject the agrarian vision of the future United States held by the Jeffersonians. He saw the country eventually becoming a traditional nation-state like the nations of Europe. His model for the United States in the 1790s was the monarchical society and government of England. Assuming as he did that societies developed progressively through stages of civilization, he thought time was on his and the Federalists' side. In time American society would naturally become more hierarchical and more unequal, more urban and more industrial—in other words, more like the refined, complex, and highly commercialized nature of eighteenth-century English society. America, he believed, ought to prepare itself for that inevitable future. More than any other American, he saw England's eighteenth-century experience as an object lesson for the new government of the United States, and he deliberately set out to duplicate England's great achievements in stabilizing its society and mobilizing its resources for the waging of war.

By the eighteenth century England had emerged from the chaos and civil wars of the seventeenth century, which had killed one king and deposed another, to become the most stable and most dominant military and commercial power in the world. That this small island on the northern edge of Europe with a third of the population of continental France was able to build the greatest empire since the fall of Rome was the miracle of the age, even surpassing the astonishing achievement of the Netherlands in the previous century. The eighteenth-century English "fiscal-military" state, in historian John Brewer's apt term, could mobilize wealth and wage war as no state in history ever had.[17] Its centralized administration had developed an extraordinary capacity to tax and to borrow from its subjects without impoverishing them. Hamilton saw that the secret of the Hanoverian monarchy's success was its system of centralized tax collection and its funded national debt together with its banking structure and its market in public securities. For a state to wage war successfully, it had to tax efficiently and borrow cheaply. As the new secretary of the treasury Hamilton aimed to copy Britain's success and turn the United States into a great power that would eventually rival Britain and the other European states on their own war-making terms. Hamilton and Washington thought this might take up to fifty years. In the meantime the country should avoid war until it was ready to take on the European powers militarily.

In light of the inexperience of eighteenth-century Americans with positive state power, Hamilton's program was truly breathtaking. He worked his remarkable program out in a series of four reports to Congress in 1790 and 1791: on credit (including duties and taxes), on a national bank, on a mint, and on manufactures. These reports, powerfully written and argued, are the source of most of Hamilton's greatness as a statesman.

Hamilton proposed that the United States government assume the obligation of paying not just the federal government's debts resulting from the Revolutionary War but all the states' debts as well—with the expectation that the creditors would be weaned away from the states and attached to the new national government. But then instead of the national government's immediately retiring either these assumed state debts or the Confederation's debts, he urged that it "fund" them—that is, transform them into a more or less permanent debt on which annual interest would be regularly paid. At the same time he proposed the creation of a national bank that could stabilize the credit of the United States and create money. Finally, he projected the eventual development of manufacturing in the United States not just to meet military requirements but also to create a more diversified and prosperous economy that would be more self-reliant and less dependent on European supplies.

Although Hamilton's financial program was designed with rich people and moneyed interests in mind, it was not intended for their benefit. They would no doubt prosper from it, but that would be incidental to his plans. All he hoped to do was use the new economic and fiscal measures to tie moneyed men and other influential individuals to the new central government. However much Hamilton contributed to the growth of American capitalism, he was anything but a businessman or entrepreneur, and he should not be celebrated as the promoter of America's later business culture. He was an eighteenth-century gentleman who, like his fellow New Yorker Aaron Burr, practiced law on Wall Street only out of financial necessity. Hamilton was willing to grant businessmen and other ordinary working people their profits and prosperity in order to make the country commercially strong, but it was aristocratic fame and glory that he wanted for himself and the United States.

Hamilton's funding program, especially the federal government's assumption of the state debts, met with stiff opposition in the 1790 Congress. This opposition was led by none other than Hamilton's former collaborator in ratifying the Constitution, James Madison, congressman from Virginia. At the same time another issue in the Congress—locating a permanent seat for the federal capital—had become as contentious as the assumption of state debts. The southern states wanted the capital on the Potomac. The New England states and New York wanted to retain the capital in New York, and the middle states wanted it in Philadelphia or at least near the Susquehanna. Fearful of disunion, people on all sides were ultimately willing to compromise. At a dinner arranged by Jefferson in June 1790 Hamilton and Madison clinched a deal in which southerners accepted the national assumption of the state debts in return for placing the permanent capital on the Potomac.

Although Hamilton's funding program was thus susceptible to compromise, this seemed less likely with the Bank of the United States. Both Jefferson and Madison believed that the creation of the bank was an unconstitutional usurpation of power; their objections troubled Washington, who asked his secretary of the treasury to write a rebuttal. Hamilton spent a week working out what became one of his masterful state papers. He carefully refuted the arguments of the bank's opponents and made a powerful case for a broad construction of the Constitution that has resounded through subsequent decades of American history. He argued that Congress's authority to charter a bank was implied by the clause in the Constitution that gave Congress the right to make all laws "necessary and proper" to carry out its delegated powers.[18] Washington was convinced and in February 1791 signed the bank bill into law.

Most Americans in 1790 were not at all familiar with banks. In 1781 the Confederation Congress had set up the Bank of North America in Philadelphia, and by 1790 there were three more banks established in

New York, Boston, and Baltimore. Yet compared with England, banking in America was new and undeveloped. There was nothing yet in America that duplicated the array of different monetary notes and the dozens upon dozens of private and county banks scattered all over eighteenth-century Great Britain. When the Bank of North America was first opened in Philadelphia in 1781, it was "a novelty," said Thomas Willing, its president. Banking in America, he said, was "a pathless wilderness, ground but little known to this side of the Atlantic." English rules, arrangements, and bank bills were then unknown. "All was to us a mystery."[19]

Few of Hamilton's fellow statesmen understood what he was doing. As we have seen, Jefferson thought that all the paper money issued by banks was nothing but a swindle, some sort of sleight of hand, and not to be compared with the "solid wealth" produced by "hard labor in the earth." How could paper not backed by an equivalent amount of specie be worth anything? It was only common sense, he said, to know "that *nothing* can produce *nothing*." John Adams agreed: "Every dollar of a bank bill that is issued beyond the quantity of gold and silver in the vaults represents nothing and is therefore a cheat upon somebody."[20]

Confronted with such ignorance of banking and finance, Hamilton in his state papers sometimes assumed the exasperated tone of the sophisticated Wall Street lawyer explaining the intricacies of banks and credit to country bumpkins. Yet with the creation of his Bank of the United States (BUS) Hamilton did not really anticipate the future of banking in America. He wanted his national bank eventually to absorb all the state banks in the country and to have a monopoly of banking. He also had a very restricted view of the bank's clients. Although he expected that the BUS would issue paper money that would pass from hand to hand, he assumed that it would make paper money available only to large merchants and others who wanted short-term loans, ninety days or less. In 1790 the several banks, including that of the United States, as yet did not want to get involved in making long-term mortgage loans to farmers; to do so would tie up money for too long a time, as the bank waited for the land-based loans to be paid back.

But that soon changed, for most farmers and entrepreneurs needed long-term credit, and in spite of opposition from Hamilton and the Bank of the United States, these mostly northern Jeffersonian Republicans went wild in chartering state banks, hundreds of them, that issued million of dollars of paper money that gave ordinary Americans the credit they wanted. Hamilton's insensitivity to the entrepreneurial needs of these common commercially minded farmers and small businessmen suggests how little he and other Federalists understood the real sources of the capitalist future of America.

In 1790, however, no one was more confident of his abilities than Hamilton, yet at the same time no one was more naive about the political effects his policies were creating. He seemed genuinely bewildered that his former collaborator Madison should become his principal opponent in the Congress. When he began setting forth his financial program—in emulation of what Great Britain had done in the eighteenth century—Madison began voicing ever more strident opposition and, with the help of his friend Thomas Jefferson, began organizing the Republican party to counter what seemed to be Hamilton's monarchlike project. Soon the two former collaborators on *The Federalist Papers* had become bitter political enemies.

Since Hamilton and Madison had very different ideas of what the new federal government should be, it is not surprising that they should eventually turn on each other. Hamilton envisioned the United States' becoming a great powerful nation like Great Britain and the other states of modern Europe, a state with a centralized bureaucracy, a professional standing army, and the capacity to wage war on equal terms with other nations. He saw himself as a realist in both domestic and foreign policy. (that is why tough-minded international scholars like Hans Morgenthau so admired Hamilton.) Hamilton had nothing but contempt for the pie-in-the-sky dreams of the Republican leaders that the natural sociability and moral sense of people might substitute for interest and the force of government as adhesives in holding society together. The idea, he said, that "as human nature shall refine and ameliorate by the operation of a more enlightened plan" based on the operation of a common moral sense and the spread of affection and benevolence, government eventually "will become useless, and Society will subsist and flourish free from its shackles," was a "wild and fatal . . . scheme." Even if the Republican "votaries of this new philosophy," like Jefferson, "do not go the whole length of its frantic creed," they go far enough to endanger human happiness.[21]

Hamilton repudiated the emerging Jeffersonian Republican view that the best government was the least government. He believed deeply in the "need" for "a common directing power" in government and had only contempt for those who thought trade and other private interests could regulate themselves. "This is one of those wild speculative paradoxes," he said, "which have grown into credit among us, contrary to the uniform practice and sense of the most enlightened nations. . . . It must be rejected by every man acquainted with commercial history."[22] He was even more contemptuous of the Jeffersonian belief that republics were naturally pacific and that economic sanctions of various sorts could replace military might in international affairs.

Given their very different views of state power and the kind of nation the United States ought to become, Jefferson and Madison were appalled at what Hamilton was doing. From the early 1790s on they sought to use their Republican party to stop him and his fellow Federalists from foisting a warmongering monarchy on America.

This struggle over the nature of the national government turned the 1790s into one of the most passionate decades in American history. Politics in such volatile circumstances could scarcely be normal, and Hamilton and other intensely engaged men sought desperately to protect their reputations from the ever-increasing scurrility and personal abuse of the time. The politics of the early national period, as historian Joanne B. Freeman has shown, can be properly understood only within this culture of personal reputation and honor.[23] Despite the emergence of political parties in the 1790s, politics still remained very much an aristocratic matter of individual loyalties and enmities subsumed by the gentlemanly code of honor, at the heart of which lay dueling. Dueling was an elaborate political ritual the negotiations of which among principals and their seconds and friends often went on for weeks or even months. These complicated political procedures resulted in many duels, most of which did not end in exchanges of gunfire.

Hamilton, acutely conscious of his honor and sensitive to every slight, was the principal in eleven affairs of honor during his lifetime. At one point during the heated struggle with the Jeffersonian Republicans over Jay's Treaty in 1795, he issued two challenges within minutes of each other and, waving his fist in the air, even offered "to fight the Whole '*Detestable faction*' one by one." Despite participating in all these affairs of honor, however, he actually exchanged fire in only one, his last fatal duel with Aaron Burr in 1804.[24]

After Hamilton left Washington's cabinet in 1795 and returned to his Wall Street practice of law in order to make some money for his family, he continued to try to control events in the nation's capital. Washington's successor, John Adams, in 1797 retained the principal members of Washington's cabinet, who were more loyal to Hamilton than to the president. As we've seen, when in 1798 it seemed as if France might invade the United States, Adams was pressured into calling Washington out of retirement as commander of an army of tens of thousands. Washington reluctantly agreed but only on condition that Hamilton be made a major general and the actual organizer and commander of the military forces. Adams was furious that Washington had compelled him to promote over the heads of more deserving men "the most restless, impatient, indefatigable and unprincipled intriguer in the United States, if not in the world to be second in command under himself."[25]

It is Hamilton's behavior in this crisis that historians have most criticized. The Republicans thought that he intended to use the army against them. Hamilton certainly intended to suppress any domestic insurrection with a massive show of force. When rumors spread that Jefferson and Madison's state, Virginia, was arming, he seemed eager to "put Virginia to the Test of resistance."[26] When an uprising actually occurred in eastern Pennsylvania early in 1799, he told the secretary of war not to err by sending too few troops. "Whenever the Government appears in arms," he wrote, "it ought to appear like a *Hercules*, and inspire respect by the display of strength."[27] He believed that the crisis of 1798 offered an opportunity to create what he had long wanted for the government, a respectable standing army. Such a permanent force would enable the United States both "to subdue a *refractory* & powerful *state*" and to deal independently and equally with the warring powers of Europe.[28] A potent standing army, however, was just the beginning of his future plans for strengthening the Union. He wanted as well to extend the judiciary, to build a system of roads and canals, to increase taxes, and to amend the Constitution in order to subdivide the larger states.

Beyond the borders of the United States his aims were even more grandiose. He thought war with France would enable the United States, in cooperation with Britain, to seize both Florida and Louisiana from Spain—in order, he said, to keep them out of the hands of an aggressive and powerful France. At the same time he held out the possibility of helping the Venezuelan patriot Francisco de Miranda to liberate South America. In all these endeavors, he told the American minister in Britain, Rufus King, in August 1798, America should be "the principal agency," especially in supplying the land army. "The command in this case would very naturally fall upon me—and I hope I should disappoint no favorable anticipation."[29] More than anything, Hamilton wanted some of the honor and glory that would come to the United States as it assumed its rightful place in the world as a great military power. All these extravagant dreams collapsed with President Adams's new peace mission in 1799 and the end of the Quasi-War with France, a move that Adams regarded as the most disinterested and important act of his career.

Many Americans, including the president, thought that Hamilton and the High Federalists had been bent on establishing a regal government allied with Britain with Hamilton as its head. There is no evidence of that, but certainly Hamilton's plans for an imperial America were out of touch with the realities of his world in 1800. Two centuries later, however, these plans do not seem so bizarre. Hamilton would be right at home in the present-day United States and present-day world. He would love our government's vast federal bureaucracy, its sprawling Pentagon, its enormous CIA, its huge public debt, its taxes beyond any he could have hoped for, and especially its large professional military force with well over a million men and women under arms spread across two oceans and dozens of countries. America has at last created the kind of powerful worldwide empire he could only dream of. In this sense Hamilton may truly be "the man who made modern America."

Chapter Five

Is There a

"James Madison Problem"?

I T IS LAMENTABLE that Americans do not remember Madison as well as they should, especially when we reflect on who he was and what he achieved: The major architect of the Constitution; the father of the Bill of Rights and one of the strongest proponents of the rights of conscience and religious liberty in American history; the coauthor of *The Federalist*, surely the most significant work of political theory in American history; the leader and most important member of the first House of Representatives in 1789; the cofounder of the Democratic-Republican party in the 1790s; the secretary of state in Jefferson's administration; and the fourth president of the United States—all this, and still he does not have the popular standing of the other founders, especially that of his closest friend, Thomas Jefferson.

Madison seems unable to escape from the shadow of Jefferson, and he seems smaller than his Virginia colleague in every way. He was after all only about five feet six inches tall compared with Jefferson's six-two or -three, and somehow that difference in height has carried over into the different degrees of popular esteem that the country has paid to these two founders. Jefferson has a huge temple erected in his honor in the nation's capital, but until 1980, with the naming of a new Library of Congress building after him, James Madison had no such memorial. Jefferson's ringing statements on behalf of freedom and democracy are inscribed everywhere, but very few of Madison's are anywhere in public view. Jefferson's home, Monticello, has been restored to Jeffersonian perfection and for decades has been a shrine, visited by thousands of people every year. By contrast Madison's home, Montpelier, has only recently been opened to visitors.

James Madison was born in 1751 into that class of Virginia slaveholding planters who dominated their society as few aristocracies have. Although his father was the wealthiest landowner in Orange County, Virginia, he was not far removed from the raw frontier, and young Madison, like most of the founding fathers, became the first of his family to attend college. In Madison's case it was the College of New Jersey (later Princeton), where he was introduced, through the president John Witherspoon, to the enlightened ideas of such eighteenth-century Scottish thinkers as Francis Hutcheson, Adam Smith, and David Hume. In college he revealed an intellectual intensity and earnestness that he never lost. His father's plantation wealth enabled Madison, who complained endlessly of his poor health, to return home to study and contemplate participating in the provincial politics of colonial Virginia. The Revolution of course changed everything.

In 1776 Madison at age twenty-five was elected to Virginia's provincial convention and became caught up in the revolutionary movement. His first great liberal passion was religious freedom, and through that concern he became friendly with Jefferson, who, eight years his senior, was already a major force in Virginia's revolutionary politics. It was the beginning of a lifelong friendship.

It is not immediately obvious why the friendship was so intimate and long-lasting. The two men after all had very different temperaments. As we've seen, Jefferson was high-minded, optimistic, visionary, and often quick to grab hold of new and sometimes outlandish ideas. Although he could be a superb politician at times, acutely sensitive to what was possible and workable, he was also a radical utopian; he often dreamed of the future and was inspired by how things might be. Madison, by contrast, had a conservative strain; he valued legitimacy and stability and was more willing than Jefferson to accept things as they were. He was often prudent and cold-eyed, if not pessimistic, analytical, and often skeptical of utopian schemes, especially if they might unleash popular passions. He never assumed an idea without questioning it, and as we've noted, he never possessed the kind of uncritical faith in the people that Jefferson had.

Both Jefferson and Madison, for example, were suspicious of governmental power, including the power of elected representative legislatures. But Jefferson's suspicion was based on his fear of the unrepresentative character of the elected officials, that they were too apt to drift away from the virtuous people who had elected them. Madison's suspicion, in contrast, was based on his fear that the elected officials were only too representative, only too expressive of the passions of the people who had elected them. Jefferson worried about the rights of the majority; Madison worried about the rights of the minority.[1] As far as Jefferson was concerned, the people could do no wrong. When Madison was wringing his hands in the late 1780s over the turbulence of Shays's Rebellion, Jefferson was writing blithely from France about the value of the spirit of popular resistance to government and the need to keep it alive. "I like a little rebellion now and then," he said. It was like a storm in the atmosphere; it cleared the air.[2]

In 1779, at age twenty-eight, Madison was elected to the Continental Congress, where he was confronted with a number of national problems besetting the Confederation. The Articles of Confederation under which Americans were conducting their Revolution had not created a real government. In fact the Confederation resembled more of an alliance among closely cooperating sovereign states than a single government, something not all that different from the present-day European Union. Each state annually sent to the Confederation Congress a delegation (called by some states "our embassy"), and each delegation had only a single vote. Under the Articles the crucial powers of commercial regulation and taxation—indeed all final ordinary lawmaking authority—remained with the states. Congressional resolutions continued to be, as they had been under the Continental Congress, only recommendations that the states were supposed to enforce. And should there be any doubts of the decentralized nature of the Confederation, Article 2 stated bluntly: "Each State retains its sovereignty, freedom, and independence, and every power, jurisdiction, and right, which is not by this Confederation expressly delegated to the United States, in Congress assembled." The Confederation therefore was intended to be and remained, as Article 3 declared, "a firm league of friendship" among states jealous of their individuality. The "United States of America" were plural and possessed a literal meaning that is hard to appreciate today.

Almost immediately after the Confederation was created, many Americans, including Madison, came to see that it was much too weak to do what they wanted. By the 1780s the problems were severe and conspicuous. The Congress could not tax and pay its bills. It could not feed, clothe, or supply the army. It could not levy tariffs to regulate trade or to retaliate against the mercantilist European empires. It was even having trouble gathering a quorum to conduct business. Attempts to revise the Articles and grant the Congress the power to levy a 5 percent impost on imported European goods were thwarted by the need to get the unanimous consent of all thirteen states. Internationally the United States were being humiliated. In the Mediterranean the Barbary pirates were seizing American ships and selling their sailors into slavery, and the Confederation was powerless to do anything. It was unable even to guarantee the territorial integrity of the new nation. Great Britain continued to hold posts in the northwestern parts of United States territory in defiance of the peace treaty of 1783. In the southwest Spain was claiming territory that included much of present-day Alabama and Mississippi and plotting with American dissidents to break away from the Union.

These glaring weaknesses of the Articles of Confederation convinced Madison and many others that some sort of reform of this first national constitution was needed. Throughout the early 1780s Madison wrestled with various schemes for overhauling the Confederation. At one point he even toyed with the idea that the government might have to make war on the states in order to compel compliance with the Congress's resolutions. By the mid-1780s almost the entire political nation was ready to change the Articles by granting the Congress a limited authority to tax and to regulate commerce. This widespread willingness to do something about the central government gave Madison and others an opportunity to do more than add a couple of powers to the Congress. By 1786 he had become convinced that the crisis of the 1780s involved more than the weaknesses of the Confederation. The real crisis lay with popular politics in the separate states.

He reached this startling conclusion not merely from poring through the bundles of books that Jefferson was sending him from Paris. More important in convincing him that the states were the source of the problems of the 1780s was his membership in the Virginia Assembly. In 1784 he was forced by the term limits for congressmen under the Articles to retire from the Congress and enter the Virginia legislature, where he spent four sessions between 1784 and 1787. They were perhaps the most frustrating and disillusioning years but also the most important years of his life, for his experience as a Virginia legislator in the 1780s was crucial in shaping his thinking as a constitutional reformer.

Although Madison in these years had some notable legislative achievements, particularly by shepherding into enactment Jefferson's famous bill for religious freedom, he was continually exasperated by what Jefferson years later (no doubt following Madison's account) referred to as "the endless quibbles, chicaneries, perversions, vexations, and delays of lawyers and demi-lawyers" in the assembly. Really for the first time Madison discovered what democracy in America might mean. Not all the legislators were going to be like him or Jefferson; many of them did not even appear to be gentlemen, never mind enlightened. The Virginia legislators seemed parochial, illiberal, small-minded, and most of them seemed to have only "a particular interest to serve." They had no regard for public honor or honesty. They often made a travesty of the legislative process and were reluctant to do anything that might appear unpopular. They postponed taxes, subverted debts owed to the subjects of Great Britain, and passed, defeated, and repassed bills in the most haphazard ways. Madison had enlightened expectations for Virginia's port bill in 1784, but the other legislators got their self-serving hands on it and perverted it. It was the same with nearly all the legislative proposals he sought to introduce, especially those involving reform of the legal code and court system. "Important bills prepared at leisure by skillful hands," he complained, were vitiated by "crudeness and tedious discussion." What could he do with such clods? "It will little elevate your idea of our Senate," he wrote in weary despair to Washington in 1786, to learn that the senators actually defeated a bill defining the privileges of foreign ambassadors in Virginia "on the principle . . . that an Alien ought not to be put on better ground than a Citizen." Those today who have to contend with New Yorkers' complaining about the parking privileges of UN diplomats might appreciate Madison's vexation.[3]

This was not what republican lawmaking was supposed to be. Madison continually had to make concessions to the "prevailing sentiments," whether or not such sentiments promoted the good of the state or nation. He had to agree to bad laws for fear of getting worse ones, and to give up good bills "rather than pay such a price" as opponents wanted. Today's legislators are used to this sort of political horse-trading, but Madison was not yet ready for the logrolling and pork barreling that eventually became the staples of American legislative politics.

He had "strong apprehensions" that his and Jefferson's hope of reforming the legal code "may never be systematically perfected." The legislature was simply too popular, and appealing to the people had none of the beneficial effects good republicans had expected. A bill having to do with court reform, for example, was "to be printed for the consideration of the public," but "instead of calling forth the sanction of the wise and virtuous," this action, Madison feared, would only "be a signal to interested men to redouble their efforts to get into the Legislature." Democracy was no solution to the problem; democracy was the problem. Madison repeatedly found himself having to beat back the "itch for paper money" and other debtor relief measures "of a popular cast." Too often Madison had to admit that the only hope he had was "of moderating the fury," not defeating it.[4]

Madison, like other enthusiastic revolutionary idealists, emerged from his experience with democratic politics in the mid-1780s a very chastened republican. It was bad enough, he wrote in his working paper "Vices of the Political System of the United States," that legislators were often interested men or dupes of the sophistry of "a favorite leader" (like Patrick Henry). Even more alarming for the fate of republican government, however, was the fact that such legislators were only reflecting the partial interests and parochial outlooks of their constituents. Too many of the American people could not see beyond their own pocketbooks or their own neighborhoods. "Individuals of extended views, and of national pride," said Madison (and he knew whom he meant), might be able to bring public proceedings to an enlightened cosmopolitan standard, but their example could never be followed by "the multitude." "Is it to be imagined that an ordinary citizen or even an assembly-man of R. Island in estimating the policy of paper money, ever considered or cared in what light the measure would be viewed in France or Holland; or even in Massts or Connect.? It was a sufficient temptation to both [the citizen and the assemblyman] that it was for their interest."[5]

Madison's experience with the populist politics of the state legislatures was especially important because of his extraordinary influence on the writing of the federal Constitution. But his experience was not unusual; indeed, the framers of the Constitution could not have done what they did if Madison's experience had not been widely shared. Many of the delegates to the Philadelphia Convention were ready to accept Madison's

Virginia Plan precisely because they shared his deep dislike of the local-ist and interest-ridden politics of the state legislatures. "The vile State gov-ernments are sources of pollution which will contaminate the American name for ages. . . . Smite them," Henry Knox urged Rufus King, sitting in the Philadelphia Convention, "smite them, in the name of God and the people."[6]

Not only Virginia but other states as well had been passing various in-flationary paper money laws and other debtor relief legislation that were victimizing creditor minorities. All this experience during the 1780s sparked new thoughts, and Madison began working out for himself a new understanding of American politics, one that involved questioning conventional wisdom concerning majority rule, the proper size for a re-public, and the role of factions in society. All these new ideas fed into the Virginia Plan, which became the working model for the Constitutional Convention that met in 1787. Crucial to this plan was the Congress's power to negative or veto all state legislation that in its opinion violated the articles of the Union.

Jefferson had no such plan in mind. During the 1780s Jefferson was minister to France and from his distant position in Paris did not share Madison's experience in democratic state politics. Although Jefferson ac-cepted the need for a new federal government, he continued to think of the United States as more of a decentralized confederation than did Madi-son. Give the national government control over foreign policy and foreign trade, he urged, but leave all domestic affairs, including taxation, with the separate states. "To make us one nation as to foreign concerns, and keep us distinct in Domestic ones," Jefferson told Madison in 1786, "gives the outline of the proper division of powers between the general and partic-ular governments."[7]

By the early 1790s Jefferson had not changed his views at all, but Madi-son had. By 1792 Madison had become fearful of the very government he had done so much to create. This change has created a "Madison prob-lem." Just as scholars used to see two different Adam Smiths, creating an Adam Smith problem, so do they see two different James Madisons.

The Adam Smith problem, or as the German scholars liked to call it, *das Adam Smith Problem*, arose out of the presumed discrepancy between the Adam Smith of the *Theory of Moral Sentiments* and the Adam Smith of the *Wealth of Nations*. Smith seemed to be two different persons with very different views of human nature. While his *Moral Sentiments* seemed to ascribe human actions to sympathy, his *Wealth of Nations* seemed to ascribe them to self-interest. Much scholarly time and energy were spent trying to account for the apparent difference between the two books. Eventually, however, more recent scholarship has shown that the problem was a figment of our scholarly imaginations and that the two books can in fact be reconciled.[8]

Can we do the same for James Madison? Can we reconcile the apparently two different Madisons?

There is the Madison of the 1780s, the fervent nationalist who feared the states and their vicious tyrannical majorities and wanted to subject them to the control of the central government. Although he did not want to eliminate the states, he seems to have wanted to reduce them to what at times are little more than administrative units that, he said, might be "subordinately useful."[9] This is the Madison who has become the so-called father of the Constitution.

By contrast there is the Madison of the 1790s, the strict constructionist, states' rights cofounder of the Democratic-Republican party who feared the national government and its monarchical tendencies and trusted the popular majorities in the states. By 1798 he was even willing to invoke the right of the states to judge the constitutionality of federal acts and to interpose themselves between the citizens and the unconstitutional actions of the central government. For the early Madison, popular majorities within states were the source of the problem; for the later Madison, these popular majorities in the states became a remedy for the problem. It is hard to see how these two seemingly different Madisons can be reconciled.

The first Madison is the author of the Virginia Plan. We often forget what an extraordinarily powerful and sweeping national government the

Virginia Plan proposed. According to Madison's plan, both branches of the bicameral national legislature would be proportionally representative, thus eliminating all semblance of state sovereignty from the national government. Moreover, this national legislature would have the power to legislate in all cases in which the separate states were incompetent and the power to negative all state laws that in its opinion contravened the Union. Madison thought this curious veto power to be "absolutely necessary and to be the least possible encroachment on the State jurisdictions."[10]

During 1789, when the new Washington administration was getting on its feet, Madison still seemed to be the quintessential Federalist—"a great friend to strong government," concluded South Carolina Federalist William Loughton Smith in August 1789.[11] Although a member of the House of Representatives, Madison was President Washington's closest confidant. He helped shape the legislation that created the departments of government and was very important in establishing the executive's independence from Congress. Even his support for a bill of rights that dealt only with individual rights and liberties was seen as a means of subverting or diverting the Anti-Federalist demand for many more substantial limits on the national government—a "tub for the whale," as the Anti-Federalists called his bill of rights.[12]

Only slowly did Madison seem to change. Although he reluctantly recognized the need for funding the national debt, he was not happy with Hamilton's proposal in January 1790 to pay only the current holders of the government's bonds. Hamilton's plan for the national government to assume all the state debts angered him even more. Finally, with Hamilton's proposal for a national bank, Madison's criticism of the secretary of the treasury's plans became even more vehement, and the political elite became severely divided.

Hamilton was not surprised by opposition to his financial plans. He knew that state and local interests would resist all efforts to strengthen national authority. But he was surprised that his harshest critic in the House of Representatives was his longtime ally Madison. He thought that Madison had desired a strong national government as much as he had.

He could not understand how he and Madison, "whose politics had formerly so much the *same point of departure*," could have diverged so dramatically.[13]

In the House Madison argued not only that the bank bill was a misguided imitation of England's monarchical practice of concentrating wealth and influence in the metropolitan capital but, more important, that it was an unconstitutional assertion of federal power. He urged a strict interpretation of the Constitution, claiming that it did not expressly grant the federal government the authority to charter a bank.

By the end of 1790 Madison and other Virginians were openly voicing their alarm at the direction the national government was taking. By 1791 Madison was privately describing the supporters of Hamilton's program not only as speculators but also as Tories, a loaded term that suggested the promoters of royal absolutism.[14] By 1792 Madison and Jefferson were emerging as the leaders of what Madison called the Republican party in opposition to what seemed to them to be Federalist efforts to establish a consolidated British-style monarchy. But so much was the Republican party the result of Madison's efforts alone that it was often referred to as "Madison's Party."[15] By May 1792 Hamilton had become convinced "that Mr. Madison cooperating with Mr. Jefferson is at the head of a faction decidedly hostile to me and my administration, and actuated by views in my judgment subversive of the principles of good government and dangerous to the union, peace and happiness of the Country."[16]

With the coming of the French Revolution and the outbreak of war between republican France and monarchical Britain in 1793, the division between the Federalists and the Republicans deepened and became more passionate. The future of the United States appeared to be tied up in the outcome of the European struggle. "None of the Republicans," writes historian James Morton Smith, "was more committed to the concept of the revolution in France as an extension of the one in America than was Madison."[17]

By this point Madison was convinced that Hamilton and the Federalists were bent on making a "connection" with Great Britain and "under her auspices" were determined to move "in a gradual approximation towards her Form of Government." Until his retirement from Congress in December 1796 Madison remained the undisputed leader of the Republican party in the Congress and its most effective spokesman in the press. When the crisis of 1798–99 came to a head, it was not surprising that Madison and Jefferson emerged as states rights' advocates against the consolidationist tendencies of the Federalists.

What happened? What could account for this apparently remarkable change of sentiment? From being the leader of the nationalist and Federalist movement in the 1780s, Madison became the leader of the states' rights and Anti-Federalist movement in the 1790s. Explaining this change seems to be a major problem, one that has bedeviled Madison's biographers and historians of the founding era.

Most biographers and historians have concluded that Madison did indeed change his mind about national power and offer a variety of explanations for his shift from being a proponent of a strong national government to a defender of states' rights. Some have described his "sudden turn" in 1790 as a matter of "political expediency," designed as "the opening move in a resumption of state-oriented politics."[18] Others have stressed his awakened loyalty to the sentiments of his Virginia constituents. Taking off from this new consciousness of Madison's Virginianess, still others have pointed to his inability to comprehend bond markets and mercantile affairs and have emphasized that his objection to Hamilton's program seemed to rest on his disgust with northern speculators and moneyed men.[19] Others have talked about his friendship with Jefferson and his willingness to defer to his older colleague, ready "always," as he told Jefferson in 1794, to "receive your commands with pleasure."[20] Still others have stressed that he "thought as a working statesman," shifting his opinion in accord with his perception of where the threats to liberty and republican government lay.[21]

Those few scholars who have stressed Madison's consistency through the 1780s and 1790s have done so by playing down his nationalism in the

1780s. They contend that he wasn't really a full-blown nationalist at the time of the Constitutional Convention.[22] But the evidence of Madison's nationalism in 1787 seems too overwhelming for this contention to be persuasive. In the 1780s Madison was very much a fervent nationalist, eager to create a national government that would control certain kinds of behavior in the states. Yet he was not the kind of nationalist that other Federalists such as Hamilton were. When he came to realize what kind of consolidated national government Hamilton was trying to create, he naturally went into opposition. His conception of what the national government ought to be was not being fulfilled.

Trying to discover consistency in a politician who lived a long life in a rapidly changing society may be a foolish and unnecessary project. Does it really matter if Madison changed his views? He certainly thought so; to the end of his life he always maintained that he was consistent in his beliefs and that it was Hamilton who had abandoned him.[23] Certainly we can never escape from the fact that the later Madison is different in many ways from the early Madison. No doubt he was a nationalist in the 1780s and a states' rights advocate in the 1790s. Yet at some basic level Madison remained in harmony with himself throughout his career. There were really *not* two James Madisons.

How to explain the consistency in Madison's thinking? First of all we have to get back to the eighteenth century to understand exactly what he was trying to do in 1787. It may be that we scholars have been attributing far more farsightedness to him than he was in fact capable of. In our eagerness to make Madison the most profound political theorist not only in the revolutionary and constitution-making period but in all American history as well, we may have burdened this eighteenth-century political leader with more theoretical sophistication than he or any such politician can bear. We want him to be one of the important political philosophers in the Western tradition. If the English have Hobbes and Locke, and the French have Montesquieu and Rousseau, then we Americans at least have Madison.

Convinced of the originality and sophistication of Madison's ideas, many scholars have been stumbling over themselves in their desire to explore the implications of his political thought, less, it seems, for understanding the eighteenth century than for understanding our own time. Since Madison was central to the creation of the United States Constitution—the founding, as we call it—he and his ideas have come to bear an exceptional responsibility for the character of American politics and society.

Political scientists have been especially eager to treat Madison as America's foremost political philosopher and have compiled a small library of works analyzing his (and Hamilton's) contributions to *The Federalist.* According to many political theorists, to understand Madison is to understand American politics. So, in Robert A. Dahl's formulation, Madison is the pluralist who unfortunately concocted our fragmented structure of government in order to protect minority rights at the expense of majority rule. Or according to Richard K. Matthews, he is the symbol of a coldhearted American liberalism that promotes a selfish individualism that has no sense of benevolence and cares only for material wealth and property. Or in Gary Rosen's hands, he is the innovative theorist of the social compact that is the foundation of natural rights and our limited constitutional government.[24]

As these studies by political scientists and political theorists become more and more refined and precious, they seem to drift farther and farther away from Madison's eighteenth-century reality. Whatever his creativity and originality may have been, we have to keep in mind that Madison was not speaking to us or to the ages. His world was not our world; indeed, our world would have appalled him. Thus, in our efforts to relate his very time-bound thinking to our present predicaments, we run the risk of seriously distorting his world and what he was trying to do. Moreover, despite all his achievements, we run the risk of exaggerating his creativity.

If we are to recover the historical Madison, we have to soften, if not discard, the traditional idea that he was the father of the Constitution. He was certainly the principal force behind the calling of the Philadelphia

Convention which drafted the Constitution in the summer of 1787. He was also the major author of the Virginia Plan, which formed the original working model for the convention. During the meeting not only did he participate vigorously in the debates, but he also took it upon himself to keep voluminous notes of the discussions; mainly because of these notes we know so much about what went on in the convention. But the Constitution that emerged from the Philadelphia Convention was not at all what he had wanted. With good reason he always contended that it was "the work of many heads and many hands."[25]

To understand Madison, we have to remove from our minds any notion that the Constitution we Americans have now or even had in the 1790s was the one he had intended to create with his Virginia Plan.

The Virginia Plan, which he introduced to the convention on May 29, 1787, was certainly original and nationalistic, but it was a quirky, even visionary kind of originality that it expressed, one that proved unacceptable to most Federalists. The Virginia Plan had grown out of Madison's view of what was really wrong with America in the 1780s. For him the weaknesses of the Confederation, which nearly everyone seemed to acknowledge, seemed secondary to the vices within the several states. Not only did the self-interested behavior of the states weaken the Union, but more important, popular politics within the states threatened the revolutionary experiment in self-government. Ever since independence, said Madison, the states had passed a host of laws whose "multiplicity," "mutability," and "injustice" called "into question the fundamental principle of republican Government, that the majority who rule in such Governments, are the safest Guardians both of public Good and private rights."[26] By 1787 Madison was convinced that these problems within the states contributed more to the calling of the Philadelphia Convention than did the obvious weaknesses of the Confederation. It was this conviction that led Madison to the peculiarities of his Virginia Plan—not only the sweeping legislative authority granted to the Congress but, more important, the extraordinary power granted to the federal government to oversee state legislation. The Virginia Plan gave the Congress the power to veto all state laws contravening the articles of union. It also created a council of revision, modeled on that of New York, composed of the executive and a convenient number of the national judiciary, to participate in legislation. It had the power not only to examine and veto all congressional laws unless the Congress repassed them but also to examine all state laws before a congressional rejection of them would be final.

Of course there were many Federalists who shared Madison's disgust with what was happening in the states and agreed with his remedy of establishing an elevated national government. But many of them did not agree with the strange judiciallike manner in which he hoped to deal with the factional politics he found in the states, a manner very much influenced by his conception of how the Privy Council of the British Crown had, or should have, operated under the empire.

Madison's proposals for checking legislation were truly odd. In the weeks leading up to the meeting of the Philadelphia Convention he imagined the national government's possessing even a stronger veto over state laws than the one that ended up being incorporated in the Virginia Plan, and in private correspondence he revealed just how much experience under the British Empire was affecting his thinking. "A negative *in all cases whatsoever* on the legislative acts of the States, as heretofore exercised by the Kingly prerogative," he told Washington a month before the meeting in Philadelphia, was "absolutely necessary" and "the least possible encroachment on the State jurisdictions."[27] As historian Jack N. Rakove has pointed out, this was an extraordinarily reactionary proposal.[28] Moreover, not only was it reactionary, but it was also bizarre. It brought to mind the infamous phrase of the British Declaratory Act of 1766 that Parliament had the right to legislate for the colonies "in all cases whatsoever." It also evoked the royal veto of colonial legislation that Jefferson had bitterly denounced in the Declaration of Independence. Madison's proposal for this national congressional power to negative all state legislation was a measure of just how eccentric his thinking actually was.

Madison envisioned a very strange kind of national government. He wanted one that was principally designed to evade popular majoritarian politics in the states in order to protect individual liberties and minority rights. He had little or no interest in creating a modern state with a powerful executive. In fact he seems to have never much valued executive authority in the states as a means of countering legislative abuses, and his conception of the executive in the new national government remained hazy at best. As late as April 1787 he told Washington that he had "scarcely ventured as yet to form my own opinion either of the manner in which [the executive] ought to be constituted or of the authorities with which it ought to be cloathed."[29] Through much of the convention he assumed that the powers over appointment to offices and the conduct of foreign affairs would be assigned not to the president but to the Senate. Only later, after the so-called Connecticut Compromise, when Madison and other nationalists became alarmed by the states' gaining equal representation in the Senate, were these powers taken away from the state-dominated Senate and granted to the president. Certainly Madison in 1787 had no inkling of the kind of presidency that Washington and Hamilton would create in the 1790s.

During the convention all Madison seemed to care about was maintaining a centralized national control over harmful state laws. When on June 6 the convention voted down his proposed council of revision, eight states to three, he became even more determined to hold on to his congressional veto over state legislation. Then the convention began undercutting his Virginia Plan in several important respects. On July 16, after a lengthy and ferocious battle, the convention agreed to the Connecticut Compromise, which gave each state two senators. For Madison this was no compromise but a serious defeat. Since he had desperately wanted proportional representation in both houses of the legislature, he was deeply depressed. Because the states commanded so much of the people's emotional loyalty, he thought giving them explicit representation in the new government and allowing their legislatures to select the senators would eventually vitiate the new central government. He even caucused the next day with his fellow Virginia delegates over whether or not to withdraw from the convention.

The next day, July 17, things got even worse, as Madison frantically sought to fend off efforts to do away with his congressional veto over improper state legislation. "A power of negativing the improper laws of the States," he declared, "is at once the most mild & certain means of preserving the harmony of the system." As a measure of his desperation he even invoked the example of "the British System" under the empire to justify his proposal. "Nothing could maintain the harmony & subordination of the various parts of the empire," he claimed, "but the prerogative by which the Crown stifles in the birth every Act of every part tending to discord or encroachment." Madison admitted that the prerogative of the king's Privy Council to disallow colonial legislation had been "sometimes misapplied thro' ignorance or a partiality to one particular part of the empire," but this, he said, was unlikely to happen in the United States, where knowledge of particular interests was more widespread.[30]

Since his odd and impractical proposal for a congressional veto over all improper state laws, as Gouverneur Morris pointed out, "would disgust all the States," it did not command much support, and on July 17 it lost, seven states to three. Madison was now deeply disheartened and convinced that the Constitution was doomed to fail. Indeed, just before the convention adjourned, he told Jefferson that the new federal government would accomplish none of its goals. The Constitution, he said, "will neither effectually answer its national object nor prevent the local mischiefs which every where excite disgusts against the state governments."[31] This extraordinary statement gives us some idea of how little the final Constitution resembled his original intentions.

Depressed as Madison may have been on July 17 over defeat of his congressional veto over state laws, he had not given up hope that some kind of revisionary power on harmful legislation might be salvaged. On July 21 he seconded and vigorously supported an effort by James Wilson, who was as concerned as he with bad popular legislation, to open up once again the question of allying the judiciary with the executive and granting them a revisionary power over legislation. In defeating the earlier motion to establish such a revisionary council, some delegates had maintained that the judiciary by itself could control improper legislation. But Wilson thought this might not be enough. "Laws," he said, "may be unjust, may be unwise, may be dangerous, may be destructive; and yet not be so unconstitutional as to justify the Judges in refusing to give them effect." (This is an indication of how rudimentary in 1787 was much of the thinking about what came to be called judicial review.)

Madison quickly endorsed Wilson's argument. Since losing the issue of proportional representation in the Senate, he was now increasingly wary of the power of a Congress in which the states as states would have such an important role. Although he mounted every argument he could think of to justify his council of revision, it was the fear of legislative power that obsessed him. He believed deeply that "experience in all the States had evinced a powerful tendency in the Legislature to absorb all power into its vortex" and that this tendency was "the real source of danger to the American Constitutions." Although many delegates agreed that a check on legislation was necessary, his council of revision raised other concerns. Opponents pointed out that such a council would mix the judicial and executive powers and give the expositors of the laws a role in framing them, "making Statesmen of the Judges." Again Madison's council of revision was lost, but this time by a narrower margin, four states to three, with two states divided.[32]

Madison clung tightly to these proposals for checking legislative power because of his conception of the judiciallike role he expected the new federal government to play in the nation, a role graphically revealed in his unusual discussion of American politics in *The Federalist*. Madison wrote twenty-nine of the eighty-five papers of *The Federalist*, and his *Federalist* No. 10 has become the most famous document in the history of American political thought. In his analysis of the sources of interest and faction in this paper, Madison seems at first to be very much the cold-eyed realist. Interest group politics, he wrote, was an ineradicable part of American social reality. People inevitably had interests, and because they wanted to protect those interests, they divided into political factions. The causes of faction, he said, were quite simply "sown in the nature of man." It was naive to expect most people to be virtuous and put aside these interests for the sake of some nebulous public good. Moreover, to try to eliminate these interests would be a denial of liberty. He thus realized that the regulation of these private factional interests was becoming the principal task of modern legislation, meaning that the spirit of party was in the future likely to be involved in the ordinary operations of government.

Even though many other Americans in 1787 were saying the same thing at this point, we scholars have generally applauded Madison for his hardheaded realism, for his unsentimental willingness to question the utopianism of some of his fellow republicans, who had hoped in 1776 that the American people would have sufficient virtue to transcend their interests and act in a disinterested manner. Yet when he continues with his analysis in *Federalist* No. 10, we begin to realize that he is not as cold-eyed and practical as we may have thought.

No government, he wrote, could be just if parties—that is, people with private interests to promote—became judges in their own causes; indeed, interested majorities were no better in this respect than interested minorities.

> No man is allowed to be a judge in his own cause, because his interest would certainly bias his judgment, and, not improbably, corrupt his integrity. With equal, nay with greater reason, a body of men are unfit to be both judges and parties at the same time; yet what are many of the most important acts of legislation but so many judicial determinations, not indeed concerning the rights of single persons, but concerning the rights of large bodies of citizens? And what are the different classes of legislators but advocates and parties to the causes which they determine? Is a law proposed concerning private debts? It is a question to which the creditors are parties on one side and the debtors on the other. Justice ought to hold the balance between them. Yet the parties are, and must be,

themselves the judges; and the most numerous party, or in other words, the most powerful faction must be expected to prevail.[33]

Since the popular colonial assemblies had often begun as courts (it is still the General Court of Massachusetts) and much of their legislation had resembled adjudication, Madison's use of judicial imagery to describe the factional and interest group politics in the state legislatures may appear understandable.[34] But it was not entirely practical and does not seem forward-looking; it tends to point back toward the colonial world, not toward our world at all.[35] For all the brilliance of Madison's diagnosis of interest-ridden popular politics in the states, his remedy for dealing with that politics was very traditional and perhaps ultimately just as utopian, just as visionary, as the views he was contesting. Madison's conception of the new national government was not modern at all. It was idealistic and in many respects harked back to older conceptions of government that prevailed in the colonial period. Madison hoped that the new federal government might transcend parties and become a kind of superjudge and arbiter. It would become, as he put it, a "disinterested & dispassionate umpire in disputes between different passions & interests" in the various states.[36] Although Madison had been unable to include in the national government an institution that resembled the British Privy Council under the empire, he continued to draw parallels between the new federal government and the British Crown. In fact he hoped that the new government might play the same superpolitical neutral role that the British king ideally was supposed to play in the empire.[37]

Madison very much desired to transcend the states and build a nation in 1787, but he had no intention of creating for this nation a modern warmaking state with an energetic and powerful executive. Instead he wanted a government that would act as a disinterested judge, a dispassionate umpire, adjudicating among the various interests in the society. That is why he, unlike his friend Jefferson, eventually came to value the position of the Supreme Court in American political life; it was the only institution that came close to playing the role that in 1787 he had wanted the federal Congress to play.[38]

With this conception of the new national government as a neutral disinterested umpire, Madison becomes something other than the practical pluralist that many scholars have believed him to be. He was not offering some early version of modern interest group politics. He was not a forerunner of twentieth-century political scientists like Arthur Bentley and David Truman. He did not envision public policy or the common good emerging naturally from the give-and-take of hosts of competing interests. Instead he turned out to be much more old-fashioned and classical in his expectations. He expected that the clashing interests and passions in the enlarged national Republic would neutralize themselves in the society and allow liberally educated, rational men—men, he said, "whose enlightened views and virtuous sentiments render them superior to local prejudices, and to schemes of injustice"—to decide questions of the public good in a disinterested adjudicatory manner.[39]

Madison, in other words, was not all as realistic and as modern as we often make him out to be. In his view, not everyone in government had to be a party to a cause. He clung to the great dream of the Revolution that virtuous politics might be possible in America. He believed that there were a few disinterested gentlemen in the society, men like Jefferson and himself, and he hoped that his system would allow these few to transcend the interest-mongering of the many in the society and be able to act as neutral judges or referees in the new national Congress. As "an auxiliary desideratum" to his scheme, Madison predicted that the elevated and expanded sphere of national politics would act as a filter, refining the kind of men who would become these national umpires.[40] In a larger arena of national politics with an expanded electorate and a smaller number of representatives, the people were more apt to ignore the illiberal, narrow-minded men with "factious tempers" and "local prejudices" who had dominated the state legislatures in the 1780s and instead elect to the new federal government only those educated gentlemen with "the most attractive merit and the most . . . established characters."[41]

His theory did not seem to have much practical effect on the character of the new national government; in fact by March 1789 Madison was already predicting that the elevated Congress would behave pretty much as the vice-ridden state legislatures had behaved.[42] In the Congress we do not hear any more talk about his notions of an extended Republic and the filtration of talent. These notions turned out to be as unrelated to reality as his idea of a congressional power to veto all state laws had been. He had other ideas now that turned out to be equally impractical. The truth is Madison was not as hardheaded a realist as we have often thought him to be. Despite the often curious and probing quality of his mind, he was at heart a very idealistic, if not a utopian, republican, perhaps in some respects not all that different from his visionary friend and colleague Jefferson.

Madison began to reveal his peculiar conception of what the national government ought to be when he gradually became aware in the early 1790s of the kind of government that Washington, Hamilton, and other Federalists were actually creating. It was not a judiciallike umpire they were after but a real modern European type of government with a bureaucracy, a standing army, and a powerful independent executive. Like Madison, other Federalists may have been concerned about too much majoritarian democracy in the states, but they had much grander ambitions for the United States than simply controlling popular politics in the states and protecting minority rights. Hamilton and his fellow Federalists wanted to emulate the state-building process that had been going on for generations in Europe and Great Britain.

As we've seen, if any of the founders was a modern man, it was not Madison but Hamilton. It was Hamilton who sought to turn the United States into a powerful modern fiscal-military state like those of Great Britain and France. Madison may have wanted a strong national government to act as an umpire over contending expressions of democracy in the states, as his Virginia Plan suggests, but he had no intention of creating the kind of modern war-making state that Hamilton had in mind. That is why he had no sense of inconsistency in turning against the state that Hamilton was building in the 1790s.

The great development of the early modern period in the Western world was the emergence of modern nation-states with powerful executives, states that had developed the fiscal and military capacity to wage war on unprecedented scales. Over the past several decades scholars have accumulated a rich historical and sociological literature on state formation in early modern Europe.[43] From the sixteenth century through the eighteenth century the European monarchies had been busy consolidating their power and marking out their authority within clearly designated boundaries while at the same time protecting themselves from rival claimants to their power and territories. They erected ever-larger bureaucracies and military forces in order to wage war, and that was what they did through most decades of three centuries. This meant the building of ever more centralized governments and the creation of ever more elaborate means for extracting money and men from their subjects. These efforts in turn led to the growth of armies, the increase in public debts, the raising of taxes, and the strengthening of executive power.[44]

Such monarchical state building was bound to provoke opposition, especially among Englishmen who had a long tradition of valuing their liberties and resisting Crown power. The country-Whig-opposition ideology that arose in England in the late seventeenth and early eighteenth centuries was essentially proto-republican. It was resisting just those kinds of monarchical state building efforts taking place belatedly in England. When later-eighteenth-century British radicals like James Burgh and Thomas Paine warned that the lamps of liberty were going out all over Europe and being dimmed in Britain itself, it was these efforts at modern state formation that they were talking about.[45] Madison, Jefferson, and many other Americans had fought the Revolution to prevent the extension of these kinds of modern state-building efforts to America. They were not about to allow Hamilton and the Federalists to turn the United States into a modern fiscal-military state burdened by debt and taxes and saddled with an expensive standing army. Such states smacked of monarchy and were designed for the waging of war. "Of all the enemies to public liberty," wrote Madison in 1795, "war is, perhaps, the most to be dreaded, because it comprises and develops the germ of every other [enemy]." As "the parent of armies," war, he said, not only promoted "debts and taxes" but also meant that "the discretionary power of the Executive is extended; its influence in dealing out offices, honors, and emoluments is multiplied; and all the means of seducing the minds, are added to those of subduing the force, of the people."[46] These sentiments, which Madison never ceased repeating, were the source of the Republicans' sometimes hysterical opposition to the Hamiltonian Federalist state-building schemes of the 1790s.

Many American revolutionaries, including Jefferson and Madison, wanted to end this kind of modern state building and the kinds of international conflicts that it promoted. Just as enlightened Americans in 1776 sought a new kind of domestic politics that would end tyranny within nations, so too did they seek a new kind of international politics that would promote peace among nations and indeed that might even see an end to war itself. Throughout the eighteenth century liberal intellectuals had dreamed of a new enlightened world from which corrupt monarchical diplomacy, secret alliances, dynastic rivalries, standing armies, and balances of power would disappear. Monarchy, unresponsive to the will of the people, was the problem. Its bloated bureaucracies, standing armies, perpetual debts, and heavy taxes were the consequence of its perennial need to wage war. Eliminate aggrandizing monarchies and all their accoutrements, and war itself would be eliminated. A world of republican states would encourage a different kind of diplomacy, a peace-loving diplomacy, one based not on the brutal struggle for power of conventional diplomacy but on the natural concert of the commercial interests of the people of the various nations. If the people of the various nations were left alone to exchange goods freely among themselves without the corrupting interference of selfish monarchical courts, irrational dynastic rivalries, and the secret double-dealing diplomacy of the past, then it was hoped international politics would become republicanized, pacified, and ruled by commerce alone. Old-fashioned diplomats might not even be necessary in this new commercially linked world.[47]

Suddenly in 1776, with the United States isolated and outside the European mercantile empires, Americans had both an opportunity and a need to put into practice these liberal ideas about international relations and the free exchange of goods. Commercial interest and revolutionary idealism thus blended to form the basis for American thinking about foreign affairs that lasted well into the twentieth century. To some extent this blending is still present in our thinking about the world.

Trade would be enough to hold states together and maintain peace in the world. Indeed, for Madison, Jefferson, and other idealistic liberals like Thomas Paine, peaceful trade among the people of the various nations became the counterpart in the international sphere to the sociability of people in the domestic sphere. Just as enlightened thinkers foresaw republican society held together solely by the natural affection of people, so too did they envision a world held together by the natural interests of nations in commerce. In both the national and international spheres monarchy and its intrusive institutions and monopolistic ways were what prevented a natural and harmonious flow of people's feelings and interests.

These enlightened assumptions lay behind the various measures of commercial coercion attempted by Madison, Jefferson, and other Republicans throughout the 1790s and the early decades of the nineteenth century. The Republicans knew only too well that if republics like the United States were to avoid the consolidating processes of the swollen monarchical powers—heavy taxes, large permanent debts, and standing armies—they would have to develop peaceful alternatives to the waging of war. Madison was not a complete utopian. He feared, as he wrote in 1792, that "a universal and perpetual peace . . . will never exist but in the imaginations of visionary philosophers, or in the breasts of benevolent enthusiasts." Nevertheless, because war was foolish as well as wicked, he still hoped that the progress of reason might eventually end war, "and if anything is to be hoped," he said, "every thing ought to be tried."[48]

The ideal, of course, was to have the world become republican—that is, composed of states whose governments were identical with the will of the people. Jefferson and Madison believed that unlike monarchies whose

wills were independent of the wills of their subjects, self-governing republics were likely to be peace-loving, a view that Hamilton had only contempt for. Madison did concede that even republics might occasionally
have to go to war. But if wars were declared solely by the authority of the
people and, more important, if the costs of these wars were borne directly
and solely by the generation that declared them, then, wrote Madison,
"ample reward would accrue to the state." All "wars of folly" would be
avoided, only brief "wars of necessity and defence" would remain, and
even these might disappear. "If all nations were to follow [this] example,"
said Madison, "the reward would be doubled to each, and the temple of
Janus might be shut, never to be opened again."[49] In other words, Madison believed that a republican world might be able to close the door on
war forever.

In a world of monarchies, however, Madison concluded that the best
hope for the United States to avoid war was to create some sort of peaceful republican alternative to it. This alternative was the use of commercial discrimination against foreign enemies backed ultimately by the
withholding of American commerce; these measures were, he said, "the
most likely means of obtaining our objects without war."[50] In other words,
Madison proposed the use of what we now call economic sanctions, something that even today we often desperately cling to as an alternative to the
direct use of military force. Given the importance Republicans attached
to commerce in tying nations together, it made sense to use it as a weapon
in international politics.

This republican idealism—this fear of the modern fiscal-military state
and this desire to find peaceful alternatives to war—is the best context for
understanding the thinking of Madison and other Republicans. It helps
explain not only their attitude toward modern state power but also their
resort to trade discrimination against Great Britain in the early 1790s.
Madison and the other Republicans were outraged by Jay's Treaty in 1795
because it took this essential weapon away from the United States. In the
same way this context helps explain Jefferson and Madison's policies in
the years following the lapse of Jay's Treaty in 1806, the several nonim-

portation and nonintercourse acts against the two European belligerents, Britain and France. These efforts came to a climax with what Jefferson called his "candid and liberal" experiment in peaceful coercion, the Republicans' disastrous embargo of all American trade in 1807 and 1808, surely the most extraordinary example in American history of ideological principles brought directly to bear on a matter of public policy.[51] (Hamilton must have turned in his grave.) Actually Madison believed in the coercive purpose of the embargo even more than Jefferson. To the end of his life Madison remained convinced that the embargo would have eventually worked if it had not been prematurely repealed.[52]

Probably the most convincing evidence of Madison's being a idealistic republican seeking to avoid a strong federal government and the state-building processes characteristic of the modern European monarchies was the way he and the other Republicans prepared for and fought the War of 1812. *Prepared for* are hardly the words to use. The Republicans in Congress talked about war, but at the same time they proposed abolishing the army. They cut back the War Department and defeated efforts to build up the navy. They abolished the Bank of the United States on the eve of hostilities, and in March 1812 they very reluctantly agreed to raise taxes, which were to go into effect, however, only if an actual war broke out.

Historians often harshly criticize Madison and the Republicans for the inept way they prepared for and conducted the war. But this criticism misses the point of what Madison and the Republicans were most frightened of. As Jefferson said in 1806, "our constitution is a peace establishment—it is not calculated for war."[53] War, the Republicans realized, would lead to a Hamiltonian monarchical type of government, with increased taxes, an overblown bureaucracy, heavy debts, standing armies, and enhanced executive power. Since war was a threat to republican principles, the Republican party and administration were determined to wage the war that began in 1812 in a manner different from the way monarchies waged war. As Secretary of the Treasury Albert Gallatin pointed out at the outset, the Republicans' dilemma was to conduct war without promoting "the evils inseparable from it . . . debt, perpetual taxation, military establishments, and other corrupting or anti-republican habits or institutions."[54]

Madison remained remarkably sanguine during the disastrous events of the war. Better to allow the country to be invaded and the capital to be burned than to build up state power in a European monarchical manner. Even during the war he continued to call for embargoes as the best means for fighting it. He knew that a republican leader should not become a Napoleon or even a Hamilton. Calm in the conviction that in a republic strong executive leadership could only endanger the principles for which the war was fought, he knowingly accepted the administrative confusion and inefficiencies and the military failures.[55]

So even though the war settled nothing, it actually settled everything. It vindicated the grand revolutionary experiment in limited republican government. As the city of Washington declared in a formal tribute to the president, the sword of war had usually been wielded at the expense of "civil or political liberty," but this had not been the case with President Madison in the war against Britain. Not only had the president restrained the sword "within its proper limits," but he also had directed "an armed force of fifty thousand men aided by an annual disbursement of many millions, without infringing a political, civil, or religious right." As one admirer noted, Madison had withstood both a powerful foreign enemy and widespread domestic opposition "without one trial for treason, or even one prosecution for libel."[56]

Historians living in a very different world, one dominated by theories of preemptive war, a vast federal bureaucracy, a sprawling Pentagon, an enormous CIA, huge public debts, taxes beyond any the founders could have imagined, and well over a million men and women under arms, may not appreciate Madison's achievement, but contemporaries did. "Notwithstand[ing] a thousand Faults and blunders," John Adams told Jefferson in 1817, Madison's administration had "acquired more glory, and established more Union than all his three Predecessors, Washington, Adams, Jefferson, put together."[57]

We historians have become so used to praising Madison the author of the tenth *Federalist* and denigrating Madison the president that we assume they must be two different Madisons. But there is no "Madison problem," except the one that we have concocted. Maybe we ought to spend less time investigating Madison the author of the tenth *Federalist* and more time investigating Madison the president. His conception of war and government, whether we agree with it or not, might help us understand better the world we have lost.

Chapter Six

The Relevance and Irrelevance of John Adams

J OHN ADAMS ALWAYS believed he was the most underrated and neglected of the revolutionary leaders. He knew, as he told his friend Benjamin Rush in 1790, that his role in the Revolution would never be properly recognized. The essence of the Revolution, he moaned, "will be that Dr. Franklin's electrical rod smote the earth and out sprung General Washington. That Franklin electrified him with his rod—and thence forward these two conducted all the policy, negotiation, legislatures and war."[1]

Adams, the Massachusetts-born patriot, had some reason to feel ignored by his fellow revolutionaries. In the Continental Congress in 1774–76 he had been in the forefront of the drive for independence, but after independence had been achieved, few made as much of that contribution as Adams thought they should have. Although he had served on the committee that drew up the Declaration of Independence, people were by the 1790s beginning to pay more attention to Jefferson's role in writing the first draft. Besides, Adams always considered the Declaration merely a document derived from the May 10 and May 15, 1776, congressional resolutions, for which he had been most responsible. The resolutions advised the colonies to adopt new governments "where no government sufficient to the exigencies of their affairs have been hitherto established," and went on to declare "that the exercise of every kind of authority under the . . . Crown should be totally suppressed," and to call for the exertion of "all the powers of government . . . under the authority of the people of the colonies." When some hesitant colleagues called the last resolution "a Machine for the fabrication of Independence," Adams jubilantly retorted that "it was independence itself." Yet as he ruefully recalled in 1805, these May resolutions were "then little known" and were "now forgotten, by all but . . . a very few."[2]

So it went. Adams always believed he never received sufficient credit for his accomplishments. True, he was appointed the first minister to Great Britain following independence, and in 1789 he was elected vice president of the United States, receiving the second-highest total of electoral votes after Washington. Still, this recognition never seemed enough; he yearned to be a great man, but only on his own terms. No one prided himself more on his independence, on being his own man, under obligation to no one. He defied his father in choosing a career as a lawyer rather than as a clergyman. In 1770 he took on the defense of the soldiers who had killed five of his countrymen in the "Boston Massacre."[3] He defied many of his fellow patriots in 1774 by defending a Loyalist victim of a mob. In Europe, negotiating the peace in the early 1780s, he defied everyone: Congress, his colleagues, and the country's French ally. He had no guile whatsoever and seemed to take a stubborn pride in the snubs and sneers that he often received for his cantankerous and outspoken opinions. His classical heroes were Demosthenes and Cicero, whose achievements came in the teeth of their defeats, their unpopularity, and their loneliness. "I must think myself independent, as long as I live," he said. "The feeling is essential to my existence."[4]

His colleagues scarcely knew what to do with him. They knew he was smart and dedicated, but his behavior often caused them to shake their heads and roll their eyes. Adams was uncommonly vain, said Jefferson during the peace negotiations in Paris in 1783, and he seemed to hate everyone. "He hates Franklin, he hates John Jay, he hates the French, he hates the English." But Jefferson conceded that Adams had integrity. "At any rate," he told his friend Madison, "honesty may be extracted even from poisonous weeds."[5] But no one summed up Adams's character better than Franklin, who famously described him as a man who "means well for his Country, is always an honest Man, often a Wise One, but sometimes and in some things, absolutely out of his senses."[6]

Still, these personal estrangements that separated Adams from his colleagues, common though they were, were nothing compared with the intellectual estrangement that he began to experience after he returned to America from England in 1788. Adams had not taken part in the drawing up of the new federal Constitution in 1787 and had not experienced the rich and wide-ranging discussions surrounding its ratification in the several states. Consequently, he did not understand the new thinking about politics that lay behind the formation and defense of the new Constitution. Indeed, it was Adams's unfortunate fate to have missed the intellectual significance of the most important event since the Revolution.

It is ironic that Adams, of all people, should have misunderstood the meaning of the Constitution, for no American was more deeply involved in the constitutionalism of the American Revolution. Certainly no one took the Revolution and its significance for politics more seriously, and no one identified his whole life and career with the Revolution and its success more completely. Politics for Adams was always the supreme science. At the beginning of and throughout his career he continually admonished himself to pursue intellectual activity. "Keep your Law Book or some Point of Law in your mind at least 6 Hours in a day. . . . Aim at an exact

Knowledge of the Nature, End, and Means of Government. Compare the different forms of it with each other and each of them with their Effects on public and private Happiness. Study Seneca, Cicero, and all other good moral Writers. Study Montesque, Bolinbroke, ... and all other good, civil Writers, etc."[7] No one read more and thought more about law and politics than John Adams.

More than any of the revolutionaries Adams represented the political and constitutional side of the American Enlightenment. At the outset of the constitution-making period his pamphlet *Thoughts on Government* (1776) became the most influential work guiding the framers of the new Republic, and in the late seventies he took an important hand in drafting the Massachusetts Constitution of 1780, widely regarded as the most consequential state constitution of the revolutionary era. He never tired of investigating politics and advising his countrymen, and he came to see, with more speed and insight than most, the mistaken assumptions about their character on which the Americans of 1776 had rested their Revolution. At the height of the intellectual crisis of the 1780s he attempted, while in England, to translate what he thought he and other Americans had learned about themselves and their politics into basic principles of social and political science that were applicable to all peoples at all times. The result was the only comprehensive analysis of American constitutionalism that the period produced, the finest fruit of the American Enlightenment, the bulky, disordered, conglomeration of political glosses on a single theme of mixed or balanced government, his *A Defence of the Constitutions of Government of the United States of America.*

If only because of his significant contributions to the revolutionary movement and to American constitutionalism, Adams deserves to be regarded as a major founder. More important, he merits special attention as a founder because of the contrasting character of his political ideas with those of other Americans in those years. For all his intense involvement in constitutionalism and for all his insight into his own and America's character, Adams never really comprehended what was happening to the fundamentals of American political thought in the years after 1776.

Throughout his life he remained the political scientist par excellence, and in the end the very intensity of his devotion to the science of politics as he understood it played him false.

Perhaps he read and remembered too much; perhaps he was too honest, too much the scientist and too little the politician. At any rate amid the intellectual turmoil of the 1780s Adams clung ever more tightly to the truths of enlightened politics as he had learned them: Government bore an intimate relation to society, and unless the two were reconciled, no state could long remain secure.

There was never anything disingenuous about Adams. He refused to pervert the meaning of language, and he could not deny or disguise, without being untrue to everything he felt within himself, the oligarchic nature of American politics. He correctly saw that no society, including America, could ever be truly egalitarian, and he attempted, as no other revolutionary quite did, to come to terms with this fact of social and political life. But he paid a high price for his honesty. For by defending more comprehensively and stridently than anyone else the traditional idea of mixed or balanced government at the very moment of its disintegration, Adams steadily isolated himself from the main line of American intellectual development.

LIKE OTHER AMERICANS, Adams began the Revolution filled with excitement and enthusiasm for the future. "America," he had written as early as 1765, "was designed by Providence for the Theatre, on which Man was to make his true figure, on which science, Virtue, Liberty, Happiness and Glory were to exist in Peace." The Revolution, he said in 1776, would be "an Astonishment to vulgar Minds all over the World, in this and in future Generations."[8] No one was more attuned to the hopes and promise of the Enlightenment than Adams.

At the same time no revolutionary leader punctured the faith of 1776 with as many doubts and as many misgivings. He had no illusions in 1776 about the difficulties that lay ahead. There would be "Calamities" and

"Distresses," he predicted on the eve of independence, "more wasting" and "more dreadfull" than any yet experienced by Americans. Such affliction, however, would have "this good Effect, at least: it will inspire Us with many Virtues, which We have not, and correct many Errors, Follies, and Vices, which threaten to disturb, dishonour, and destroy Us."[9] Adams knew full well the dependence of republicanism on the character of the people. History had taught that "public Virtue is the only Foundation of Republics." No republican government could last, he said, unless there was "a positive Passion for the public good, the public Interest, ... established in the Minds of the People, ... Superiour to all private Passions." Yet could America attain this Spartan sense of sacrifice? "Is there in the World a Nation, which deserves this Character?"

Americans, Adams noted, possessed as much public spirit as any people in the modem world. Nevertheless, he had seen all through his life "such Selfishness and Littleness even in New England" that the cause seemed doubtful, not for lack of power or wisdom but for lack of virtue. The Revolution had unleashed a bundle of passions, "Hope, Fear, Joy, Sorrow, Love, Hatred, Malice, Envy, Revenge, Jealousy, Ambition, Avarice, Resentment, Gratitude," creating a whirlwind up and down the continent. There was, he told Mercy Warren in January 1776, "so much Rascallity, so much Venality and Corruption, so much Avarice and Ambition such a Rage for Profit and Commerce among all Ranks and Degrees of Men" that republicanism seemed indeed a precarious experiment. It was as if Adams were carrying in his own mind all the promise and all the anxiety engendered by the Revolution.[10]

More so perhaps than any other revolutionary in 1776 Adams rested his hopes for the future on the regenerative effects of republican government and on the emergence of politicians who could mold the character of the people, extinguishing their follies and vices and inspiring their virtues and abilities. As early as 1765 he had observed that Americans alone among the peoples of the world had learned that liberty could not be preserved without "knowledge diffused generally through the whole body of the people." In the excitement of the early days of the Revolution, Adams, like others, clung to this trust in education and republicanism to curb the violent passions of men. They, he hoped, would give a "decisive Colour to the Manners of the people," and thereby produce "Strength, Hardiness, Activity, Courage, Fortitude and Enterprise," along with a pervasive belief in the principle "that all Things must give Way to the public." If "pure Virtue," "the only foundation of a free Constitution . . . ," he explained in June 1776, "cannot be inspired into our People, in a greater Measure, than they have it now, they may change their Rulers, and the forms of Government, but they will not obtain a lasting Liberty.— They will only exchange Tyrants and Tyrannies." The reliance that Adams placed on the ameliorative power of republicanism may have been illusory, but given his deep apprehension of the American character, an apprehension that sprang from his knowledge of himself, he had little choice. The Revolution had to reform the culture, or it could not succeed.[11]

Within a few years after independence, however, whatever optimism Adams had had for the betterment of the American character was gone. The American people could no more change than he himself could. By the 1780s what he had feared all along was too evident to deny: Americans had "never merited the Character of very exalted Virtue," and it was foolish to have "expected that they should have grown much better." He now saw and expressed more vividly than anyone that if the new American republics were to rely simply on the virtue of the people, they were destined, like every previous republic, for eventual destruction. By the time he came to write his *Defence* in 1787 he had become thoroughly convinced that his countrymen were as corrupt as any nation in the world. Unlike Jefferson's mission abroad, Adams's long stay in Europe had only confirmed his anxiety about America's character. For Jefferson, Europe made American simplicity and virtue appear only dearer by contrast, but for Adams, Europe represented only what America had already become.

It was now clear that there was "no special providence for Americans, and their nature is the same with that of others." Once the hopes of 1776 had disappeared, Adams set for himself the formidable task of convincing his countrymen that they were after all "like all other people, and shall do like other nations." Since he was denying the emerging myth of America's exceptionalism, his divergence from his countrymen could not have been more fundamental.[12]

Americans, Adams now believed, were as driven by the passions for wealth and precedence as any people in history. Ambition, avarice, and resentment, not virtue and benevolence, were the stuff of American society. Those who argued that Americans were especially egalitarian were blind to reality. "Was there, or will there ever be," asked Adams, "a nation, whose individuals were all equal, in natural and acquired qualities, in virtues, talents, and riches?" Every people, he contended, possessed inequalities "which no human legislator ever can eradicate." Such inequalities did not have to be legal or artificial—hereditary dignities symbolized by titles or ribbons—in order to be real. They were rooted in nature, in wealth, in birth, or in merit. Because of greater industry or because of a bountiful legacy, some were richer than others. Some were better born than others, inheriting from their families' position and prestige in the community. Some were wiser, bolder, more talented than others, displaying courage or learning in such a way as to command respect. All such distinctions produced inequality in the society, and all these inequalities were "common to every people, and can never be altered by any, because they are founded in the constitution of nature."[13]

The inevitability of these distinctions lay at the heart of Adams's image of society. All life, he believed, was a scramble for them, for wealth, for power, for social eminence, that people hoped would be everlasting, passed on to one's descendants. "We may call this desire of distinction childish and silly," said Adams, "but we cannot alter the nature of men." The desires of man, especially those Adams called the "aristocratical passions," were unlimited and consuming. "The love of gold grows faster than the heap of acquisition." The love of praise was worse. Man so desired it that he "is miserable every moment when he does not snuff the incense." Ambition, the most powerful of the aristocratic passions, so intensified that it "at last takes possession of the whole soul so absolutely, that a man sees nothing in the world of importance to others or himself, but in his object."[14]

Only a handful made their way to the top in this ferocious struggle for superiority, but unfortunately there was little guarantee that these few would be men of talent and virtue. The republican hope that only real merit should govern the world was laudable but hollow. How could it be arranged, asked Adams, "that men ought to be respected only in proportion to their talents, virtues, and services. . . ? How shall the men of merit be discovered? . . . Who shall be the judge?" The republican reliance on elections had hardly worked out. The voters had repeatedly been deceived by the chicanery and falsehoods of pretended merit. The numbers who thirsted for respect and position were "out of all proportion to those who seek it only by merit." Men thus disguised their lack of talent "by displaying their taste and address, their wealth and magnificence, their ancient parchments, pictures, and statues, and the virtues of their ancestors," any artifice, any hypocrisy, that would convince others that they were designed to rule. "What chance has humble, modest, obscure, and poor merit in such a scramble?"[15]

It seemed that there was nothing meritorious in those who reached the pinnacle of the society except their ability to get there. And once on top the few would seek only to stabilize and aggrandize their position by oppressing those below them. Those on the bottom of the society, meanwhile, driven by the most ambitious, would seek only to replace and to ruin the social leaders they hated and envied. Those especially "whose fortunes, families, and merits, in the acknowledged judgment of all" seemed closest to those on the top "will be much disposed to claim the first place as their own right." No matter that the few were not happy in their superiority. Men were driven by inscrutable passions to supplant those above them. "To better their condition, to advance their fortunes, without limits, is the object of their constant desire, the employment of all their thoughts by day and by night." They want to share in that pleasure "which they presume those enjoy, who are already powerful, celebrated, and rich."[16]

Hence arose, concluded Adams, that inevitable social division between "the rich and the poor, the laborious and the idle, the learned and the ignorant," a division neither rigid nor secure, grounded in the irrationalities and passions of men, a division, moreover, from which America, however republican, however simple, could never escape. "Perhaps it may be said," remarked Adams, "that in America we have no distinctions of ranks, and therefore shall not be liable to those divisions and discords which spring from them." But this was a futile hope. "All that we can say in America is, that legal distinctions, titles, powers, and privileges, are not hereditary." The desire for distinction, rooted in all human nature, still prevailed. Were not, asked Adams, the slightest differences of rank and position, between laborers, yeomen, and gentlemen in America, "as earnestly desired and sought, as titles, garters and ribbons are in any nation of Europe?"[17]

In fact, he argued, almost a half century before Tocqueville made the same penetrating observation, the urge for distinction was even stronger in America than elsewhere. "A free people are the most addicted to luxury of any." Americans would inevitably seek to set themselves off one from another, yet because their republican commitment to equality would give them no sanctions for such distinctions, they would create deep and bitter resentments throughout the society. In a democratic society "there can be no subordination." A man would see his neighbor, "whom he holds his equal," with a better coat, hat, house, or horse. "He cannot bear it; he must and will be upon a level with him." Following the Revolutionary War, noted Adams, America "rushed headlong into a greater degree of luxury than ought to have crept in for a hundred years." Indeed, because America was "more Avaricious than any other Nation that ever existed," it would be madness, concluded Adams, to expect the society to be free of luxury and the desire for distinction. The English Crown had not been, as many in 1775 had believed, the source of colonial America's corruption and factionalism after all. Social struggle and division were endemic to every society, and America possessed no immunity.[18]

THIS, THEN, was the America John Adams felt and saw, a ceaseless scrambling for place and prestige, a society without peace, contentment, or happiness, a society in which "the awful feeling of a mortified emulation" ate at everyone's heart and made failure unbearable. Adams gave Americans as grim and as dark a picture of themselves as they have ever been offered. Indeed, so pessimistic was Adams's conception of American society that despair seemed inevitable. What possibly could keep this restless society from tearing itself to pieces? What could restrain these brutal and selfish passions that threatened to destroy their possessors? Nature had "wrought the passions into the texture and essence of the soul," and man could never destroy them. "To regulate and not to eradicate them," said Adams, "is the province of policy." But how could these unruly passions be regulated?

By the 1780s Adams had lost his former faith in the inspirational and ameliorating qualities of republicanism. He no longer shared the continuing faith of other Americans like Jefferson and Benjamin Rush in the capacity of education to discipline the emotions of men. People could not be taught to submerge their individual desires into a love for the whole. No nation could so educate its people. "Millions must be brought up, whom no principles, no sentiments derived from education, can restrain from trampling on the laws." It was impossible, said Adams, to reconcile the "diversity of sentiments, contradictory principles, inconsistent interests, and opposite passions" of America "by declamations against discord and panegyrics upon unanimity." Education, religion, superstition, oaths—none of them could control human appetites. "Nothing," he said, "but Force and Power and Strength can restrain them." Nothing "but three different orders of men, bound by their interests to watch over each other, and stand the guardians of the laws" could maintain social order.[19]

A balanced or mixed constitution—only such a classical scheme could restrain the furies and passions of men and keep the society together. The political solution Adams offered was essentially the ancient mixed polity, the traditional eighteenth-century English constitution, which Adams called "the most stupendous fabric of human invention," refined and refurbished in the manner of the Swiss observer, Jean Louis de Lolme, "whose book," said Adams, "is the best defence of the political balance of three powers that ever was written."[20]

It was not, however, the English constitution as most eighteenth-century Englishmen had understood it. By the 1780s Adams's balance was no longer that between the monarchy and the people, the equipoise of the Glorious Revolution, which pitted the ever-encroaching power of the Crown against the liberty of the people, mediated by a nobility that in the Whig scheme of history had interceded on the side of the people as much as it had aided the king. Adams, like other Americans in these years, reconstructed this traditional Whig balance to fit what seemed to be a new social situation, a new appraisal of the nature of American society.

It was not a jumbling of diverse passions that Adams pictured. Society was not for him the hodgepodge of various interests and factions that it was for Madison in *The Federalist*, No. 10. The passions may have been varied, but there was no doubt in Adams's mind that the interests in the society could be reduced to a duality, the few and the many, those that had attained superiority and those who aspired to it, a conclusion that was by no means unique to him. Others too in the 1780s were increasingly describing politics as a contest between "men of some, but small property, much embarrassed and devoured by the interest of their debts," and "men of large estates, especially those which consist in money," in short, between the democracy and the aristocracy.[21]

Especially in Massachusetts references to this social polarity attained an intensity that was not duplicated elsewhere in the 1780s. As early as 1778 Theophilus Parsons in *The Essex Result* had suggested a bicameral legislature that would represent in its separate houses the persons and the property of the state.[22] This stark distinction was later embodied in the Massachusetts Constitution of 1780, which Adams largely composed. No other state in the period so boldly interpreted the bicameral principle in this way. By the middle 1780s the Massachusetts press was filled with talk of the struggle between the rich and the poor, the patricians and the plebeians, and some radicals were even urging that the stronghold of property, the Senate, be abolished.

From 1784 to 1786 Benjamin Lincoln, Jr., the son of the Revolutionary War general and a recent Harvard graduate, explained in a series of articles in the *Boston Magazine* and the *Independent Chronicle* the natural and historical basis of the Massachusetts Constitution. In his essays he anticipated John Adams's *Defence* at every major point. Although Adams was abroad when Lincoln's writings were published and was probably not directly influenced by them, he was certainly familiar with the intellectual and political atmosphere that produced them. His *Defence* grew out of the same Massachusetts cultural climate that shaped the writings of both Parsons and Lincoln.[23]

"A balance," Lincoln had written in 1785, "supposes three things, the two scales, and the hand that holds it." Adams himself could not have put it better. Only "orders of men, watching and balancing each other," could preserve the constitution. The legislature must provide separate chambers for those on the top and those on the bottom of the society, one for the aristocracy and another for the people, an organizing, segregating, and a balancing of the warring social elements, mediated by an independent executive who shared in the lawmaking. The perfect constitution, echoed Adams, was "the tripartite balance, the political trinity in unity, trinity of legislative, and unity of executive power, which in politics is no mystery."[24]

The aristocracy, "the rich, the well-born, and the able," with its heightened sense of avarice and ambition, was especially dangerous, yet Adams also believed that it generally represented the best that society could offer in honor and wisdom. How then, asked Adams, "shall the legislator avail himself of their influence for the equal benefit of the public? and how, on the other hand, shall he prevent them from disturbing the public happiness?" Only by arranging this natural aristocracy or the most conspicuous of its members, together in a separate legislative house, isolating them from the rest of the nation, would the state "have the benefit of their wisdom, without fear of their passions."[25]

In a like manner the popular mass of the society must also be restrained in a separate legislative house. Just as Adams feared the overweening passions of aristocracy because he experienced them in his own tormented soul, so too did he perceive the voracious character of the common people because he once had been one of them. The many were just as dangerous to liberty and the public good as were the few: "They are all of the same clay; their minds and bodies are alike." "The people will not bear a contemptuous look or disrespectful word." Indeed, the aristocracy at least had the advantage of wisdom derived from education and breeding, while the people were generally inconstant and ignorant. Unchecked, the people not only would turn on the aristocrats, robbing them and ruining them without hesitation, but also would despoil and plunder among themselves. All history, said Adams, offered irrefutable proof that the people, unrestrained, "have been as unjust, tyrannical, brutal, barbarous, and cruel, as any king or senate possessed of uncontrollable power." Yet without the people's representation in the constitution the government would surely be oppressive. "There can be no free government," wrote Adams, "without a democratical branch in the constitution." In fact the absence of the people's voice in the governments of Europe had rid the Old World of liberty. The people needed to be institutionalized in a separate legislative chamber not only to curb their passions but also to counter the wiles and greed of the aristocracy. Their houses of representatives became the bulwark against the exploitation of the many by the few.[26]

However, a balance between these two social elements was not enough, indeed, "in the nature of things, could be no balance at all" but only a perpetually swinging pendulum. Only an independent executive power, the one, the monarchical element of the society, said Adams, could mediate and balance these clashing passions of the democracy and the aristocracy. The executive with a veto over all lawmaking could then throw its weight against the irrational and oppressive measures of either branch of the legislature, particularly, said Adams, against the usurpations of the aristocracy. "If there is one certain truth to be collected from the history of all ages," he argued, it is "that the people's rights and liberties, and the democratical mixture in a constitution, can never be preserved without a strong executive." The executive for Adams, as it was for de Lolme and Lincoln, was the mainstay of the entire mechanism, the indispensable balancer, "the essence of government," that kept the social forces in equilibrium. If the passions and parties of society were to be controlled, the only alternative to the balance he proposed, declared Adams, was an absolute monarchy with a standing army.[27]

No aspect of Adams's thinking had changed more since 1776 than his new appreciation of the role of the executive. He coupled that change with a significant shift in his conception of the principal antagonists of politics. In his *Thoughts on Government* Adams, like most Whigs in 1776, had assumed that politics was essentially a struggle between the ruler, or chief magistrate, and the people, in which the aristocracy sitting in an upper house would act as mediator. Now, in the *Defence*, Adams described the basic struggle as one between the people and the aristocracy in which the magistracy or executive took on the function of balancer. Whereas earlier Adams, like other Americans, had conceived of the aristocracy as simply the ablest and wisest men in the society, different from the people but by no means opposed to the people's welfare, he now saw the aristocratic interest set in opposition to the people's or the democratic interest. Between these two antagonistic social elements now stood the executive as an independent social entity representing the monarchical interest and as such obliged to share in the lawmaking of the state.

"Among every people, and in every species of republics," said Adams, "we have constantly found a first magistrate, a head, a chief, under various denominations, indeed, and with different degrees of authority." Yet for all their differences of titles and power these single magistrates were fundamentally similar: They all sprang from the basic need of every society to realize its monarchical impulse. Hereditary and elective rulers were essentially alike; the American state governors, despite their elective dependency and their lack of hereditary sanctity, fulfilled the same social role in politics as did the king of England. Therefore to Adams most states could never be categorized intelligibly as either monarchies or republics. Massachusetts was actually as much a monarchy as England was a republic. The only meaningful method of classifying governments was by their degree of mixture, and the only good government was a properly mixed one, a regal republic.

For Adams this balancing of the forces inevitable in every society was the Enlightenment fulfilled—a principle of political science discovered to be applicable to all times and all peoples. Only by "combining the great divisions of society in one system," only by forming an "equal, independent mixture" of the three classic kinds of government, "monarchy, aristocracy, and democracy," could stability and order in any state be achieved. These "three branches of power have an unalterable foundation in nature. . . . If all of them are not acknowledged in any constitution of government, it will be found to be imperfect, unstable, and soon enslaved."[28]

ADAMS'S CONSTITUTIONAL remedy could scarcely have been more disproportionate to the severity of the social ills he described. Adams assumed that his balanced constitution—a bicameral legislature and an independent executive—could somehow be overlaid on the fiery and ferocious scramble he saw in the society and then restrain and control that scramble. Not only was his view of American society darker and more pessimistic than that of any other of the founders, but his political solution to the social problems he described, though similar in form, was fundamentally contrary to the central thrust of American political thinking in 1787. Too immersed in the climate of opinion of his own state of Massachusetts, too involved in Europe, and too cut off from the whirling broader currents of American thinking, Adams never quite perceived what his fellow Americans had done in 1787 to the conventional theories of politics and a balanced constitution.

Adams aimed in his *Defence*, he said, "to lay before the public a specimen of that kind of reading and reasoning which produced the American constitutions," particularly the Massachusetts Constitution of 1780. As a result, he was initially uninterested in the efforts of Madison and the other Federalists to create a new national government in place of the Articles of Confederation. As late as 1787 the states remained for him the source of American salvation, "whatever Imperfections may remain incurable in the Confederation." While he was cautiously willing to grant some additional powers to the Confederation Congress, he believed, as he

wrote in the *Defence*, that the American people had decided "that a single assembly was every way adequate to the management of all their federal concerns; and with very good reason, because congress is not a
legislative assembly, nor a representative assembly, but only a diplomatic
assembly."[29]

However, when the new federal Constitution was created in 1787,
Adams at once saw the similarity of its internal structure to his own proposals for balance and immediately became a fervent advocate of it. But
because he remained unaware of the originality of the new American
thinking about federalism, divided power, representation, and popular
sovereignty that came out of the debates in the ratifying process, he was
convinced that the new Constitution necessarily had created a "wholly national" government and not a federal one at all. "Federal," he said, was an
"improper Word" to describe it. Sovereignty, "the Summa imperil," he had
learned from both history and experience," was "indivisible." Sovereignty,
he said, could not be divided or shared. He knew from the experience of
the imperial debate with Britain in the 1760s and 1770s "that imperium
in imperio is a solecism, a contradiction in terms" and that the final
supreme lawmaking power in government had to be located in either the
national or the state governments, but not in both. In other words, said
Adams, two legislatures could not operate simultaneously over the same
community; one or the other had to be supreme—precisely the position
that British officials had taken in the 1760s and 1770s. This doctrine of sovereignty over which the British Empire had broken thus inevitably made
the new American government, said Adams, "not a confederation of independent Republicks" but "a monarchical republic."[30]

Perhaps nothing was more symptomatic of Adams's divergence from
the mainstream of American thought than his inability to understand
what the defenders of the new Constitution, the Federalists, had done to
this concept of sovereignty. Instead of locating sovereignty in either the
national government or the state governments, the Federalists had located it in the people at large. By asserting that all sovereignty rested with
the people, the Federalists were not simply saying, as theorists had for

ages, that all governmental power was derived from the people. Instead they were saying that sovereignty, the final supreme indivisible lawmaking authority, remained always with the people and that government was only a temporary and limited agency of the people—lent out to the various government officials, so to speak, on a short-term, always recallable loan. No longer could any parts of the state and federal governments, even the so-called popular houses of representatives, ever fully represent the people; instead all elected parts of the governments—senators and governors and presidents—were now regarded in one way or another as simply partial agents of the people. Some were suggesting that even judges were agents of the people.

This new thinking made nonsense of the age-old theory of mixed or balanced government in which monarchy, aristocracy, and democracy were set against one another—the very theory that Adams was devoutly committed to. Even though the American governments, both state and federal, contained monarchlike executives and aristocratic senates, most Americans no longer regarded them as classically mixed or balanced governments embodying the various orders of the society. Thus most Americans, but not Adams, now began to call their governments unmixed democracies or representative democracies. With the process of election becoming the sole criterion of representation, most Americans, but not Adams, now began to think of all elected governmental officials, including senators and executives, as equal agents of the people. Moreover, if judges were agents of the people, maybe they too ought to be elected.

All this new thinking passed Adams by. He had written his *Defence* to counter French criticism of the American revolutionary state constitutions drafted between 1776 and 1780. Many liberal Frenchmen, like Adams, were preoccupied with the relation of estates or orders to the institutions of government and thus had concluded that the bicameral legislatures of most of the American state constitutions conceded too much to the aristocratic order at the expense of the third estate of the people. If the people were all that counted in the society, then by rights the government ought to embody only them—that is, it ought to have a unicameral legislature like the Pennsylvania government, with only a house of representatives and no senate and no monarchlike governor.

Confronted with this radical French thinking, Adams clung ever more tightly to the classical English idea of mixed or balanced government without, however, breaking with the French assumption that the government bore some relation to the orders or estates of the society. Indeed, like most Englishmen, Adams assumed that a proper government had to embody not just the people but all the social orders; it was what gave the British government of the king-in-Parliament its ultimate sovereignty.

But Adams's fellow Americans had moved beyond the English and French notions of estates or orders and were creating an entirely new and modern notion of the relation of government to the society, and it was this new and modern notion that Adams never fully grasped.

As he was writing his book, however, he did begin to sense the eccentric character of his ideas and his divergence from the mainstream of American political thinking. The *Defence*, he told Benjamin Franklin in 1787, "contains my confession of political faith, and, if it is heresy, I shall I suppose be cast out of communion. But it is the only sense in which I am or ever was a Republican." He told James Warren in 1787: "Popularity was never my Mistress, nor was I ever, or shall I ever be a popular Man. This Book will make me unpopular."[31]

It did not, however, at least not immediately. Adams's advocacy of a two-house legislature with an independent executive sharing in the lawmaking power coincided with the Federalist remedy for the constitutional problems of the 1780s and so obscured the obsolescence of the reasoning behind his scheme. The response to his three-volume work was thus confused. Because of the seeming identity of his system with the Constitution proposed by the Philadelphia Convention, the *Defence* was generally warmly praised as proof "that," as a Rhode Island newspaper declared in 1787, "a people cannot long be free under a government that consists of a single legislature." The timing of the first volume was fortunate, and although it was actually an apology for America's balanced state constitutions, the book and the new federal Constitution became linked in people's minds.[32]

Those who took the time to probe Adams's reasoning, however, soon found many contradictions with radical American thought as it had developed by 1787. Some even in their admiration saw that the book, as William Davie of North Carolina pointed out, was "rather an encomium on the British Constitution than a defence of American systems." Instead of explaining the principles of the American constitutions, critics observed, Adams seemed to be "insidiously attempting, notwithstanding now and then a saving clause, to overturn our Constitutions, or at least to sow the seeds of discontent." Perhaps, it was said, Adams's "optics have been too weak to withstand the glass of European Courts." It was not long before the *Defence* was being "squibbed at in almost every paper" and being called "one of the most deep wrought systems of political deception that ever was penned by the ingenuity of man."[33]

Everywhere critics pounced on Adams's talk "of the awful distance which should be maintained between some and others" and on his declamations "upon the necessity of one of his three balancing powers, consisting of the *well born*, or of those who are distinguished by their descent from a race of illustrious ancestors. In what part of America are those well born to be found? or, if there are any, did they come into the world with coronets upon their heads, or with any other marks of preeminence above the poorest of our species?" In every society, and particularly in America, declared Samuel Bryan of Pennsylvania, there existed "so great a disparity in the talents, wisdom and industry of mankind" that no "corresponding weight in the community" with distinct views and interests could be isolated so as to allow Adams's three orders "to exercise their several parts" in the government. Even in England, said Bryan, where there was "a powerful hereditary nobility, and real distinctions of rank and interests," such a balanced scheme as Adams proposed had not worked.[34]

None of these criticisms, however, was as fully developed as that of John Stevens, a prominent New Jersey "Farmer." Like others, Stevens was particularly bothered by Adams's obsession with aristocracy. America, he argued, was peculiar in its equality. "We have no such thing as orders, ranks, or nobility; and . . . it is almost impossible they should ever gain any footing here." Only immense accumulations of wealth in a few hands could breed an aristocracy. Yet because of America's republican laws of descent, its prohibitions on monopolies and privileges in any one set of men, and its extensive commercial and social mobility, "there is little danger to be apprehended from this source of wealth being confined to a few places, or to a few persons: in all probability it will be diffused every where." Of course, Stevens admitted, Adams had denied that America possessed at this time different orders of men. But Stevens correctly realized that Adams was at bottom arguing for the recognition of an aristocracy in America, however inchoate.

There could be no mistaking Adams's meaning: Despite the absence of an hereditary nobility, America was no freer of aristocracy than Europe, and the only way to control and to use this aristocracy properly was to ostracize it in a separate house of the legislature. No doubt Stevens was less well read in political theory than Adams, but he was much more attuned to current American thinking and knew instinctively that Adams's old-fashioned classical idea of mixed or balanced government—orders of government derived from constituents of the society—was inapplicable to America. "Not a single scruple of this universal and so much boasted political nostrum," said Stevens, "is to be found in any one of the governments of the United States." If Adams's arguments were correct, Stevens said, America's grand experiment in republicanism was not unique after all, and "we have hitherto been only in pursuit of a phantom." Yet Stevens was convinced that Adams was wrong. The American republics were different and were not mere copies of the English constitution. They were, emphasized Stevens, all "democratic forms of government."[35]

And they were democracies, said Stevens, even though they balanced powers and possessed upper houses and independent executives. Stevens was not quarreling with the structure of government that Adams defended; he was only contesting Adams's reasoning and his justifications for a bicameral legislature and an independent executive. For Stevens the purpose of instituting an upper house was not social but functional. Senates were designed not to confine or embody the aristocracy but rather to lessen the problems of having only a single house of representatives. To prevent these problems, said Stevens, "another representative branch is added: these two separate houses form mutual checks upon each other." As a further means of curbing legislative inconstancy and usurpation, continued Stevens, the executive and judiciary became additional checks.

Adams's analogy of government as a set of two scales held by a third hand, said Stevens, was inapplicable for America. He suggested a more appropriate mechanical analogy: a jack, which represented the machinery of government, controlled by a weight, which was the people, "the power from which the motion of all parts originates." For Stevens the people were not really part of the government at all. He did not see the people as an order in the government balanced against the aristocracy; instead he saw the sovereign people standing outside the entire government, distributing and delegating bits and pieces of their power to various agents. "The several component powers of government," said Stevens, "should be so distributed that no one man, or body of men, should possess a larger share thereof than what is absolutely necessary for the administration of government." Stevens's balance of powers was intended not to embody and confine the major constituents of the society but only to separate, diffuse, and check a mistrusted political authority delegated by the people. For Stevens the parts of the government had lost their ancient social roots. All had become more or less equal agents of the people. Thus the institutions of government for both Adams and Stevens were identical, but the rationale was quite different.[36]

Other Americans kept stumbling over Adams's statements. They were bewildered by the contradiction between his political structures—bicameral legislatures and independent executives—which appeared so consistent with the American governments, and his reasoning, which seemed so out of touch with what many Americans had come to believe by 1790. Although Adams conceded that the people were the source of all authority, he still clung to the classical notion of balanced government that the people could participate in only one part of the government. They were in effect an estate or order that merely partook of the sovereignty (as the people did in England through the House of Commons), and they could exercise the whole sovereignty only in a single-house legislature like that of Pennsylvania.

"Whenever I use the word republic with approbation," he told Samuel Adams, "I mean a government in which the people have collectively, or by representation, an essential share in the sovereignty." Samuel Adams, like most Americans by 1790, accepted wholeheartedly the desirability of a two-house legislature, yet he had no doubt that the entire sovereignty of government remained in the people, "a political doctrine which I have never heard an American politician seriously deny." He just could not make sense of his cousin's statement that the people only shared in the supreme power of government. "Is not the whole sovereignty, my friend, essentially in the people?" he asked. They had the power to amend or even to abolish their forms of government whenever they pleased. They exerted their sovereignty continually, said Samuel, by electing their representatives, senators, and governors; "they delegate the exercise of the powers of government to particular persons, who, after short intervals, resign their powers to the people, and they will reelect them, or appoint others, as they think fit."[37]

It was as if John Adams were speaking a language different from that of other Americans. Why couldn't his countrymen understand him? "How it is possible," he lamented, "that whole nations should be made to comprehend the principles and rules of government, until they shall learn to understand one another's meaning by words?" Roger Sherman, for example, was thoroughly perplexed by Adams's statements. He could not comprehend Adams's unusual definition of a republic as "*a government whose sovereignty is vested in more than one person*," a peculiar definition that made England as much a republic as America, "a monarchical republic it is true, but a republic still; because the sovereignty, which is the legislative power . . . is equally divided, indeed, between the one, the few, and the many, or in other words, between the natural division of mankind in society,—the monarchical, the aristocratical, and democratical." For Sherman a republic was the antithesis of a monarchy, a commonwealth without a king, a government under the authority of only the people, consisting of a legislature, with one or more branches that, together with an executive, were elected by the people. What especially denominated a state "a republic," said Sherman, "is its dependence on the public or people at large, without any hereditary powers."[38]

Yet to Adams this definition was just another example of the "peculiar sense in which the words republic, commonwealth, popular state" were being used by men "who mean by them a democracy, or rather a representative democracy." Adams could not understand that in America by 1787 the chief magistrates and the senates no longer embodied estates in the society as they did in Britain; they had become somehow as representative of the people as the houses of representatives. Therefore a government wholly in the hands of the people, or a democracy, did not for many Americans signify, as it did for Adams, a government in "a single assembly, chosen at stated periods by the people, and invested with the whole sovereignty." To Adams, thinking in traditional classical terms, the mere presence of a governor and a senate inevitably made the government something other than a democracy. Since the governor of Massachusetts was "a limited monarch," so "the Constitution of the Massachusetts is a limited Monarchy." So too, said Adams, was the new national government "a limited Monarchy" or "a monarchical republic" like that of England.

While many Americans by 1787 had moved away from the classical assumptions behind the balanced constitutions they had created in 1776, Adams for ten years had sought to bring those assumptions to the surface and to reconcile them with the English conception of a mixed monarchy, recently made most famous by de Lolme. "The duration of our president," Adams told Sherman, "is neither perpetual nor for life; it is only for four years; but his power during those four years is much greater than that of an avoyer, a consul, a podesta, a doge, a stadtholder; nay, than a king of Poland; nay, than a king of Sparta." And because America was a monarchical republic, its president's being a kind of elective king and an embodiment of the "one" in the society, "it is essential to a monarchical republic, that the supreme executive should be a branch of the legislature, and have a negative on all the laws." Without a proper share in the legislature by the monarchical order, he told Sherman, the desired balance of the state "between the one, the few, and the many" could not be preserved.[39]

By 1790 this explanation of the executive veto was totally out of touch with American thinking. The veto in America had nothing to do with representing the monarchical element in the society, said Sherman; the qualified veto given to American executives was designed "only to produce a revision" of the laws and to prevent hastily drawn legislation. In fact the more Sherman thought about it, the more Adams's ideas seemed to be unrelated to the new government. Its bicameral legislature, for example, had nothing to do with social divisions. "As both branches of Congress are eligible from the citizens at large, and wealth is not a requisite qualification, both will commonly be composed of members of similar circumstances in life." Indeed, all the branches of the government were equal agents of the people, "directed to one end, the advancement of the public good."[40]

As most Americans came to view their state and federal governments and the various parts of these governments as merely agents of the people exercising different functions, Adams, seemingly immune to the new thought around him, moved back into history and grasped the classical theory of the mixed polity even more firmly. His friends' reservations and objections were no match for his vitriolic and gushing passion. For every statement of conventional American republicanism timidly offered by Benjamin Rush, Adams had a fiery retort that left Rush aghast. In Rush's opinion, Americans were different from other people, freer of faction, and peculiarly qualified for republicanism, which, said Rush, had never before in history had a fair trial. For Adams this was absurd. Boston, New York, and Philadelphia were as vicious and profligate as London.

"How can you say," he demanded of Rush, "that Factions have been few in America? . . . Have not our Parties behaved like all Republican Parties? is not the History of Hancock and Bowdoin, the History of the Medici and Albizi?" To Rush's horror Adams even praised hereditary institutions not only for possessing "admirable wisdom and exemplary Virtue in a certain stage of Society in a great Nation" but also for being "the hope of our Posterity," to which Americans must eventually resort "as an Asylum against Discord, Seditions and Civil War, and that at no very distant Period of time." Even titles and symbols of distinction now seemed necessary, indeed beneficial, for America. It was in fact Adams's 1789 proposal of a monarchlike title for the president that got him in trouble.

The widening separation from his countrymen frustrated and frightened him but only compelled him to proclaim his diverging beliefs more shrilly than ever. He saw himself as a Promethean figure, cast aside and punished for his knowledge, while his fellow Americans went on "bawling about a Republicanism which they understand not."[41]

OLD AGE brought no rest. At seventy-nine Adams had to contend with the most penetrating and devastating attack ever written against his *Defence of the Constitutions of the United States*. No one perceived more acutely how he had diverged from the mainstream of American revolutionary thinking than John Taylor of Caroline, the intellectual spokesman for Jeffersonian democracy. In his *An Inquiry into the Principles and Policy of the Government of the United States* (1814) Taylor accused Adams of misunderstanding the exceptional character of America's governments. The American Revolution, declared Taylor, had finally freed men's minds from the "numerical analysis" of politics, the classification of governments into the one, few, and many, into monarchy, aristocracy, and democracy, that had inhibited political thinking since antiquity. At the outset of the Revolution, America had observed only the elevation of the mixed British constitution, yet "through the telescope, necessity, new principles were discovered," and a new way of looking at politics was found. America, de-

clared Taylor, had moved more rapidly in twenty years toward an understanding of political science than the world had in twenty centuries.[42]

Yet Adams seemed unaccountably oblivious of these breakthroughs in
political thinking. His "very language" was "strange" to Americans. He did
not appear to understand the new basis of the American states; he thought
like an Englishman and considered American society to be made up of
orders created by nature. He had arranged "men into the one, the few and
the many" and had attempted to bring the political system of America
within the pale of this tripartite classification "by modifying our temporary, elective, responsible governors, into monarchs; our senates into aristocratical orders; and our representatives, into a nation personally
exercising the functions of government." But the American governments
had nothing to do with these ancient categories of politics. Americans,
said Taylor, did not think of society as made of orders or estastes embodied in the government but "as made of individuals," existing outside all
governments, distributing various portions of their sovereign power, but
not all, "into a multitude of hands."

In England, unlike America, the people gave up their full sovereignty
to their legislature. In the English constitution, the model of the mixed
polity favored by Adams, "the nation and the government is considered
as one, . . . ; whereas, by ours, the nation and the government are considered as distinct." A government of orders was believed sovereign "because
the orders composing it, consider themselves as composing the society."
In England the idea of complete representation assumed by Adams "helps
to take sovereignty from the people, and bestows it upon the government." The English people ceased to exist politically until the next election. The American governments were different. They were never full
embodiments of the society. "All our governments are limited agencies"
of the people, said Taylor, and the electoral process that created them did
not eclipse the continued existence of the sovereign people. The political
assumptions Taylor set forth later made possible the introduction of ref-
erenda, ballot initiatives, the recall of elected officials, and the other extraordinary characteristics of America's democracy.[43]

In Taylor's opinion, Adams had been hopelessly wrong, his system antiquated. Because Adams had never understood America's unique system of politics and had made the "radical errour" of confounding "our division of power . . . with his balance of orders," his great work, concluded Taylor, was in no way a defense of the American constitutions; it was instead "a caricature or travesty" of them.[44]

What could the old man reply? Adams had embraced his political principles too long and too tightly to allow one more attack, however powerful, to shake them loose. For Adams the "analysis of antiquity" was still the "eternal, unchangeable truth." He answered Taylor, of course—in more than thirty letters. But age had mellowed his passion, and the correspondence, he told Taylor, was "intended for your amusement and mine." He only reiterated his deep-felt belief in the inevitability of inequality in society and scarcely showed that he had read, let alone comprehended, Taylor's book. The gulf separating him from his countrymen was saddening. He felt misunderstood and persecuted, and it seemed it had been so from the beginning. "From the years 1761, now more than Fifty years," he lamented to Benjamin Rush in 1812, "I have constantly lived in an enemies Country."[45] For too long and with much candor he had tried to tell his fellow Americans some truths about themselves that American values and American mythology would not abide.

Chapter Seven

Thomas Paine, America's First Public Intellectual

I N 1805 John Adams was as cantankerous as ever. He was continually looking back at the wild and tumultuous age he had lived through and wondering what to call it. Perhaps, he said, it might be called "the Age of Folly, Vice, Frenzy, Brutality, Daemons, Buonaparte, . . . or the Age of the Burning Brand from the Bottomless Pit." Call it "anything," he said, but don't call it "the Age of Reason."

It couldn't be the Age of Reason because it had been dominated by Thomas Paine. Adams doubted "whether any man in the world has had more influence on its inhabitants or affairs for the last thirty years than Tom Paine." But this influence was far from a good thing. Indeed, said Adams, "there can be no severer satyr on the age. For such a mongrel between pig and puppy, begotten by a wild boar on a bitch wolf, never before in any age of the world was suffered by the poltroonery of mankind, to run through such a career of mischief. Call it then the Age of Paine."[1]

Despite Adams's bitter sarcasm, Paine would have loved the title; he was nothing if not vain. Why shouldn't the age be named after him? Who deserved it more? "With all the inconveniences of early life against me," Paine once wrote, "I am proud to say, that with a perseverance undismayed by difficulties, a disinterestedness that compelled respect, I have not only contributed to raise a new empire in the world, founded on a new system of government, but I have arrived at an eminence in political literature, the most difficult of all lines to succeed and excel in, which aristocracy, with all its aids, has not been able to reach or to rival."[2] Paine thought he had as much claim to being a founder of the United States as Franklin, Adams, or Jefferson.

Can we honestly say he was wrong in this view? Didn't Jefferson say in 1801 that Paine had labored on behalf of liberty and the American Revolution "with as much effort as any man living"?[3] Yet somehow Paine's qualifications as a founder have not impressed many Americans. We can imagine the "Age of Jefferson," but despite Adams's quirky comment, it is unlikely that Americans will ever call the period of their Revolution the Age of Paine. Most Americans have never been able to make Paine a central figure in even the American Revolution, never mind the age as a whole. Indeed, for most of our history we have tended to ignore him. We let him die in obscurity in 1809 and ten years later even allowed William Cobbett to take his bones away to England. Even the revolutionary leaders eventually came to ignore him. Although they all knew him, none of them publicly eulogized him upon his death. Most who had known him were embarrassed by the connection and wanted only to forget him. His papers were scattered and destroyed, and memory of him was allowed to fade.

To this day Americans have never mounted any serious campaign to publish a complete and authoritative collection of his writings, a collection that would match in aim, if not in size, those monumental multivolume editions of the revolutionary leaders that are presently being published. The early biographies Americans wrote were muckraking diatribes that pictured Paine as an arrogant, drunken atheist. Despite a few feeble attempts in the nineteenth century to refute this image of Paine, not until the end of the nineteenth century, with Moncure D. Conway's two-volume *The Life of Thomas Paine* (1892), was an authoritative laudatory treatment finally written. The place of Paine in the American pantheon of revolutionaries has improved considerably since then, of course. But it was not until the 1970s that modern historians, as distinct from literary scholars, attempted a biography.

Even with all the studies of Paine we have had over the past several decades, the man still does not quite fit in. Paine ranked himself "among the founders of a new Independent World," but most Americans have not agreed. Everyone senses that he is not like the other revolutionaries, not like Franklin, Washington, Adams, or Jefferson. We cannot quite bring ourselves to treat him as one of America's founders. This neglect is actually astonishing, especially when we consider the breadth of his influence. His most thorough and recent biographer, Englishman John Keane, in his biography *Tom Paine: A Political Life* calls Paine "the greatest public figure of his generation." Paine, writes Keane, "made more noise in the world and excited more attention than such well-known European contemporaries as Adam Smith, Jean-Jacques Rousseau, Voltaire, Immanuel Kant, Madame de Staël, Edmund Burke, and Pietro Verri." His important works—*Common Sense, The Rights of Man*, and *The Age of Reason*— "became the three most widely read political tracts of the eighteenth century." His vision of a decent and happy life for ordinary people in this world is still "alive and universally relevant, . . . undoubtedly more relevant than that of Marx, the figure most commonly identified with the nineteenth- and twentieth-century political project of bringing dignity and power to the wretched of the earth." In fact, says Keane, "not only is Paine's bold rejection of tyranny and injustice as far-reaching as that of his nineteenth-century successor, but his practical proposals . . . are actually more radical than Marx's, mainly because they managed to combine breathtaking vision, a humble respect for ordinary folk, and a sober recognition of the complexity of human affairs."[4]

Paine's origins were as obscure as any of the founders. He was born in Thetford, England, in 1737, five years after Washington and six years before Jefferson. His father was a Quaker, his mother an Anglican, a mixture that was bound to give him an oblique view of religion. Although some biographers believe that Paine regarded himself as a Quaker through most of his life, he probably chose to become neither a Quaker nor an Anglican but borrowed the moral teachings of both. After a half dozen years of education in the local grammar school, where he learned no Latin, Paine at age twelve or thirteen was apprenticed to his father in the corset or stay making trade. With his father's business declining, Paine moved to London for a while. In 1757 he ran away to sea as a privateersman for six months. He returned to stay making in Dover and later in Sandwich and married, but a year later in 1760 he lost his wife and child in childbirth. In 1761 the young widower returned to Thetford. Several years later he secured a position as an excise tax collector, one of the most hated government officials in Great Britain. A year or so later he was dismissed, presumably for laxity, and was forced to try teaching and even preaching for a time, until being reinstated in 1768 as an exciseman in the Sussex town of Lewes. In 1771 he married again, but this marriage was probably never consummated, and he and his wife soon separated. Actually since the death of his first wife Paine had become cold and uncomfortable with women and remained so for the rest of his life.

In Lewes Paine became interested in politics and local affairs and joined a discussion club similar to the one the young Benjamin Franklin had belonged to in Philadelphia. In a campaign to get the salaries of excise officers raised, Paine in 1772 moved to London, where he fell in with Newtonian popularizers and met Franklin, who was busy trying to hold the British Empire together. Paine's campaign on behalf of the excise officers collapsed, and in 1774 he was again dismissed from the excise service and compelled to declare himself bankrupt. The future scarcely looked promising; at the age of thirty-seven he had failed at everything he had ever tried.

Franklin must have seen something in Paine, however, for in September 1774 he wrote a letter of introduction for Paine to his son-in-law

Richard Bache to help the twice-dismissed excise officer get a new start in America "as a clerk, or assistant tutor in a school, or assistant surveyor," all of which Franklin thought him "very capable" of doing.[5]

PAINE HAD SCARCELY landed in the New World in November 1774 before he began writing short pieces for the newspapers, taking the American position in the imperial crisis. It was as if the first thirty years of his life, spent in poverty and obscurity and pressed close to the bottom of English society, had primed him to think like an American. At any rate, after only fourteen months in America, most of which he spent helping edit a Philadelphia magazine, Paine in January 1776 suddenly burst upon the world with his pamphlet *Common Sense.* His life and the world would never again be the same.

Common Sense is the most radical and important pamphlet written in the American Revolution and one of the most brilliant ever written in the English language. It went through dozens of editions and sold at least 150,000 copies, at a time when most pamphlets sold in the hundreds or a few thousand at best. Although the pamphlet, published in January 1776, did not *cause* Americans to think of declaring independence, it did express more boldly and eloquently than any other writing what many of them had already come to think about America's tie to the British Crown. Paine dismissed the king as the "Royal Brute" and called for American independence immediately. "For God's sake, let us come to a final separation . . ." he implored. "The birthday of a new world is at hand."[6]

There is no doubt that, as his friend Benjamin Rush said, "its effects were sudden and extensive upon the American mind."[7] Nearly everyone knew it was a work of genius, and it immediately made Paine an American celebrity. From such a high point his reputation in America could only decline. Franklin's daughter, Sarah Franklin Bache, later said of Paine that "the most rational thing he could have done would have been to have died the instant he had finished his Common Sense, for he never again will have it in his power to leave the World with so much credit."[8]

During his many years in England Paine had mingled in radical circles and had picked up from pamphlets and lectures a substantial understanding of the most liberal and radical thinking in the English-speaking world. Although he was not an original thinker, he did have the uncanny ability to put into readable form what others had conceived of. In *Common Sense* Paine may not have uttered new thoughts, but he did set forth in lucid prose much of what constituted radical, enlightened Anglo-American thinking during the last quarter of the eighteenth century. Like fellow radical Thomas Jefferson, Paine optimistically believed that every person had a natural moral or social sense that compelled him to reach out to others. Indeed, both he and Jefferson thought that the natural sociability of people might replace much of governmental authority. If only the natural moral tendencies of people to love and care for one another were allowed to flow freely, unclogged by the artificial interference of government, particularly monarchical government, Paine and other optimistic republicans believed, society would hold itself together and prosper.

Unlike liberals of the twenty-first century, Paine and other liberal-minded thinkers of the eighteenth century tended to see society as beneficent and government as malevolent. Social honors, social distinctions, perquisites of office, business contracts, legal privileges and monopolies, even excessive property and wealth of various sorts—indeed all social inequities and deprivations—seemed to flow from connections to government, in the end from connections to monarchical government. "Society," wrote Paine in a brilliant summary of this liberal view in the opening paragraph of *Common Sense*, "is produced by our wants and government by our wickedness." Society "promotes our happiness *positively* by uniting our affections," government "*negatively* by restraining our vices." Society "encourages intercourse;" government "creates distinctions." The emerging liberal Jeffersonian view that the least government was the best was based on such a hopeful belief in the natural harmony of society."[9]

But Paine and other liberals went further in their radicalism. In that new and better world that Paine and some other revolutionaries envisioned, war itself might be abolished. Just as enlightened liberal Americans sought a new kind of republican domestic politics that would end tyranny, so too did many of them seek a new kind of international republican politics that would promote peace among nations. Paine very much shared this enlightened international vision.

Throughout the eighteenth century, as we have seen, liberal intellectuals had looked forward to a new republican world in which corrupt monarchical diplomacy, secret alliances, dynastic rivalries, and balances of power would be abolished. Since the dynastic ambitions, the bloated bureaucracies, and the standing armies of monarchies were related to the waging of war, the elimination of monarchy promised the elimination of war. War, said Paine, "from its productiveness, as it easily furnishes the pretence of necessity for taxes and appointments to places and offices, becomes a principal part of the system of Old Governments; and to establish any mode to abolish war, however advantageous it might to be Nations, would be to take from such Government the most lucrative of its branches." Monarchies encourage war simply "to keep up the spirit of the system." The reason republics were not plunged into the waging of war was that "the nature of their Government does not admit of an interest distinct to that of the Nation."[10] A world of republican states would encourage a peace-loving diplomacy, one based on the natural concert of international commerce. If the people of the various nations were left alone to exchange goods freely among themselves—without the corrupting interference of selfish warmongering monarchical courts, irrational dynastic rivalries, and the secret double-dealing diplomacy of the past—then, it was hoped, international politics would become republicanized and pacified.

"Our plan is commerce," Paine told Americans in *Common Sense*, "and that, well attended to, will secure us the peace and friendship of all Europe, because it is the interest of all Europe to have America a free port."[11] America had no need to form political connections with any part of Europe. Such traditional military alliances were the legacies of monarchies, and they only led to war. "It is the true interest of America," said Paine, "to steer clear of European contentions." Trade between peoples alone would be enough to tie states together.[12] Paine shared the view of Jefferson and Madison and other enlightened liberals that trade among the peoples of the various nations in the world corresponded to the sociability of those within each nation.

After *Common Sense* had established his reputation, Paine came to know nearly all the political leaders of the United States, including Washington, Jefferson, and Franklin, and he continued to write on behalf of the American cause. The most important of these writings was his *American Crisis* series, essays that appeared throughout the war with Britain. The most famous was the first, published on December 19, 1776, which opens with the memorable lines "These are the times that try men's souls: The summer soldier and the sunshine patriot will, in this crisis, shrink from the service of their country; but he that stands it *now*, deserves the love and thanks of man and woman."[13] Washington had this essay read to his troops at Christmas 1776 on the eve of their first victory at Trenton.

When during the Revolutionary War the French philosophe Abbé Raynal criticized the French monarchy for allying itself with a republic and the new United States for not having a justifiable cause to revolt from the British Empire, it was left to Paine to formulate a powerful reply. In his *Letter to the Abbé Raynal on the Affairs of North America* (1782), he dismissed the idea that the American Revolution was a mere colonial rebellion; instead he turned it into a world-historical event and the harbinger of world citizenship and world peace. Other Americans conceived of the Revolution in these grandiose universalist terms, but no one was able to say it as he did.

IF THESE IMPORTANT contributions were not sufficient to immortalize Paine as one of the founders of the United States, then we have his extraordinary book *The Rights of Man* (1791–92), which became one of the most important works of political thought in the history of the Western world. Although the book was written after Paine had left the United States in 1787 and was intended as a refutation of Burke's *Reflections on the*

Revolution in France (1790), it actually sums up what he had learned about constitutionalism and political theory during his years in America. In fact *The Rights of Man* is the best and most succinct expression of American revolutionary political thinking ever written.

Paine himself noted how "American" were his reactions to events in Europe. In *The Rights of Man* he laid out with great clarity the new assumptions about politics and society that the American Revolution had recently made manifest: that the age of hereditary monarchy and aristocracy was over; that people were citizens, not subjects, and were born with equal natural rights; that the people created written constitutions that defined and limited their governments; that these written constitutions could not be changed by the governments but only by the sovereign people themselves; that the rulers had no rights of their own but were only temporary agents of the people, who must continually watch and empower their agents through electoral consent; that because people are naturally sociable, society is practically autonomous and self-regulating; and that people were free and independent to pursue happiness in their own way. Indeed, if Jefferson had ever written out in any systematic way what he believed about politics, it would have resembled much of *The Rights of Man.*

Despite these great intellectual contributions, however, Paine apparently never quite has had what it takes to get admitted to the sacred temple of American founders. Perhaps it is because he never became president of the United States as some of the other founders did. But neither did Franklin and Hamilton, and their credentials as founders seem solid. There seems to be something else at work to account for America's relative neglect of Paine and its inability to think of him as one of its founders.

Perhaps he has been neglected because he was a recent immigrant to America. Paine spent the first thirty-seven years of his life in England and came to America in late 1774. Yet other important revolutionary leaders were also recent immigrants. James Wilson arrived from Scotland in 1765, just at the beginning of the imperial crisis, and Alexander Hamilton came from the West Indies to New York only in 1772. As Paine himself said in

1778, "In a country where all men were once adventurers, the difference of a few years in their arrival" could not make them less American.[14]

Maybe the explanation of Paine's peculiarity lies in the fact that he was not born a gentleman. But most of the founding fathers were not born gentlemen either. They had to achieve that important eighteenth-century status, usually by getting a liberal arts education at Harvard, Princeton, or some such college. Of the revolutionary leaders, Franklin's origins were most similar to Paine's. Both were born of obscure parents, both were apprenticed as artisans, and both received only a few years of education, neither attending college. But Franklin became a very different person from Paine. As we've seen, Franklin became a very wealthy man, and long before the Revolution he had become fully acculturated and assimilated to gentlemanly status. Because of Franklin's great literary legacy to us, his *Autobiography* (which was never published in his lifetime), we are too apt to think of him as Poor Richard, the hardworking middling printer who made it. But after ostentatiously retiring from his printing business in 1748 at the age of forty-two, Franklin never again worked a day in his life. He became a full-fledged leisured gentleman with all his time and energy devoted to science, philanthropy, and public service. Although he never achieved his hopes of becoming a member of the upper levels of the English government, he eventually moved pretty much at ease in the highest aristocratic circles of England and France, even dining with kings. Franklin in fact played the social game of courtier as well as anyone in Anglo-American society and, until the Revolution, built his career on cultivating the right people. While no doubt many in London and Philadelphia could never hide their contempt for him as a parvenu, he seldom let his origins show. He was a man superbly of the eighteenth century, wearing masks as that century taught men to do. So he always appeared in the character of a gentleman.

In this respect Paine was different from Franklin and all the other founders. There was something direct and earthy about Paine. He wore no masks over his fiery black eyes. His appearance was careless and slovenly, with a large nose reddened from too much drink. His dress was drab and coarse, his wig worn and tattered. One observer noted in 1792, "He is the very picture of a journeyman tailor who has been drunk and playing at nine pins for the first three days of the week, and is returning to his work on Thursday."[15] Paine was never quite able to shed his lowly corset maker origins and the effects of all those years living in poverty and obscurity near the bottom of English society. No wonder people said that "he is better in print than in the flesh."[16] Paine never really assimilated to gentry status the way Franklin did. To be sure, he moved in aristocratic and gentlemanly circles, especially after his fame had been established in 1776. His writings became an entrée into liberal gentry society and enabled him to mingle with Washington, Jefferson, and Lafayette. Yet as much as he joined in their conversations he was never fully accepted as a gentleman.

Something about Paine bothered members of the America's gentry, particularly the aristocratic likes of William Smith of Philadelphia and Gouverneur Morris of New York. These sorts of gentlemen called Paine many things, but one of the most common and opprobrious terms they could think of to abuse him with was to say that he lacked connections. Smith charged Paine in 1776 with having neither "character nor connection." Morris in 1779 called him a "mere adventurer *from England*, without fortune, without family or connections, ignorant even of grammar."[17]

To be "without connections" hardly strikes us today as much of an insult, but for the vertically organized and patronage-dominated social world of the eighteenth century it said a lot. Paine seemed to be someone floating loose in this hierarchical world, coming out of nowhere and tied to no one, a man without a home and even without a country. Paine's initial response to this sort of criticism was defensive. In his debate in the press with Smith in 1776 he felt compelled to deny that he was a mere piece of debris that had washed up on America's shores. The culture's emphasis on connections forced him to emphasize that when he sailed from England to America in 1774, he had possessed a letter of introduction from none other than Benjamin Franklin.

After the explosive success of *Common Sense* Paine had no further need for such letters of introduction in America. His reputation was made at once, and no one needed to be told who he was. Of course he continued to rely on patronage of one sort or another. In 1777 friends got him a position as secretary to the Committee of Foreign Affairs of the Continental Congress, which only drew him into one political dispute after another, culminating in his forced resignation in 1779. Increasingly he seemed at odds with everyone, and he complained endlessly of his poverty and America's neglect of him. Although friends eventually secured for him a three-hundred-acre farm in New Rochelle and a three-thousand-dollar congressional grant, his complaints of poverty and neglect continued. He felt unwanted, unattached. Soon, however, he began to turn the criticism of himself as a person "without connections" into a positive attribute. As early as 1778, in *The American Crisis, No. 7*, he declared that he wrote for no personal advantage, not even for America. "My principles are universal. My attachment is to all the world, and not to any particular part, and if what I advance is right, it is right no matter where or who it comes from."[18]

He became passionate about his lack of connections. He boasted that he owned no property, had no residence, had never voted, and could "view the matter rather than the parties, and having no interests, connection with, or personal dislike to either, shall endeavor to serve all." He talked of being "a citizen of the world," one who "never had nor ever would have anything to do in private affairs."[19] He had no personal interests to promote. "If there is any one circumstance in my character which distinguishes itself from all the rest," Paine wrote in 1782, "it is personal disinterestedness, and an anxiety to serve a public cause in preference to myself."[20]

Of course much of this was conventional eighteenth-century liberal rhetoric. All the American founders at one time or another talked of being disinterested citizens of the world. All enlightened gentlemen were supposed to be impartial members of the cosmopolitan "republic of letters" that transcended all national boundaries. But Paine gave this traditional notion a special emphasis. The other revolutionary leaders may have considered themselves citizens of the world, but America was still home to them. But for Paine this was always much in doubt. Perhaps Americans did not know, he wrote in 1779 with some bitterness, "that it was neither the place nor the people but the Cause itself that irresistibly engaged me in its support; for I should have acted the same part in any other country could the same circumstances have arisen there which have happened here." He saw himself as little better than a "refugee, and that of the most extraordinary kind, a refugee from the Country I have befriended." He became a man without a home, without a country, truly a citizen of the world.[21]

THUS IT WAS inevitable that sooner or later he would return to the Old World. In 1787 he sailed for Europe to promote a wrought-iron bridge he had designed; he first visited France, then traveled back and forth between England and France. By 1789, with the outbreak of the French Revolution, he had come to see himself as the intellectual progenitor of revolutions. "A Share in two revolutions is living to some purpose," he excitedly told Washington in October 1789.[22] When things began heating up in Paris, he left England for France in order to participate directly in its Revolution. He was optimistic and had no idea what he was getting into. "With respect to the French Revolution," he reported to Benjamin Rush in 1790, "be assured that every thing is going on right—little inconveniences, the necessary consequence of pulling down and building up, may arise, but even these are much less than ought to have been expected."[23] Like Jefferson, Paine thought that the French Revolution marked the beginning of the breakup of the Old World and was "a forerunner to other revolutions in Europe."[24]

He returned to London in order to take on Edmund Burke and to write the first part of his *Rights of Man* in what he called "a style of thinking and expression different to what had been customary in England."[25] In August 1792 the French National Assembly conferred French citizenship on Paine. A month later he was elected to a seat in the National Convention that abolished the French monarchy and established a republic. He was assigned to a nine-man committee to design a new constitution for France. Paine supported the trial of Louis XVI for treason, but he opposed the deposed king's execution. He was shouted down by Jean-Paul Marat. At the end of the year he was expelled from the Convention and arrested. During 1794 he was held for ten months in prison, where he continued work on *The Age of Reason*. Even after these harrowing experiences in France and his persistent inability to learn to speak French, he hesitated to leave France for the United States, whose citizenship he had claimed while in prison. The United States was not home, but just a symbol for him, and from the time he returned to America in 1802 until his death in 1807, he was not happy.

By then it was clear how Paine's status differed from the founders. He was not a political leader; he was exclusively a writer who stood in an adversarial relationship to the dominant political culture. In 1802 Paine described himself as having achieved "an established fame in the literary world."[26] Today we might most accurately describe him as a "public intellectual," as someone who spent his life writing and criticizing his society.

He was not simply someone who wrote for money, a hired pen. Although he did sometimes write on commission, he was not really like those eighteenth-century Grub Street scribblers hired by English officials to turn out political propaganda. But as a "public intellectual" neither was he a man of letters involved in the belletristic tradition. Paine was not a literary figure in the sense that the novelist Charles Brockden Brown or the poet John Trumbull aspired to be. He was a modern intellectual, America's first modern intellectual, an unconnected social critic, who, as he said in 1779, knew "but one kind of life I am fit for, and that is a thinking one, and of course, a writing one."[27]

This goes to the heart of the important differences separating Paine from the other revolutionary luminaries. As much as Jefferson, Madison, Adams, and others wrote, they do not resemble modern critical intellectuals in the way that Paine does. They were gentlemen attached in various ways to their society, and their writing was very different from Paine's. They were not social critics; in fact they were amateurs at writing, meaning that their writings were only by-products of their careers as lawyers, planters, or political leaders. Writing was only one of their many duties or accomplishments as gentlemen. They were amateur writers in the same way that they were amateur politicians. For all the time and energy the revolutionary leaders devoted to politics, most of them cannot be described accurately as professional politicians, at least not in any modern sense of that term. Their relationship to public life and their conception of public service were very different from those of today. Their political careers, like their literary careers, did not create but rather followed from their previously established social positions as important gentlemen. Paine's status was very different from any of them.

Some of this difference between him and the other revolutionary leaders is revealed in the different kinds of audiences they wrote for and in the different tone and style of their writings. Most of the revolutionary leaders—Adams, Jefferson, John Dickinson—spoke and wrote for one another, for rational, enlightened, restricted audiences of educated men like themselves. Their speeches and writings were generally reasonable affairs that aimed to persuade or explain. Their works were often highly stylized by rhetorical rules and were usually very erudite, filled with Latin quotations, classical allusions, and historical citations, multitudes of references to every conceivable figure in the heritage of Western culture from Cicero, Sallust, and Plutarch to Montesquieu, Pufendorf, and Rousseau. The revolutionary leaders delighted in citing authorities and in displaying their scholarship, sometimes crowding or even smothering the texts of their pamphlets with quantities of footnotes.[28]

Paine's writing was very different. Much of the consternation and awe aroused by his writings came from his deliberate rejection of the traditional apparatus of persuasion in his determined effort to reach a wide audience and to express feelings—revulsions and visions—that the existing conventions of writing would not allow. Paine looked for readers everywhere, but especially in the tavern- and artisan-centered worlds of the cities. So he relied on his readers' knowing only the Bible and the Book of Common Prayer. He scorned "words of sound" that only "amuse the ear" and used simple, direct—some critics said coarse, barnyard—imagery drawn from the commonplace world that could be understood even by the unlearned. Nature obviously disapproved of monarchy, he wrote in *Common Sense*; "otherwise she would not so frequently turn it into ridicule, by giving mankind an *ass for a lion.*"[29] He wanted to write for ordinary people. "As it is my design to make those that can scarcely read understand," he said, "[I] shall therefore avoid every literary ornament, and put it in language as plain as the alphabet."[30] He aimed to break through the usual niceties and forms of rhetoric and to reach people with a simple common style.

What was frightening to authorities about Paine's writings was not so much what he said but how he said it and to whom. In the 1790s the British attorney general warned radical writers like Paine to publish their suspect works in an expensive edition, "so as to confine it probably to that class of readers who may consider it coolly." If it were to be "published cheaply for dissemination among the populace," declared this law officer of the Crown, "it will be my duty to prosecute."[31] Paine of course ignored such advice, and consequently in 1792 the English government charged him with sedition for writing *The Rights of Man.* In it he had spoken to ordinary people about issues of government and religion as no one in history ever had. In fact he saw it as his mission to make political and religious criticism accessible to the common reader. But even more important than his accessibility was the fact that he spoke with a rage that few writers before him had ever expressed; certainly none of the American founders ever wrote as he did. Paine spoke out of a deep anger shared in those years by many common people—artisans, shopkeepers, traders, petty merchants—who were at long last tired of being scorned and held in contempt by a monarchical and aristocratic world. The American revolutionary gentry leaders, liberally educated graduates of Harvard or Princeton, could not really represent the indignation of these ordinary people, but Paine could. He spoke out of a tradition of radical republicanism that ran deeper and was more bitter yet more modern than the balanced and reasonable classical republicanism of most of the founders. Some of the revolutionary leaders were uneasy over the anger that Paine was stirring up among ordinary folk, but because they themselves spoke in the name of the people, they were in no position to resist his fiery language. Only in the 1790s, when artisans and small farmers like Matthew Lyon and William Manning began voicing their own resentments and rage against the leisured aristocracy, did many of the founders come to realize what the Revolution and Paine's rhetoric had released: a democratic revolution of ordinary working folk that went well beyond what the revolutionary leaders of 1776 had anticipated.

UNFORTUNATELY for Paine's reputation, most of the common people whom he emotionally represented brought with their democratic revolution and their antiaristocratic attitudes an intense religiosity and an evangelical Christianity that he never shared. Paine had very radical religious views. In *The Age of Reason* (1794) he vehemently attacked Christianity, the Bible, and orthodox religion and said things that most ordinary folk found unforgivable. "Of all the systems of religion that ever were invented," he concluded, "there is none more derogatory to the Almighty, more unedifying to man, more repugnant to reason, and more contradictory in itself than this thing called Christianity."[32] Although such statements led people to call him, in the infamous words of Theodore Roosevelt, that "filthy little atheist," Paine was no atheist. Indeed, in *The Age of Reason* he went out of his way to set forth his deistic belief in God the creator and harmonizer of the world. But in the fearful times of the French Revolution most Americans could see only infidelity, and the label of "atheist" stuck.

Of course one would be hard put to demonstrate the ways Paine's rationalistic religion or deism differed from the religious views of his contemporaries Franklin or Jefferson. In fact Paine's religious opinions were common among liberal-thinking gentlemen of the era. Jefferson and other elites usually had enough discretion to confine their deistic religious views to the privacy of their dining rooms. Paine, however, spoke openly to the people in the streets, and that made all the difference. In America *The Age of Reason* went through seventeen editions between 1794 and 1796. Many people became frightened that Paine and his radical religious ideas were undermining the entire moral order of the society.

Upon his return to America in 1802, Paine was attacked everywhere in the press as a "lying, drunken, brutal infidel." Even former friends and sympathizers like aged Samuel Adams grieved over what they took to be Paine's efforts to "unchristianize the mass of our citizens."[33] Paine denied truthfully that he was ever an atheist, but it was to no avail. Every defense he made only made matters worse. He had lived by the pen, and in the end he died by the pen. By the end of the eighteenth century Paine had become one of the most notable victims of an increasingly scurrilous and powerful press. He was always a man out of joint with his times, and he has remained so ever since.

Chapter Eight

The Real Treason
of Aaron Burr

A ARON BURR is not normally considered one of the founders of the nation. Yet he was an important revolutionary, and he did become the third vice president of the United States at a time when the vice president was a significant figure. His relation to the founders, however, is really one of contrast. It's his difference from the others—Washington, Franklin, Jefferson, Hamilton, Madison—that makes him interesting. By examining Burr's eccentric and extraordinary career, we can begin to understand better the character of the major founders. His behavior challenged the basic premises of their thinking and violated the fundamental values of their experiment in republicanism. Because Burr's behavior ultimately threatened the meaning of the Revolution, the major founders could not allow him to continue.

Burr was tried for treason in 1807. He was acquitted of the charge largely because of the narrow constitutional interpretation of treason set forth by Chief Justice John Marshall, sitting on the federal circuit court in Richmond. So Burr in his mysterious adventures in the West was judged not guilty of treason against the United States. But that was never the real treason of his career anyhow. Burr did not fall out of favor with the leaders of the country because of his shenanigans in the West. He fell out of favor well before 1806 and 1807 and his western ventures. Burr was a traitor not to his country but to his class. That was the real treason of Aaron Burr.

Burr is no ordinary historical figure. His life is scarcely credible. He was a man who skyrocketed to the vice presidency of the United States and almost seized the presidency; who challenged and killed the leader of the opposition, Alexander Hamilton; who organized his venture into the West perhaps to break up his own country or at least to dismember the Spanish Empire; who allied himself in this venture with James Wilkinson, who was both the commanding general of the United States Army and at the same time a paid agent of the Spanish. Burr was a man who was eventually accused of sedition by this same General Wilkinson, ordered seized by President Thomas Jefferson, chased, captured, and brought back to the East to stand trial for treason in Jefferson's home state; who, though finally acquitted by Jefferson's enemy Chief Justice Marshall, fled his country in disgrace, returning years later only to live out his life in obscurity.

Add to this the fact that Burr was a freethinking, free-spending aristocrat who lived always on the edge of bankruptcy; who had lynxlike eyes that charmed everyone he met; who was a notorious womanizer who left broken hearts (and numerous offspring) scattered over two continents; and who at the age of seventy-seven married a fifty-eight-year old widow, the famous Madame Jumel, who was both a former prostitute and the richest woman in America. The New Yorker Philip Hone noted the marriage in July 1833 in his famous diary. It was "benevolent" of the "celebrated Mrs. Jumel," he wrote two days after the wedding, "to keep the old man in his latter days." Unfortunately, the marriage didn't last. A year later Madame Jumel sued Burr for divorce, on the ground of his infidelity. He had also run off with about thirteen thousand dollars' worth of her property, which he quickly dissipated.[1]

With such an amazing career, it is no wonder that Burr has become the most romanticized and vilified historical character in American literature. He has been the subject of countless poems, songs, sermons, and semifictional popular biographies and the central character in nearly three dozen plays and more than four dozen novels and stories, the most entertaining being Gore Vidal's *Burr: A Novel* (1973).[2]

Amid all the literary extravagances and inflated fantasies about Burr there has not been much room for the plodding prosaic historian. Not that Burr himself had any illusions about what historians would do, especially when they dealt with "great statesmen." He reportedly said just before his death in 1836, "Historians are partisans, on one side or the other," and, "No confidence can be placed in their statements, except as to dates, or [whether] some great events such as the battle was fought, etc."[3] Still, historians have seemed especially scared to touch a person so much under the spell of sensationalist fiction and melodramatic romance. During the nineteenth century there were several publications by Burr's political associate and executor Matthew L. Davis and a sympathetic biography by James Parton, but not much else.[4] Only within the last several decades have modern scholars given Burr anything approaching serious dispassionate attention, particularly with Milton Lomask's reliable and readable two-volume biography (1979–82).[5]

But it has not been just the romantic brouhaha surrounding Burr's life that has kept historians away. The documentary record of his career is so incomplete and dispersed that historians have had little to work with. Some of Burr's papers were with his remarkable daughter, Theodosia Alston, when her ship was lost in 1813. (Burr had a very unusual relationship with his daughter, very different from the relationship that, say, Jefferson had with his daughters. Burr taught Theodosia to think like a man. Vidal in his novel implies an incestuous relationship.) Others of Burr's papers were willed to Davis, who scarcely could have been more negligent about what he was entrusted with. Davis did publish a two-volume *Memoirs of*

Aaron Burr in 1836 and portions of Burr's *Private Journal* two years later, both of which contained many of Burr's letters.[6] But many other letters, even those that were "interesting" and "amusing," Davis chose not to print, particularly the "voluminous" correspondence, which he said "in no manner develops any other views than such as relate to land speculation." Eventually Davis destroyed or otherwise disposed of all the papers left in his care. Those numerous letters written or received by Burr over a long lifetime that revealed, said Davis, "no strict morality in some of his female correspondents" were especially the ones "with my own hands I committed to the fire."[7] By the late nineteenth century what remained of Burr's papers were scattered throughout the world.

Only within the past several decades have the remnants been brought together, first in a microfilm collection of several dozen reels and then, in 1983, in a letterpress edition of two volumes edited by Mary-Jo Kline and her associates.[8] Presumably Burr ought to be satisfied with small favors, but he must be smiling knowingly at the contrast between his meager two volumes and the magnificent editions of the papers of the founders that are currently being published. Each of the lavish publishing projects of the Jefferson, Franklin, Madison, Washington, Hamilton, and the Adams family papers number or will number in the dozens of volumes, and each, with the exception of the Adams family, has been virtually exhaustive in what it has printed about its subject.

By contrast, Burr's editors in the 1980s were highly selective in what they printed from his papers. Not that it matters much. On the surface his papers do not seem to have much of importance to reveal, at least not about the great events of his life. His two published volumes do not tell us anything startlingly new about the major controversies in which he was engaged: his Western conspiracy, his presidential electoral tie with Jefferson in 1801, his duel with Hamilton, or his trial for treason in 1807. What Burr's correspondence does reveal, however, are the more humdrum day-to-day events of his career. His papers contain hundreds of very mundane letters relating to his workaday life in politics and business, and cumulatively they reveal an image of Burr that is very different from the great romantic hero or villain pictured by playwrights and novelists. He seems not at all like the other revolutionary statesmen.

Burr's correspondence certainly differs markedly from that of Washington, Jefferson, Madison, or Hamilton. Many of the letters to and from Burr deal either with patronage and influence or with speculative moneymaking schemes of one sort or anther. It is extraordinary to think that his friend Davis threw away all of Burr's letters dealing with land speculation, since so many that remain also deal with speculative schemes of one sort or another.

At any rate, one searches Burr's papers in vain for a single thoughtful letter about political philosophy or government or, indeed, for a carefully developed letter of any sort. Many of the letters seem to be the hastily scribbled notes of a very busy man who did not have the time or the desire to put much on paper. Here is a not untypical sample written in 1795, when he was a United States senator, to Timothy Green, one of his New York business partners:

> Dr Sir
> Your letter of the 24th is just come in—I will be your Bail to any amount & have written to Mr. Prevost to that effect—he will do what may be necessary—
> I do expect Mr Schultze will be this Day appointed—nothing has been left undone on my part—but there is competition.
> On Sunday I shall have the pleasure to see you in NYork—
> Yr. Ob. St
>
> Aaron Burr
>
> [P S]
> Say nothing to Mr. Brauer abt Schultze—if I succeed I would choose to announce it to him & would not wish to flatter him with expectations which may not be realized.[9]

This is the character of much of Burr's correspondence. Burr did not much care about what posterity thought of him. Burr, said Hamilton, in his most damning indictment, "never appeared solicitous for fame."[10] The love of fame for the founders, in Hamilton's words, was "the ruling passion of the noblest minds," and Burr seemed free of this particular noble passion. He didn't care about his correspondence in the way that, say, Jefferson and Washington did. Both were meticulous about their letters. In 1781, for example, Washington got a captain and several clerks to copy all his letters and put all his papers in order. His instructions were demanding, to say the least. "That there may be a similarity and Beauty in the whole execution," Washington told his aides, "all the writing is to be upon black lines equidistant. All the Books [are] to have the same Margin, and to be indexed in so clear and so intelligent a manner, that there may be no difficulty in the references."[11]

The contrast with Burr could not be more glaring. Burr's files were a mess: he could not find his past letters or be sure if he had answered a correspondent. His letters were for the moment and for particular people. At one point in 1801 he told the acting secretary of the navy, "Have the goodness to recollect that my letters are not official letters to be filed in the Navy office for the benefit [of] present clerks & future Ministers!"[12] Burr certainly had no sense of a future public audience for his letters in the way, say, Jefferson did. After receiving a long, informative, and polished letter from Jefferson in 1797, for example, Burr wrote a brief reply, apologizing that "it would not be easy neither would it be discreet to answer your enquiries or to communicate to you my ideas with satisfaction to either of us, in the compass of a Letter—I will endeavor to do it in person."[13]

Writing out his thoughts was not Burr's way. As he once warned his law clerks, "Things written remain."[14] Because he always worried that his letters might "miscarry," he tried to avoid saying anything in them too implicating. "If it were discreet to write plainly," he said once, but in his conspiratorial world it was rarely possible to write plainly. He repeatedly appended warnings to his letters: "Say nothing of this to any other person," and "Let no suspicion arise that you have any knowledge of these matters," and "The recommendation must not appear to have been influenced by me," and "You & I should not appear to act in concert." It was a highly secretive, suspicious world he moved in. As he told one business associate, as a member of the New York Assembly he could not give any opinion on how a piece of pending legislation might influence the businessman's company, "except confidentially"—that is, orally in person.[15]

But the peculiar character of Burr's correspondence goes deeper than just his preoccupation with haste and secrecy. Burr never developed any ideas about constitutionalism or governmental policy in the way the other revolutionary statesmen did because in truth he was not much concerned about such matters. If he had an idea about the new federal Constitution of 1787, we do not know about it. Nor did he have much to say about the Federalists' great financial program of the early 1790s. He mentioned Hamilton's plan for a national bank at one point in 1791 but confessed he had not read Hamilton's arguments. He recalled that Hume had "some ingenious thoughts" on banking in his essays, "but I have not the leisure to turn to them."[16]

Unlike the other revolutionary leaders, Burr offered his countrymen little in the way of political principles or a public vision. He had "*no theory*," it was said; he was "a mere matter of fact man."[17] Although such pragmatism is supposed to be the source of success for American politicians, in Burr's case it was the source of his failure and ultimately the source of his real treason.

THAT BURR'S CAREER would end in failure seemed highly unlikely at its outset. He seemed born for political leadership. He had everything going for him: looks, charm, extraordinary abilities, a Princeton education, distinguished revolutionary service, and, above all, a notable lineage. John Adams said that he had "never known, in any country, the prejudice in favor of birth, parentage, and descent more conspicuous than in the instance of Colonel Burr." Burr was the son of a president of Princeton and the grandson of another Princeton president, none other than Jonathan Edwards, the most famous theologian in eighteenth-century America. Burr, said Adams, "was connected by blood with many respectable families in New England."[18] Unlike the other leaders of the revolutionary generation—Jefferson, Washington, Adams, Hamilton, Madison, and Franklin—Burr was born fully and unquestionably into whatever nobility and gentility eighteenth-century America had. Unlike the other revolutionary leaders, Burr never thought he had to earn his aristocratic status. Aristocracy was in his veins, and he never forgot it.[19] He always had an air of superiority about him, and though he could condescend in the best aristocratic manner, he always considered himself more of a gentleman than other men.

He certainly sought to live the life of an eighteenth-century aristocratic gentleman. He had the best of everything—fine houses, elegant clothes, lavish coaches, superb wines. His sexual excesses and his celebrated liberality flowed from his traditional European notions of gentility. Since real gentlemen were not supposed to work for a living, he could not regard his law practice or indeed even money—that "paltry object"—with anything but distaste.[20] Like a perfect Chesterfieldian gentleman, he was always polite, charming, and reserved, and he almost never revealed his inner feelings. He publicly vented his pent-up passions only twice in his career, and the outbursts are revealing. The first was his challenge to Hamilton, which grew, most immediately, out of his frustration over the loss of the gubernatorial campaign in New York in 1804. "He was determined," Charles Biddle, one of his closest friends, reported, "to call out the first man of any respectability concerned in the infamous publications concerning him." The second came, in 1815, in an explosive letter about James Monroe that contained the most disparaging remarks ever written by one gentleman of another. "The Man himself," he said of Monroe, "is one of the Most improper & incompetent that could have been selected [as a candidate for president]—Naturally dull & stupid—extremely illiterate—indecisive to a degree that would be incredible to one who did not know him—pusillanimous & of course hypocritical—has no opinion on any subject & will be always under the Govt of the worse Men—pretends as I am told, to some Knowledge of Military Matters, but never commanded a platoon nor was ever fit to command one." This extraordinary letter released all Burr's accumulated frustration over what the "Virginia dynasty"—Jefferson, Madison, Monroe—had done to him.[21]

What is most notable about Burr's gentility in comparison with the other revolutionary leaders is its lack of the one characteristic that his peers always stressed, virtue or devotion to the public good. Burr seems remarkably free of the strain of opposition Whig and classical republican thought that colored the ideas of the other revolutionaries. It was once said of him that the only virtue he ever had was not claiming any. Certainly Burr made little pretense of being public-spirited in the fulsome way the other revolutionaries did. The other founding fathers always made a great deal of their virtue and disinterestedness. Burr never did. There was nothing self-righteous and hypocritical about him. Perhaps because he was so sure of his aristocratic lineage, he did not have the same emotional need as the other revolutionary statesmen had to justify his gentlemanly status by continually expressing an abhorrence of corruption and a love of virtue.

Nearly all the revolutionary leaders were first-generation gentlemen. That is to say, nearly all were the first in their families to attend college, the first to acquire a liberal arts education, and the first to display the marks of an enlightened gentleman. Unlike Burr, most of the revolutionary leaders could never claim ancestry as the source of the gentility they aspired to. Indeed, their revolutionary ideology condemned all claims of family and blood and celebrated virtue and other enlightened values as the only proper source of a republican aristocracy.[22] Burr, whose status was clearly ascribed and inherited, had no such need to talk about virtue as the measure of a gentleman.

Although Burr had eagerly joined the Revolutionary War in 1775 as a glory-seeking nineteen-year-old, his participation appears more personal than patriotic. He wrangled with Washington over inferiors' being promoted over him, and in 1779, after several threats to do so, he finally resigned his commission. He gave ill health as his reason, but it was clear that he could no longer bear the slights he felt he had received from the commander in chief. In the post revolutionary political struggles he could have gone in several different directions; only a series of accidents in the early 1790s and his own trimming temperament threw him into the Republican party. But despite becoming its vice presidential candidate in 1800, he was never committed to it or its beliefs, and he continually flirted with the Federalists. It is not surprising that people at the time accused him of being "unsettled in his politics" and of having "no fixed principle, no consistency of character."[23]

Burr probably should have been a Tory at the Revolution; in fact his ties to the Loyalists in his wife's family remained strong. He viewed politics largely in traditional, prerevolutionary, ancien régime terms: as contests between "great men" and their followers, tied together by strings of interest and influence. He expected that someone with his pedigree and his high social standing and talent was due high office as a matter of course and that public office was to be used to maintain his position and influence. Beyond what politics could do for his friends, his family, and him personally, it had little emotional significance for him. Politics, as he once put it, was "fun and honor & profit."[24]

Of course other politicians of the early Republic viewed politics in much the same way as Burr did, especially in New York. But Burr was special. We are apt to forget just how prominent a political leader he was. He was at one time or another a U.S. senator, a vice president (at a time when you had to be somebody to be vice president), and an aspirant for the presidency. Not only did he receive the same number of electoral votes as Jefferson in the election of 1800, but in the election of 1796 he received thirty electoral votes, which put him fourth after John Adams's seventy-one, Jefferson's sixty-eight, and Thomas Pinckney's fifty-nine, all of whom had accomplished some great service to the country, Pinckney's being his negotiating the 1795 treaty with Spain that established the Florida boundary and opened the Mississippi to American trade. The remaining forty-eight votes were distributed among nine other candidates, only one of whom received as many as fifteen. Burr in the 1790s was regarded as a distinguished and promising figure. Yet no political leader of his prominence in the period ever spent so much time and energy so blatantly scheming for his own personal and political advantage. And no one of the other great revolutionary statesmen was so immune to the ideology and the values of the Revolution as Burr was.

He certainly had little of the aversion to the use of patronage, or what was often called corruption, that a revolutionary ideologue like Jefferson had. Jefferson's pained scrupulousness over throwing out Federalist officeholders and putting in Republicans after his presidential victory in 1801 was incomprehensible to Burr, who was utterly shameless in recommending for an office anyone and everyone—even in the end himself. Jefferson recalled that he had first met Burr when the latter was senator from New York in the early 1790s and had mistrusted him right away. He remembered that when the Washington and Adams administrations in the 1790s were about to make a major military or diplomatic appointment, Burr came quickly to the capital "to shew himself" and to let the administration know, in Jefferson's words, "that he was always at market, if they had wanted him."[25] Burr's zealousness over patronage was crucial in convincing Jefferson that Burr was not Jefferson's kind of Republican.[26] At last in 1807, when Jefferson as president had an opportunity to get Burr, he moved heaven and earth, and the legal principles of the Constitution, in trying to have him convicted of treason.

Burr showed no embarrassment in promoting friends for office or doing favors for them in the legislature because for him that was the way politics and society worked, befriending people and creating personal loyalties and connections. Aristocrats were patrons, and they had clients who were obliged to them. Hence Burr sought to patronize as many people as he could. His celebrated liberality and generosity grew out of this need. Like any "great man" of the age, he even patronized young artists, including John Vanderlyn, whom he sent on a grand tour of Europe. In fact, in bustling republican America no opportunity to create an obligation or interest could be overlooked. When Burr in 1802 learned that a French agent in New York was to purchase provisions for the French troops in the West Indies, he quickly wrote to the French agent to recommend

"Winship the Butcher as a Man on whose ability & punctuality he may rely for any supplies of meat." Not surprisingly, "Winship the Butcher" was one of Burr's loyal political lieutenants.[27]

The great flaw in Burr's desire to be an eighteenth-century aristocrat was that he lacked the money to bring it off. Money was "contemptible," he said, but he needed it.[28] Despite being one of the most highly paid lawyers in New York, he was perpetually in debt and often on the edge of bankruptcy because of his lavish living and his aristocratic liberality. He borrowed and borrowed over and over again and created complicated structures of credit that always threatened to come crashing down. It was this insecure financial situation coupled with his grandiose expectations that led to his wheeling and dealing and self-serving politics.

So from Burr's papers—the few that remain—we have this remarkable picture of a self-assured aristocrat using his public office in every way he could to make money. When his efforts in 1796 to become vice president proved futile, he lost all interest in his Senate seat; he stopped attending the Senate's sessions and devoted all his attention to making money through speculation. He next entered the New York legislature with the hope of aiding his business associates and restoring his personal fortune. He pushed for tax exemptions, bridge and road charters, land bounties, alien rights to own land—any scheme in which he and his friends had an interest. In 1798 and 1799 his manipulations of the Manhattan Company, in which he used a state charter to provide water for the city of New York as a cover for the creation of a bank, was only the most notorious of his self-interested shenanigans.[29] When he became vice president in 1801, he even toyed with the idea of continuing to practice law. Would it be all right, he asked a friend, for him to "go into Courts with the Weight & influence of office & thus retail out these"? Only when the friend told him it would be improper for the vice president to go into court and argue cases—Burr would overawe the court, his friend said—did he abandon the idea.[30] The more desperately he sought to establish his financial independence with one great scheme or another, the more he violated what the rest of his aristocratic peers thought was the proper role for a gentlemanly leader in postrevolutionary America.[31]

Burr could never be the leisured aristocrat, the independent country gentleman living off the rents of tenants on his landed estate. The income of the eighteenth-century English landed gentry, said Adam Smith, came without exertion; it "costs them neither labour nor care, but comes to them, as it were, of its own accord, and independent of any plan or project of their own." The lack of direct involvement in the marketplace is what gave the English landed gentry their capacity for impartiality and disinterestedness; that was why Smith believed that these gentry made the best political leaders.[32] In classical republican thinking, only such gentlemen were free from the petty concerns of the marketplace, free of occupations (by which every male in the society, except gentlemen, was designated). Only such gentlemen were capable of disinterestedness and ideally equipped to lead the society and promote the public good. In America finding this kind of gentleman whose income came without exertion was not easy. Many thought that only in the South was this ideal image of the independent country gentleman even partially realized, and there of course gentleman farmers like Jefferson had hundreds of slaves to keep them in leisure and wine.

Alexander Hamilton tried to argue that members of the learned professions, by which he mainly meant lawyers, somehow resembled the landed gentry and thus could likewise play the role of impartial umpires among the conflicting interests of the society. It may have been true, he wrote in *The Federalist*, No. 35, that mechanics, merchants, and farmers were deeply involved in the marketplace and that because they had interests to promote, they could never be trusted in politics to make disinterested judgments. This was not the case, however, said Hamilton, with members of the learned professions. They made the best kind of political leader. They "will feel a neutrality to the rivalships between the different branches of industry" and therefore will be most likely to be "an impartial arbiter" among the diverse interests and occupations of the society.

Hamilton thus reinforced a notion that has carried into our own time: that lawyers and other professionals are somehow free of the marketplace, are less selfish and interested and therefore better equipped for disinterested political leadership than are merchants and businessmen.[33]

But Burr, even though he was a talented lawyer and gentleman, didn't seem to care about all this. What he was doing was beyond the pale of any sort of ideal disinterested republican leadership, and it appalled Hamilton. Burr was not even pretending to stand above the different partial interests of the society and arbitrate among them; he was right down in the pits with all the narrow, self-seeking factions and interests.

Like Burr, Hamilton had a continual need for money, and he knew that many public officials like Burr were using their political connections to get rich. He did not want to be one of them. In 1795, at a time when Hamilton was financially pressed and out of public office, his close friend Robert Troup pleaded with him to get involved in business, especially in speculative land schemes. Everyone else was doing it, said Troup. "Why should you object to making a little money in a way that cannot be reproachful? Is it not time for you to think of putting yourself in a state of independence?" He even joked to Hamilton that such moneymaking schemes might be "instrumental in making a man of fortune—I may say—a gentleman of you. For such is the present insolence of the World that hardly a man is treated like a gentleman unless his fortune enables him to live at his ease."[34]

Hamilton refused. "Saints," he told Troup, might get away with such profit making, but he knew he would be denounced by his Jeffersonian Republican opponents as just another one of those "speculators" and "peculators." He had to refuse "because," as he sardonically put it, "there must be some public fools who sacrifice private to public interest at the certainty of ingratitude and obloquy—because my vanity whispers I ought to be one of those fools and ought to keep myself in a situation the best calculated to render service."[35] (In 1797 Hamilton was accused of having been involved in corruption, using his office for private purposes, when he was secretary of the treasury earlier in the decade. In order to explain why he had paid money to a Mr. Reynolds in 1791, he had to reveal that he had had an affair with Mrs. Reynolds and that Mr. Reynolds was blackmailing him. Hamilton sacrificed his reputation for private virtue, and hurt his wife deeply, rather than allow his reputation for public virtue to be tarnished. Better to be thought a private adulterer than a corrupt public official.)

Because Hamilton clung as long and as hard to the classical conception of leadership as anyone in postrevolutionary America, it is not surprising that he should turn on Burr with a special vengeance, for it was that classical conception of leadership that Burr, so able and so promising, was violating.

IT WAS NOT THAT Burr's behavior itself was uncommon in American politics of the early Republic. Indeed, it was precisely the prevalence of this kind of self-interested politics in the state legislatures and even in the Congress that made the aristocratic Burr's behavior so alarming to his peers. Madison had foreseen that legislative politics would be a competition among various selfish factions. In the 1780s he had come to realize that state politics were dominated by obscure, middling, narrow-minded, and parochial politicians who could not see beyond their own neighborhoods and responded only to the selfish interests of their constituents. But Madison and the other founders also expected that someone of Burr's cosmopolitan background, education, and talents would rise above this localism and these special interests and act differently, act in a disinterested manner and promote the common good. Madison in fact had designed the new Constitution in 1787 with the hope of encouraging the election to the national government of these sorts of cosmopolitan and liberally educated gentlemen. With the elevated government, the enlarged arena of politics, and the smaller number of representatives at the national level, only those possessing, as Madison put it in *The Federalist*, No. 10, "the most attractive merit and the most diffusive and established characters" were likely to be elected to high office.[36]

Burr's behavior was a direct challenge to this revolutionary hope that enlightened gentry leaders would play the role of impartial umpires among the various interests. It was bad enough when ungenteel merchants, money-hungry stockjobbers, or narrow-minded artisans and business-men scrambled in the political arena for their parochial interests. But when obviously distinguished and liberally educated gentlemen like Burr, men who, Hamilton said, should have the "commanding eminence . . . to look down with contempt upon every mean and interested pursuit," be-haved like moneymaking, interest-mongering scramblers, then there was no one left to reconcile these narrow, selfish interests and look after the good of the whole society.

No wonder then that Burr's behavior filled many of his fellow "great men" with horror. Both Hamilton and Jefferson, from opposite ends of the political spectrum, were scared to death by what Burr was doing—and this well before his wild adventures in the West. In the election of 1800 both Jefferson and Burr happened to receive the same number of electoral votes, seventy-three, and the election was thrown into the House of Rep-resentatives, with each state's congressional delegation having a single vote. The Federalists were in a position to throw the election to Burr. Many of them, including John Marshall, who had just become chief jus-tice of the United States and did not know Burr at all but knew and hated Jefferson intensely, wanted to. The Federalists were very frightened of what Jefferson would do to national authority, to their commercial and banking systems, and to American foreign policy. They figured that Jef-ferson was a doctrinaire democrat who wanted to take the country back to something resembling the Articles of Confederation, that he was in the pocket of France and would likely go to war with Great Britain. Burr posed no such threat.

Theodore Sedgwick of Massachusetts summed up much Federalist thinking. Burr, he said, was no democrat, was not attached to any foreign nation, and was not an enthusiast for any sort of theory. He was just an ordinary selfish politician who promoted whatever would benefit him and get him reelected. But, added Sedgwick, Burr's "very selfishness" was his saving grace. It would prevent him from doing harm to the Federalists' national and commercial systems. Burr had personally benefited so much from these systems, said Sedgwick, that he would do nothing to dismantle them. He was therefore safer than Jefferson.[37]

Hamilton disagreed violently. To him (and to Jefferson), Burr's reputation for "selfishness" was precisely the problem. Burr may have represented what most American politicians would eventually become—pragmatic, get-along men—but to Hamilton and Jefferson he violated everything they had thought the American Revolution had been about. There was "no doubt" in Hamilton's mind that "upon every virtuous and prudent calculation" Jefferson was to be preferred to Burr. It was a matter of character, he said: Burr had none, and Jefferson at least had "pretensions to character."[38]

While the issue of the presidency was in doubt in the House of Representatives, Hamilton spared no energy in trying to convince his fellow Federalists to support Jefferson over Burr. Over five or six weeks' time in December 1800 and January 1801, he wrote letter after letter in what one historian has called a "hysterical" campaign to prevent Burr from becoming president. "For heaven's sake," Hamilton pleaded with Sedgwick, "let not the Federal party be responsible for the elevation of this Man." He told his correspondents over and over: "Burr loves nothing but himself. . . . He is sanguine enough to hope every thing—daring enough to attempt every thing—wicked enough to scruple nothing."[39] Hamilton preferred Jefferson even though he knew that he and Jefferson were personal enemies; indeed, he said, "if there be a man in the world I ought to hate, it is Jefferson." He knew too that the opposite was true with Burr. He had always gotten along well with him personally, but, he said, his personal relations should not count in this matter. The country's survival was at stake, and, he said, "The public good must be paramount to every private consideration."[40] He convinced his fellow Federalists not to vote for Burr, and after thirty-five ballots in the House, Jefferson was finally elected president.

"Never in the history of the United States," Henry Adams wrote in his great history of the Jefferson administration, "did so powerful a combination of rival politicians unite to break down a single man as that which arrayed against Burr." Burr had not just Jefferson, Madison, and the whole Virginia legion making up the circle against him, but, said Adams, Hamilton himself, the "strangest of companions," joined "hands with his own bitterest enemies to complete the ring."[41] Adams in his *History of the United States of America* seems puzzled that such bitter enemies could unite in a circle of hostility against Burr, but he should not have been. In their minds, Burr posed far more of a threat to the American Revolution than either of them ever thought the other did. Burr threatened nothing less than the great revolutionary hope, indeed, the entire republican experiment, that some sort of disinterested politics, if only among the elite, could prevail in America. Because of this threat, Hamilton and Jefferson together eventually brought Burr down. To both men the treason that Burr committed to his class was far more serious than any supposed treason to his country. It was the real treason of Aaron Burr.

Epilogue:

The Founders and the
Creation of Modern
Public Opinion

T he intellectual creativity of the founding generation has never been in doubt. Samuel Eliot Morison and Harold Laski both believed that no period of modern history, with the possible exception of the Civil War decades of seventeenth-century England, was as rich in political ideas and contributed as much in such a short period of time to Western political theory.[1] In the Americans' efforts to explain the difference of their experience in the New World and ultimately to justify their Revolution and their new governments, they were pressed to speak and write both originally and extensively about politics, using a wide variety of eighteenth-century instruments, newspapers, pamphlets, state papers, poetry, plays, satire, and, of course, letters. Indeed, their phenomenal reliance on personal correspondence for the communication of their thoughts made the revolutionary years the greatest letter-writing era in American history. (Without Jefferson's letters, what would we know of his mind?) It is a remarkable body of political literature that the revolutionaries created, and what is most remarkable about it is that this political theory was generally written by the very men responsible for putting it into effect.

Despite the intellectual creativity and productivity of the revolutionary leaders, however, it is obvious that they were not professional writers. They bore no resemblance to the Grub Street hacks turning out political propaganda. Nor were they only men of letters, "intellectuals" like the eighteenth-century French philosophes or the Tory satirists of Augustan England, writers fully engaged in political criticism who used their pens to gain money and position. To be sure, there were American writers like John Trumbull and Philip Freneau who sought to make careers as litterateurs, but they were exceptions. Most of the intellectual leaders of the Revolution were amateurs at writing, clergymen, merchants, planters, and lawyers deeply involved in their separate occupations. Thomas Paine, as we've seen, was the great exception.

No doubt writing was important to the founders. Indeed, it was often through their writing that they first gained a reputation. Both John Adams in the Stamp Act crisis and Jefferson in 1774 captured the attention of their peers by something they wrote. Even Washington first caught the eyes of people with the publication of his account in 1754 of his adventures with the French and Indians in the West. Still, they were not writers by profession. Writing was simply a by-product of their careers and one of their many accomplishments or duties as gentlemen. Because they were gentlemen, they never wrote for money and often avoided putting their names on what they wrote for publication. They thought of their writing, even the belletristic sort, as a means to an end, to make a polemical political point or to demonstrate their learning and gentlemanly status.

Yet men like James Otis, Richard Bland, Thomas Jefferson, and John Adams were not only amateur writers but in an important sense amateur politicians as well. For all the time and energy these revolutionary leaders devoted to politics, most of them cannot accurately be described as professional politicians, at least not in any modern meaning of the term. As we've seen, their relationship to public life and their conception of public service were different from those of today: Their political careers did not create, but rather followed from, their established social positions; their political leadership, like their intellectual leadership, was a consequence, not a cause, of their social leadership. Some of them, Washington most notably, even refused salaries for their offices, protesting that it was unbecoming for gentlemen to be paid for public service.

As gentlemen they thought they had an duty to lead the society, serve in government, and build consensus. Franklin certainly felt this obligation. "Let not your love of philosophical amusements have more than its due weight with you," he admonished his friend and New York royal official Cadwallader Colden in 1750. Public service was far more important than science. In fact, said Franklin, even the "finest" of Newton's "Discoveries" could not have excused his neglecting to serve the commonwealth if the public had needed him.[2]

Because public office was seen as an obligation, the founders often described it—sometimes wrongly, of course, but sincerely—as an unhappy burden, as a wretched responsibility thrust upon them by the fact of their high social rank. Few of Jefferson's letters are as revealing and filled with emotion as his 1782 protest to Monroe over the social pressures making him engage in public service despite the miseries of office and his longing for private repose.[3] We smile today when we hear politicians complaining about the burdens of public office, but precisely because the eighteenth-century leaders were not professional politicians, such disavowals of public office and such periodic withdrawals from politics as they habitually made possessed a meaning that is difficult for us today to recapture.

BECAUSE THE revolutionary leaders were cultivated gentlemen with special privileges and responsibilities, tied to the people through lines of personal and social authority, they believed that their speeches and writings did not have to influence directly and simultaneously all the people but only those who were rational and enlightened, who in turn would bring the rest of the populace with them through the force of deferential respect. The politically minded public in eighteenth-century America may have been large compared with contemporary England, but most of the political literature of the period, unlike much of the religious literature, showed little evidence of a broad reading public.[4] The revolutionary leaders for the most part wrote as if they were dealing with reasonable and cultivated readers like themselves. Of course, by publishing their writings, they realized they were exposing their ideas to the vulgar, and therefore often resorted to pseudonyms, but before the Revolution they made very few concessions to this wider public. They were aware of the term *public opinion*, which had first arisen in the English-speaking world in the early 1700s, but they conceived of the public as a very limited sphere.[5]

For many gentlemen this sphere was in fact the restricted arena where gentlemanly affairs of honor took place. Honor was an aristocratic conception. It essentially meant reputation, but the only reputation that counted was the one that existed in the eyes of one's fellow gentlemen. Gossip was everywhere, and every gentleman was fearful of being slandered by other gentlemen. Consequently, insults to one's honor provoked responses that sometimes ended in duels. Although ritualized affairs of honor became very common in the last quarter of the eighteenth century, most of them, as we saw in the eleven duels Hamilton was involved in, did not result in actual exchanges of fire.[6]

It was this genteel public that the revolutionary leaders generally thought of when they wrote and spoke, a public that was roughly commensurate with their social world. "When I mention the public," wrote John Randolph in a 1774 political pamphlet, "I mean to include only the rational part of it. The ignorant vulgar are as unfit to judge of the modes, as they are unable to manage the reins of government."[7] Such bluntness in public was rare and became even rarer as the Revolution approached. Although few of the revolutionaries shared Randolph's contempt for the mass of the populace—indeed, most had little reason as yet to fear or malign the people—they vaguely held to a largely unspoken assumption that the only public opinion worth worrying about was that of their cultivated peers.[8]

Actually the reading public for genteel literature in the mid-eighteenth century may have been more limited than we have generally assumed. Certainly the prevalence of literacy is no measure of it. The price of both newspapers and pamphlets was itself restricting. Although a pamphlet cost no more than a shilling or two, that put it beyond the reach of most. (In 1789 even Senator William Maclay of Pennsylvania thought he could not afford to buy a copy of *The Federalist*; he wanted to read it and hoped that someone would lend him a copy.)[9] Indeed, the practice of reading some pamphlets before groups of Sons of Liberty or town meetings indicates not the general breadth but the usual limits of their circulation. Even members of the elite relied extensively on passing pamphlets from hand to hand as if they were letters.[10]

Yet there is no doubt that the intellectual climate was changing in the half century before the Revolution. In the 1720s there were fewer than a half dozen newspapers in the colonies, with a limited number of subscribers; by 1764 there were twenty-three newspapers, each with double or triple the earlier circulation. Between 1741 and 1776 men had experimented with at least ten magazines, and although none of them lasted longer than a few years, the effort was promising. Since most of the publications emphasized governmental matters, there was bound to be some raising of political consciousness, and printers were becoming important public figures. The number of political pamphlets multiplied at an ever-increasing rate, and in some urban areas in the years before the Revolution such writings were being used with particular effectiveness in election campaigning. Indeed, three-quarters of everything published in America between 1639 and 1800 occurred in the last thirty-five years of the eighteenth century.[11] All these developments were bringing Americans to the edge of a vast transformation in the nature and size of their politically conscious reading public.[12]

Regardless of the actual extent of the American reading public, what is crucial is the revolutionary leaders' belief that the public for which they wrote was cosmopolitan and cultivated. We know they conceived of their audiences or readership as restricted and aristocratic, as being made up of men essentially like themselves, simply by the style and content of what they wrote. They saw themselves and their readers as mutual participants in an intellectual fraternity, the "republic of letters," a view that gave them a confidence in the homogeneity and the intelligence of their audience, which in turn decisively influenced the particular qualities of their literary productions.[13]

In addition to being extraordinarily learned, their newspaper essays and pamphlets were often mere extensions of the kinds of speeches that they might present in legislative halls, devices by which gentlemen, in the absence of published reports of legislative debates, might tell other gentlemen what they said, or would like to have said, within the legislative chamber. Thus Stephen Hopkins's *The Rights of Colonies Examined* was first read before the Assembly of Rhode Island, which then voted that it should appear in pamphlet form.[14] Even more indicative of the limited elitist conception of the audience was the extraordinary reliance on personal correspondence for the circulation of ideas. It is often difficult to distinguish between the private correspondence and the public writings of the revolutionaries, so alike are they. Sometimes the published writings even took the form of letters or, like John Adams's pamphlet *Thoughts on Government*, grew out of what were originally letters to colleagues and friends.[15]

It is not just the prevalence of scholarship and the personal form of the literature that reveal the limited and elitist nature of the audience. Even the character of the invective and polemics suggests a restricted reading public in the minds of the authors. Much of the polemics was highly personal, a succession of individual exchanges between gentlemen who were known to one another, quickly becoming unintelligible to an outsider and usually ending in bitter personal vituperation. Since such abuse was designed to destroy the gentlemanly reputation of one's enemies, no accusation was too coarse or too vulgar to be made, from drunkenness and gambling to impotence and adultery.[16] The vitriolic burlesques, like the satiric closet dramas of Mercy Otis Warren, derived much of their force from the intimate knowledge the author presumed the audience or readers had of the persons being ridiculed or satirized. Without such familiarity on the part of the audience, much of the fun of the pieces—the disguised characterizations, the obscure references, the private jokes, the numerous innuendos—is lost.[17]

It is the prevalence of satire in the revolutionary literature that as much as anything suggests the elite nature of the audience. Satire as a literary device depends on a comprehending and homogeneous audience with commonly understood standards of rightness and reasonableness. Since the satirist can expose to instantaneous contempt only what is readily condemned by the opinion of his readers, he must necessarily be on intimate terms with them and count on their sharing his tastes and viewpoint. If this intimacy should break down, if the satirist's audiences should become heterogeneous and the once-shared values become confused and doubtful, if the satirist has to explain what his ridicule means, then the satire is rendered ineffectual.[18] But most revolutionary writers, at least at the outset, presumed the existence of these universal principles of right behavior and expected a uniformity of response, supposing that their audience either was, or would like to be, part of that restricted circle of men of good taste and judgment.

Nearly all the literature of the revolutionary leaders thus suggests—in its form, its erudition, its polemics, its reliance on satire—a very different intellectual world from ours, a world dominated by gentlemen who were both amateur writers and amateur politicians, essentially engaged, despite their occasional condescension toward a larger public, in either amusing men like themselves or in educating men to be or think like themselves. More than any of these characteristics, however, what decisively separates the literature of the revolutionary generation from ours was its highly elevated rhetorical character. In fact the revolutionaries' obsession with rhetoric and with its requirement of effectively relating to the audience in the end helped contribute to the transformation of American intellectual life.

Rhetoric today no longer means what it meant to the eighteenth century. To us, rhetoric suggests at best elocution or at worst some sort of disingenuous pleading, hyperbolic bombast lacking the sincerity and authenticity of self-expression that we have come to value so highly. To the revolutionary generation, rhetoric, briefly defined as the art of persuasion, lay at the heart of an eighteenth-century liberal education. It was regarded as a necessary mark of a gentleman and an indispensable skill for a statesman, especially for a statesman in a republic.[19] Language, whether spoken or written, was to be deliberately and adroitly used for effect, and since that effect depended on the leader's conception of his audience, any perceived change in that audience could alter drastically the style and content of what was said or written.

In retrospect we know that this eighteenth-century neoclassical world of civic-minded philosopher-statesmen was passing even as it expressed itself most forcefully and brilliantly. While the revolutionary gentry were still busy creating their learned arguments to persuade reasonable men of the need for resistance or of the requirements of government, there were social processes at work that in time undermined both their political and intellectual authority. A new democratic society was developing, becoming both a cause and a consequence of the Revolution. As egalitarian as American society was before 1776, as broad as the suffrage was in the several eighteenth-century colonies, the republican society and culture that gradually emerged after the Declaration of Independence were decidedly different from what had existed earlier. The older hierarchical and homogeneous society of the eighteenth century—a patronage world of personal influence and vertical connections, whose most meaningful horizontal cleavage was that between gentlemen and common people—weaker in America and never as finely calibrated as in England, beset by forces released and accelerated by the Revolution, now finally fell apart, to be replaced over the subsequent decades with new social relationships

and ideas and attitudes, including a radical blurring of the distinction between gentlemen and the rest of society. New men, often obscure ordinary men, were touched by the expanding promises of opportunity and
wealth in postrevolutionary America and clamored for a share in the new
governments and in the economy. The "people" were now told repeatedly
that they rightfully had a place in politics, and lest they should forget,
there were thousands of new rising popular tribunes, men who lacked the
traditional attributes of gentlemanly leaders, to remind them, cajole them,
even frighten them into political and social consciousness. Under such
pressures, the old eighteenth-century world was transformed within a
generation or so after independence. The gentry, at least outside the
South, gradually lost its monopoly of politics and intellectualism as the
audience for politicians, writers, and orators swelled to hitherto unimag-
inable proportions.

Although few of these changes actually began with the Revolution, it
was during the Revolution that they became evident. Before the revolutionary movement only a few Americans, mostly royal officials and their
connections, had worried about the expanding size of America's political
society. But the imperial controversy had the effect of making all Americans more conscious of the power of the people out of doors. Political
leaders, in their contests with royal authority, vied with one another in
demonstrating their superior sympathy with the people—and in the
process considerably widened and intensified their public audiences.[20]
Given the Whig tradition of celebrating the people against the Crown,
it was a tendency most American leaders found difficult to resist. In 1766
the Massachusetts House of Representatives erected a public gallery for
the witnessing of its debates, a momentous step in the democratization
of American culture. The Pennsylvania Assembly followed reluctantly in
1770, and eventually the other legislatures, usually provoked by the desire
of Whig leaders to build support among the people for opposition to
Great Britain, began to reach out to a wider public.[21]

Yet old habits died hard, and it was difficult to shed the conception of
assembly proceedings' being in the nature of private business among gen-

tlemen. Votes in the legislatures continued to remain unrecorded, and reports of debates were rarely carried to the outside world. When in 1776 the revolutionaries met in their conventions to discuss the forms of their new state constitutions, they felt no need either to report what they said or to extract vows of secrecy to prevent leaks of what they said to the people out of doors. As a result, we know very little of what went on during those momentous closed meetings in the months surrounding the Declaration of Independence. Apparently the leaders believed that nearly everyone who counted and ought to hear what was said was within the legislative or convention halls.

A decade later, however, by 1787, the situation had become very different. In many of the states, particularly Pennsylvania and Massachusetts, legislative debates had begun to be reported by a growing number of newspapers (which now included dailies), and political leaders had developed a keen, even fearful awareness of a larger political society existing outside the legislative chambers. Politics no longer seemed an exclusively gentlemanly business, and consequently gentlemen in public discussions increasingly found themselves forced to concede to the popular and egalitarian ideology of the Revolution, for any hint of aristocracy was now pounced upon by emerging popular spokesmen eager to discredit the established elite leaders. Under these changed circumstances the delegates to the Philadelphia Convention in 1787 thought it necessary to take extraordinary measures to keep their proceedings private: No copies of anything in the journal were allowed, nothing said in the convention was to be released or communicated to the outside society, and even sentries were to be posted to prevent intruders, all out of a sensitivity to a public out of doors that had not existed ten years earlier.

By the late 1780s gentlemen in the convention had become convinced not only that this public—"the too credulous and unthinking Mobility," one delegate called it—was now interested in what went on within doors but that, if allowed access to the debates through publication by "imprudent printers," this hovering presence of the people would inhibit the delegates' freedom of expression.[22] Events bore out the significance of this deliberate decision to impose secrecy. The delegates to the Philadelphia convention showed a remarkable degree of candor and boldness in discussing what were now sensitive issues, like aristocracy and the fear of popular power, that was notably missing from the debates in the various ratifying conventions held several months later. Since the ratifying conventions were open and their proceedings widely publicized in the press, the difference in the tone and character of the respective debates is revealing of just what a broader public could mean for the intellectual life of American politics. Madison later reportedly declared that "no Constitution would ever have been adopted by the convention if the debates had been public."[23] As it was, the defenders of the proposed Constitution knew very well that "when this plan goes forth, it will be attacked by the popular leaders. Aristocracy will be the watchword; the Shibboleth among its adversaries.[24] Hence the proponents of the Constitution found themselves in the subsequent public debates compelled to stress over and over the popular and "strictly republican" character of the new federal government. Men who only a few months earlier had voiced deep misgivings about popular rule now tried to outdo their opponents in expressing their enthusiasm for the people. "We, sir, idolize democracy," they said in answer to popular critics of the Constitution.[25]

Although aspects of this public exuberance by supporters of the Constitution over the democratic character of the Constitution appear disingenuous and hypocritical to us in light of their private fears of popular power and majority rule, in the debates they were doing only what their liberal education in rhetoric had taught them: adapting their arguments to the nature and needs of their audience. Still, the demands of rhetoric were not supposed to lead to dishonesty and duplicity by a political and intellectual leader, particularly if his audience was the people. Such a gap between private and public feelings as was displayed in the debates over the Constitution only raised in a new form an issue that had been at the heart of American public discussions throughout the eighteenth century and never more so than at the time of the Revolution.

During that entire century, and even earlier, enlightened men everywhere had been obsessed by what was often called Machiavellian duplicity, the deliberate separation between men's hidden feelings or motives and their public faces, an obsession that the rhetorical attitude only enhanced. It was often feared that some dishonest men would assume roles and play falsely with their audience or public. The worst villain was the one who, like Iago, achieved his end through plots and dissembling; indeed, the enlightened eighteenth century was incapable of locating evil anywhere else but in this kind of deceiving man.[26]

Assumptions like these lay behind the character of American political life in the eighteenth century and eventually became central to the decision to revolt in 1776. Time and time again, opposition spokesmen against royal authority in the colonies had emphasized the duplicity and flattery of courtiers who selfishly sought the favor of great men while they professed service to the public. Dissimulation, deception, and design were thus accusations quickly made, and suspicion of men in power pervaded the political climate. The alternative to the courtier, opposition spokesmen said, was the true patriot, a man like themselves, who did not need to dissemble and deceive because he relied solely on the people. As the conventional theory of mixed government pointed out, the people may have lacked energy and wisdom, but they made up for these deficiencies by their honesty and sincerity. Hence writers and critics, themselves gentlemen, delighted in posing as simple farmers in attacking the aristocratic pretensions and duplicity of other gentlemen who acted condescendingly or seemed to possess privileges and powers they had no right to have, all the while citing in support of their arguments eighteenth-century writers, from Richardson to Rousseau, who were increasingly celebrating the moral virtue of sincerity or the strict correspondence of appearance and reality, action and intention.

As a young man in the 1760s John Adams, for example, had celebrated equality, and writing as Humphrey Ploughjogger, he had done battle on behalf of all those ordinary humble people who were "made of as good Clay" as the so-called "great ones of the World." He had wondered, "Who are to be understood by the better Sort of People?" and concluded that there was "no Difference between one Man and another, but what real Merit creates." He was thinking of Lieutenant Governor Thomas Hutchinson and his genteel crowd, with their "certain Airs of Wisdom and Superiority" and their "Scorn and Contempt and turning up of the Nose," and he believed passionately that they were no better than he was. Let the people decide who are the better sort, said Adams, in his naive and youthful republican enthusiasm; they would be the best judges of merit.[27]

At the beginning of the Revolution few American Whig gentlemen had any deep awareness that in drawing these contrasts between the aristocratic guile and pretensions of the rank they belonged or aspired to and the sincerity and honest hearts of the body of common people, they were unleashing a force they could not control. In 1776 many of them, including the likes of John Adams and Thomas Jefferson, watched with equanimity and indeed enthusiasm the displacement in political office of proud and insolent grandees by new men "not so well dressed, nor so politely educated, nor so highly born. . . ." There was little to fear from such a "political metamorphosis," to use Jefferson's term, for these new men were "the People's men (and the People in general are right). They are plain and of consequence less disguised, . . . less intriguing, more sincere."[28]

Out of these kinds of changes in values, fed by the vast social transformation taking place on both sides of the Atlantic, elite leaders began sentimentalizing the common man and natural and spontaneous speech. Already in the mid-eighteenth century theorists of rhetoric were responding to the need for a language that could move and influence the passions of audiences, calling for a more natural speech that would avoid ornamentation and formality and would express the plain and naked truth of the speaker's inner feelings.[29]

We saw these changes in rhetorical style in the writings of Thomas Paine. They were equally visible in the oratory of Patrick Henry, who, like Paine, sought to reach out to wider and deeper layers of the population and in the process aroused the awe and consternation of his gentlemanly colleagues. Henry was a failure as a planter and storekeeper, but at the age of twenty-three he taught himself law and soon emerged as the gentle-manly spokesman in the Virginia House of Burgesses for the poor and middling farmers and religious dissenters of southwestern Virginia. Like the evangelical preachers he listened to as a youth, Henry was the master of the oral culture in which most ordinary people still lived.

Like Paine, Henry deliberately rejected the customary classical apparatus of persuasion and sought to express to ordinary people the kinds of feelings—both revulsions and visions—that the traditional elitist conventions of speech and writing did not allow. Also like Paine, he lacked formal schooling and was accused of using ungrammatical language and coarse and vulgar idioms. Henry ignored all this criticism of his pronunciation and speaking style, for as his fellow burgess Edmund Randolph pointed out, he discovered that an irregular and homespun language "which might disgust in a drawing room may yet find access to the hearts of a popular assembly."[30] Again like Paine, he aimed to break through the usual niceties and formalities of rhetoric and meant to declare, as Randolph said, that "it was enough to feel."[31]

To both Paine and Henry fancy words and learned citations no longer mattered as much as honesty and sincerity and the natural revelation of feeling. In this atmosphere the use of Greek and Latin as the exclusive property and ornament of gentlemen was disparaged, and the written and spoken word itself became suspect, as men, taking off from Locke's mistrust of imagery, increasingly urged that what was needed in communication were things, not words.[32] And since words, not to mention the classical languages, were associated with cultivated learning and with aristocracy, it was the common man, the simple untutored farmer, or even, in the eyes of some like Jefferson, the uncorrupted Indian with his natural gift of oratory who became consecrated.

By the final decade of the eighteenth century the implications of what was happening were becoming clear to some American gentry. Growing apprehensions over the abuses of popular power had contributed to the movement to create the new federal government, and such fears of democracy eventually became the fixation of the Federalist party in the 1790s.

Most Federalist leaders, at least those old enough to be politically conscious at the time of the Revolution, had not anticipated becoming afraid
of the people. Like other good Whigs, they had assumed that the people,
once free of English influence, would honor and elevate the country's
true patriots and natural aristocracy in ways that the English Crown had
not. But when in the decades following the Revolution the people seemed
to succumb to the deceit and flattery of mushroom demagogues, who
were the popular counterparts of courtiers, the Federalists became bewildered and bitter.

The Federalist writers and speakers of the 1790s responded as
eighteenth-century gentlemen would: with the traditional elitist weapons
of satire and invective, saturating the political climate with vituperation
and venom the likes of which have never been equaled in our national history. But such verbal abuse and ridicule—against democracy, demagoguery, vulgarity—were rhetorical devices designed for a different culture
from that which America was creating. Such calumny and invective as the
Federalists expressed were supposed to be calculated and deliberately exaggerated, not a genuine expression of the satirists' inner emotions, and
were justifiable because they were the result of the righteous indignation
that any gentleman would feel in similar circumstances.[33] Hence, to be effective, such rhetorical anger and abuse were dependent on an instantaneous uniformity of recognition by the audience of the universal principles
of truth and reasonableness to which the satirist appealed. However, the
democratization of American society and culture that was occurring in
these years was not only broadening and diversifying the public, weaken-
ing those common standards of rightness and good behavior that under-
lay the potency of satire, but also destroying the ability of the Federalist
writers to maintain a rhetorical detachment from what was happening.
The Federalists thus groped during the next decade or so to discover a
rhetoric that could persuade their audience without at the same time
alienating it.

Most of the revolutionary gentry soon came to realize that the people
in America were beyond public criticism; they could not, as in the past,

refer to them as the common "herd." During the Virginia ratifying convention in June 1788 Edmund Randolph had used just this term in reference to the people, and Patrick Henry had immediately called him on it. By likening the people to a "herd," Henry charged, Randolph had "levelled and degraded [them] to the lowest degree," reducing them "from respectable independent citizens, to abject, dependent subjects or slaves." Randolph was forced to rise at once and defensively declare "that he did not use that word to excite any odium, but merely to convey an idea of a multitude."[34] Clearly he would not use it again in public.

This exchange marked an important point in the transformation of American culture. The Federalists found it increasingly difficult to speak publicly the truth as they saw it and not get punished for it. Anonymity was now resorted to, less because it was unseemly for a gentleman in the eyes of other gentlemen to expose his writings to the vulgar than because it was harmful for a gentleman's public career in the eyes of the vulgar (who could vote) to be caught writing, especially if that writing contained anything unpopular.[35] "In democracies," the Federalists concluded, "writers will be more afraid of the people, than afraid for them." Thus the right principles of political science, like those that had been discovered by the revolutionary leaders, would become "too offensive for currency or influence," and America's intellectual contributions to politics would cease.[36]

Some Federalists, regarding scorn by the people as a badge of honor and counting on posterity to vindicate their reputations, took a stubborn pride in their growing isolation from the public.[37] Other Federalists, however, could not easily abandon their role as gentlemanly leaders and sought desperately to make their influence felt, some eventually concluding that they too must begin flattering the people, saying that if they could not achieve their ends "but by this sort of cant, we must have recourse to it." They came to realize, in Hamilton's words, that "the first thing in all great operations of such a government as ours is to secure the opinion of the people." But in competition with their Republican opponents, the Federalists, said Fisher Ames, were like "flat tranquillity against passion; dry leaves against the whirlwind; the weight of gunpowder against its kindled force."[38] They could not shed fast enough their traditional eighteenth-century rhetorical and elitist techniques. They continued to rely on a limited audience of reasonable gentlemen like themselves who alone could respond to their satirical blasts against democracy and vulgarity. They also preferred private correspondence among "particular gentlemen" to dealing with the unlettered multitude through the newly developing media of communication, especially the newspapers.[39]

In the 1790s both the Federalists and their opponents, the Jeffersonian Republicans, recognized the changing role that popular media of communication were coming to play in American public life.[40] The sale of every sort of printed matter—books, pamphlets, handbills, periodicals, posters, broadsides—multiplied, and through new channels of distribution these publications found their way into hands that were not used to such literature. In New York City alone the number of booksellers increased from five in 1786 to thirty by 1800.[41] No vehicle of communication was more significant than newspapers; in time men of all persuasions came to believe that the press was almost single-handedly shaping the contours of American political life. The number of newspapers grew from fewer than 100 in 1790 to over 230 by 1800; by 1810 Americans were buying more than 22 million copies of 376 newspapers annually, the largest aggregate circulation of newspapers of any country in the world.[42] With this increase in readership came a change in the newspaper's style and content. Although much of the press, especially that in Federalist control, retained its eighteenth-century character, other papers began responding to the wider democratic public. Prices were reduced, new eye-catching typography was used, cartoons appeared, political information replaced advertisements on the front pages, political speeches, debates, and rumors were printed, editorials were written, and classical pseudonyms were dropped as "A Friend of the People" or "One of the People" became more attractive signatures. In most public writing there was a noticeable simplification and vulgarization. The number of footnotes, the classical and literary allusions, the general display of learning all became less common, as authors sought, in the way Paine had, to adapt to the new popular character of their readers.[43]

Not all gentlemen in the 1790s became Federalists, of course, nor did they all become apprehensive over what was happening. Jefferson and the other gentlemen who came to constitute the leadership of the Republican party retained a remarkable amount of the earlier Whig confidence in the people and in what Jefferson called the "honest heart" of the common man. Part of this faith in democracy on the part of Jefferson and his Republican colleagues in the South can be attributed to their very insulation from it, for most of the southern planters remained comparatively immune to the democratic electoral politics that were beginning to disrupt northern society seriously and to eat away the popular deference to the "better sort" that the southern gentry took for granted.[44] Moreover, because these democratic developments in the North—not only the new popular literature and the broadened public but also the expanded suffrage, the new immigrants, the mobilization of new men into politics—all tended to support the Republican cause, they seemed unalarming to Republican gentlemen everywhere and only vindications of their trust in the people and fulfillments of the Revolution.

Nevertheless, the Republican political and intellectual leaders at first showed little more knowledge than the Federalists in dealing with an expanded American public. To be sure, Jefferson, in good Enlightenment manner, had always favored the full exchange of ideas and almost alone among the founders had disliked the Philadelphia Convention delegates' "tying up the tongues of their members," a decision, he said, that only reflected "their ignorance of the value of public discussion." Moreover, at the outset of the 1790s Madison had urged as being favorable to liberty and republican government the development of "whatever facilitated a general intercourse of sentiments," such as roads, commerce, frequent elections, and "particularly a circulation of newspapers through the entire body of the people."[45] Yet during the 1790s, when the popularization of American culture was proceeding rapidly, Jefferson persisted in believing that political pamphlets were for "the thinking part of the nation," which would "set the people to rights," and he continued to rely extensively on private correspondence for the dissemination of his views.[46] At the same time, despite his recognition of an expanded public, Madison kept on writing learned pieces, like his *Helvidius* essays, for a restricted audience of educated gentlemen.

Others, however, dozens of writers and speakers, common, ordinary, obscure men, men without breeding, without learning, without character—in short, persons who were not gentlemen—were now presuming "without scruple, to undertake the high task of enlightening the public mind." By 1800, wrote the Reverend Samuel Miller in his elaborate compendium of the Enlightenment entitled *A Brief Retrospect of the Eighteenth Century*, much of the political and intellectual leadership of America had very recently fallen into "the hands of persons destitute at once of the urbanity of gentlemen, the information of scholars, and the principles of virtue."[47] Over the previous decade or so middling men had taken over increasing amounts of America's political and intellectual life. They were men such as Jedediah Peck, described as "illiterate but a shrewd cunning man," whose "language was low and he spoke with a drawling, nasal twang, so that on public speaking he was almost unintelligible," and Matthew Lyon, who came from Ireland in 1764 as an indentured servant but became a wealthy businessman and editor in Vermont.[48]

Unlike the Federalists, who stood for office by writing one another letters and lining up influential gentlemen as supporters, these plebeian politicians, who were invariably Jeffersonian Republicans, began promoting their own candidacies and campaigning for office openly. They used the newspapers to reach out to other common people in order to challenge the Federalist assumption that only well-to-do, educated gentlemen were capable of exercising political authority.[49]

These new men identified, as Peck did, with their "brother farmers, mechanicks and traders," and they wrote in the newspapers as "A Friend of the People" or as "A Ploughjogger." The classical signatures that Hamilton and Madison used were not for them. They began assaulting in the legislatures and newspapers all those "lawyers, and men of learning and money men, that talk so finely, and gloss over matters so smoothly."[50] Since lawyers were especially disliked by common folk, they bore the brunt of this middling criticism. Lawyers, it was said, "have wooled up the practices of the law in such a heap of formality on purpose so that we cannot see through their entanglement to oblige us to employ them to untangle them, and if we go to them for advice they will not say a word without five dollars."[51]

Everywhere in the northern parts of America the Federalist gentry were frightened by these rough and enterprising upstarts who were supplying many of the leaders and much of the support for the Jeffersonian Republican party in the North. But it was not social mobility itself that the Federalists feared. They were long used to men of obscure origins rising up in America and becoming gentlemen; indeed, many of the Federalists themselves were the products of this sort of social mobility, Hamilton and Adams being conspicuous examples, as we've seen. But traditionally those who moved up socially had shed their humble beginnings and become assimilated to gentry status, often by attending college or by strenuously acquiring the attributes of gentility.

Nor were the Federalists' feelings of anger and resentment toward the Republican parvenus of the 1790s new. As we've also seen, many of the revolutionary generation had felt the same resentment toward the Tory aristocrats who had dominated the royal governments. John Adams had posed as a ploughjogger in order to express his anger at the aristocratic pretensions of Thomas Hutchinson and his crowd. But his solution to the difference between them and him was not to celebrate his lowly origins but to outdo Hutchinson and his ilk at their own game. Although Adams may have begun his career writing as a hick farmer, he had no intention of remaining one of the humble people. Instead he had determined to become more learned, more genteel, and, most important, more virtuous and public-spirited than Hutchinson and his sort, who lived only by their lineage.[52]

Many of the Republican upstarts of postrevolutionary America behaved quite differently. They were not afraid of becoming what Benjamin Franklin in the 1730s had ridiculed as "Molatto Gentlemen," referring to all those ordinary folk, mechanics and tradesmen, who sought to become gentlemen when they weren't really ready for the status. This new generation of ambitious commoners was moving in a very different world from that of Franklin in the 1730s. They had the advantage of a postrevolutionary republican climate that celebrated equality in a manner that Franklin's earlier generation had never known. Moreover, despite the large numbers of middling sorts who continued to buy and read etiquette manuals in order to become polite and genteel, many of the new Republican leaders avoided becoming one of Franklin's "Molatto Gentlemen" by openly defying the traditional attributes of gentry rank.

Sick and tired of being humiliated by the college-educated leaders for being unrefined or for not having read Montesquieu, the middling upstarts threw their deficiencies back at their critics, who by the 1790s were usually Federalists. In their writings and rhetoric the Republican parvenus began ridiculing book learning, genteel manners, and aristocratic arrogance and, to the amazement of the Federalist gentry, won popularity in the process. Instead of becoming half-baked gentlemen, they chose to flaunt their lowly origins and their plebeian tastes and manners, a radical stance that shocked the traditional-minded Federalists.

To the Federalist the upstart nature of both authors and audience was precisely the point of their frenzied response to the literature of the 1790s. It was one thing to endure calumny and abuse from one's own social kind. That had been a constant part of Anglo-American political life for a century or more. It was quite another thing to suffer such invective from social inferiors, from nongentlemen, from "uneducated printers, shop boys, and raw schoolmasters," and to have such criticism and vituperation carried down to the lowest levels of the society.[53]

All this demagoguery, all this criticism of the enlightened standards of gentility that the revolutionary leaders had done so much to promote had a withering effect on traditional political authority. By the mid-1790s no gentleman's character, even Washington's, seemed immune to the crassest and crudest criticism from the press. In the aftermath of Jay's Treaty Washington was charged with tyranny and the "Machiavellian policy" of fomenting a monarchy in America. He was called "the scourge and misfortune of our country," whose name gave "a currency to political iniquity and to legalized corruption." Some even said that he had been a secret British agent during the Revolution. This vilification of the first president climaxed with an open letter to him in July 1796 written by none other than the great pamphleteer of the Revolution, Thomas Paine, who accused Washington of "cold and unmilitary conduct" during the Revolution. "You slept away your time in the field, till the finances of the country were completely exhausted, and you have but little share in the glory of the final event." He went on to charge Washington with ingratitude, vanity, and Stuart-like pride; he was a man whose integrity was questionable, whose politics was duplicitous, and whose character was "chameleon-colored." It wasn't that Washington professed indifference to moral principles, said Paine; it was just that he was "prudent enough to conceal the want of them."[54]

If someone as great and as celebrated as Washington could be criticized in this outrageous manner, then it seemed to many Americans, especially to the Federalists of the 1790s, that the world was being turned upside down. All respectability, all learning, all character—the very idea of a gentleman as a political leader—were under assault.

Like freethinking and deistic religious views, personal abuse of the political leaders was socially harmless as long as it was confined to the gentlemanly ranks. But when it spread to the lower orders, as it was doing in the 1790s at the hands of Republican publications, it was very serious indeed. If all the Republicans' smear campaigns against the government had been read by gentlemanly elites alone, they might have been tolerable to the Federalists. Instead the Republicans' slanders against public officials were reaching down to new popular levels of readers, and that was intolerable. In other words, more important than what one said was the person to whom it was said. Anything that undermined the public's confidence in their leaders' capacities to rule was by that fact alone seditious.[55]

It was one thing to libel a private individual who was not in government, but quite another to libel someone who was holding government office. Such libels against political officials were doubly serious, indeed under the common law were seditious, because they brought into question the officeholders' authority to rule. Even Republican Thomas McKean, chief justice of the Pennsylvania Supreme Court, agreed. Libels against public officials, McKean declared, involved "a direct tendency to breed in the people a dislike of their governors, and incline them to faction and sedition."[56]

Because politics was still very personal, the honor and reputation of the political leaders seemed essential to social order and stability. It was difficult in this early modern world for men to conceive of anyone's becoming a political leader who did not already have an established social and moral superiority. Today a politician's reputation and social status are often a consequence of his political office; in the eighteenth century the process was reversed: An individual's social position and reputation were thought to be the necessary prerequisites to political officeholding. In other words, important offices of government were supposed to be held only by those who had already established their social and moral superiority. They at least ought to be "gentlemen," and preferably gentlemen of talent, education, and character.

The reasons seemed obvious to many American leaders of the time, both Federalists and Republicans. Since early modern governments lacked most of the coercive powers of a modern state—a few constables and sheriffs scarcely constituted a police force—officeholders had to rely on their social respectability and their reputation for character to compel the obedience of ordinary people and maintain public order. It is not surprising therefore that public officials should have been acutely sensitive to criticism of their character. "Whatever tends to create in the minds of the people, a contempt of the persons who hold the highest offices in the state," declared the conventional eighteenth-century wisdom, whatever convinces people that "subordination is not necessary, and is no essential part of government, tends directly to destroy it."[57]

In the Federalists' eyes much of the Republican press in the 1790s was indeed creating contempt for authority and undermining the due subordination of society. President Adams was especially vulnerable to criticism. Washington had been so widely popular that all the royal pomp and circumstance that surrounded him seemed fitting and natural. But Adams was different. Lacking Washington's popularity and stature, he was ill equipped to play the role of the republican monarch, and efforts to bolster his authority with formal ceremonies and elaborate rituals made him seem only absurd and open to ridicule, which the Republican press was more than willing to supply.[58] After suffering criticism that he was "a mock Monarch" who was "blind, bald, toothless, querulous" and "a ruffian deserving of the curses of mankind," Adams concluded that he had become the victim of "the most envious malignity, the most base, vulgar, sordid, fishwoman scurrility, and the most palpable lies" that had ever been leveled against any public official.[59]

IT WAS THESE CONSIDERATIONS—the belief that the channels of communication between governors and governed were rapidly becoming poisoned by mushroom intellectual leadership and the fear that the stability of the entire political order was at stake—that lay behind the Federalists' desperate resort to coercion, the sedition law of 1798, an action that more than anything else has tarnished their historical reputation. The Federalists' attempt to stop up the flow of malice and falsehood from the Republican presses by the use of state power may have been desperate, but it was not irrational, as the subsequent debate over the Sedition Act showed. For at issue in the debate was not simply freedom of the press but the very nature and structure of America's intellectual life.

The debate over the Sedition Act marked the crucial turning point in the democratization of American intellectual life. It fundamentally altered America's understanding not only of its intellectual leadership but of its conception of public truth. The debate, which spilled over into the early years of the nineteenth century, drew out and articulated the logic of America's intellectual experience since the Revolution, and in the process it undermined the foundations of the elitist eighteenth-century classical world on which the founders stood.

Americans believed in freedom of the press and had written it into their Bill of Rights. But they believed in it as Englishmen did. The English had celebrated freedom of the press since the seventeenth century but had meant by it, in contrast with the French, no prior restraint or censorship of what was published. Under English law people were nevertheless held responsible for what they published. If a person's publications were slanderous and calumnious enough to bring public officials into disrespect, then under the common law the publisher could be prosecuted for seditious libel. The truth of what was published was no defense; indeed, it even aggravated the offense. Furthermore, under the common law, judges, not juries, had the responsibility to decide whether or not a publication was seditious. Although this common law view of seditious libel had been challenged by the Zenger trial in New York in 1735, it had never been fully eradicated from American thinking or practice in the state courts.

The Federalists in their Sedition Act of 1798 thought they were being generous by changing the common law conception of seditious libel and enacting the Zenger defense into law. They not only allowed juries to determine what was seditious but made truth a defense, stating that only those statements that were "false, scandalous, and malicious" would be punished. But the Republican polemicists would have no part of this generosity. In the debate over the sedition law the Republican libertarian theorists rejected both the old common law restrictions on the liberty of the press and the new legal recognition of the distinction between truth and falsity of opinion that the Federalists had incorporated into the Sedition Act. While the Federalists clung to the eighteenth century's conception that "truths" were constant and universal and capable of being discovered by enlightened and reasonable men, the Republicans argued that opinions about government and governors were many and diverse and their truth could not be determined simply by individual judges and juries, no matter how reasonable such men were. Hence they concluded that all political opinions—that is, words as distinct from overt acts—even those opinions that were "false, scandalous, and malicious," ought to be allowed, as Jefferson put it, to "stand undisturbed as monuments of the safety with which error of opinion may be tolerated where reason is left free to combat it."[60]

The Federalists were incredulous. "How ... could the rights of the people require a liberty to utter falsehood?" they asked. "How could it be right to do wrong?"[61] It was not an easy question to answer, as we continue to discover even in our own time. The Republicans thought they could not deny outright the possibility of truth and falsity in political beliefs and thus fell back on a tenuous distinction, developed by Jefferson in his first inaugural address, between principles and opinions. Principles, it seemed, were hard and fixed, while opinions were soft and fluctuating; therefore, said Jefferson, "every difference of opinion is not a difference of principle." The implication was, as Benjamin Rush suggested, that individual opinions did not count as much as they had in the past, and for that reason such individual opinions could be permitted the freest possible expression.[62]

What ultimately made such distinctions and arguments comprehensible was the Republicans' assumption that opinions about politics were no longer the monopoly of the educated and aristocratic few. Not only were true and false opinions equally to be tolerated, but everyone and anyone in the society should be equally able to express them. Sincerity and honesty, the Republican polemicists argued, were far more important in the articulation of ultimate political truth than learning and fancy words that had often been used to deceive and dissimulate. Truth was actually the creation of many voices and many minds, no one of which was more important than another and each of which made its own separate and equally significant contribution. Solitary individual opinions may thus have counted for less, but in their numerous collectivity they now added up to something far more significant than had ever existed before. Mingled together, they resulted into what was called *public opinion*. But this public opinion was no longer the small intimate entity it had been for the revolutionary leaders; it was huge and impersonal, modern and democratic, and it included everyone's opinion. This new expanded idea of public opinion soon came to dominate all of American intellectual life.[63]

Public opinion is so much a part of our politics that it is surprising that we have not incorporated it into the Constitution. We constantly use the term, seek to measure whatever it is and to influence it, and worry about who else is influencing it. Public opinion exists in any nation, but in our democracy it has a special power. The Revolution in America transformed it and gave it its modern significance. By the early years of the nineteenth century Americans had come to realize that public opinion, "that invisible guardian of honour—that eagle eyed spy on human actions—that inexorable judge of men and manners—that arbiter, whom tears cannot appease, nor ingenuity soften and from whose terrible decisions there is no appeal," had become "the vital principle" underlying American government, society, and culture.[64] It became the resolving force not only of political truth but of all truth, from disputes among religious denominations to controversies over artistic taste. Nothing was more important in explaining and clarifying the democratization of American culture than this new conception of public opinion. In the end it became America's nineteenth-century popular substitute for the elitist intellectual leadership of the revolutionary generation.

Although the will of the people, the vox populi, was an old idea in Western culture, it took on enhanced significance in the latter half of the eighteenth century in response to the steady democratization of Western society. During the revolutionary era many American leaders, echoing David Hume and other enlightened thinkers, had become convinced that public opinion ought to be the "real sovereign" in any free government like theirs. Yet when Madison in 1791 referred to public opinion, he was still thinking of it as the intellectual product of limited circles of gentlemen rulers. That is why he feared that the large extent of the United States made the isolated individual insignificant in his own eyes and made easier the counterfeiting of opinion by a few.[65] Other Americans, however, were coming to see in the very breadth of the country and in the very insignificance of the solitary individual the saving sources of a general opinion that could be trusted.

Because American society was no longer an organic hierarchy with "an intellectual unity," public opinion in America, it was now argued, could not be the consequence of the intellectual leadership of a few learned gentlemen. General public opinion was simply "an aggregation of individual sentiments," the combined product of multitudes of minds reflecting independently, communicating their ideas in different ways, causing opinions to collide and blend with one another, to refine and correct themselves, leading toward "the ultimate triumph of Truth." Such a product, such a public opinion, could be trusted because it had so many sources, so many voices and minds, all interacting, that no individual or group could manipulate or dominate the whole.[66] Like the example of religious diversity in America, a comparison many now drew upon to explain their new confidence in public opinion, the separate opinions allowed to circulate freely would by their very differentness act, in Jefferson's word, as "a Censor" over one another and the society, performing the role that the ancients and Augustan Englishmen had expected heroic individuals and satiric poets to perform.[67]

The Americans' belief that this aggregation of individual sentiments, this residue of separate and diverse interacting opinions would become the repository of ultimate truth required in the end an act of faith, one that was not much different from a belief in the beneficent workings of Providence. In fact this conception of public opinion as the transcendent consequence of many utterances, none of which deliberately created it, was an aspect of a larger intellectual transformation taking place in those years. It was related to a new appreciation of the nature of the social and historical process being developed by Western intellectuals, particularly by that group of brilliant Scottish social scientists writing at the end of the eighteenth century. Just as numerous economic competitors, buyers and sellers in the market, were led by an invisible hand to promote an end that was no part of their intent, so too could men now conceive of numerous individual thinkers, makers and users of ideas, being led to create a result, a public opinion, that none of them anticipated or consciously brought about.

In such a world, a democratic world of progress, Providence, and in-numerable isolated but equal individuals, there could be little place for the kind of extraordinary political and intellectual leadership the revolution-ary generation had demonstrated. All these obscure and anonymous in-dividuals resembled Washington's "broomsticks," who he complained were replacing as political leaders men of distinction and character. Because, Americans now told themselves over and over, "public opinion will be much nearer the truth, than the reasoning and refinements of speculative or interested men"; because "public opinion has, in more instances than one, triumphed over critics and connoisseurs" even in matters of artistic taste; because, the Federalists warned, public opinion was "of all things the most destructive of personal independence & of that weight of character which a great man ought to possess"; because of all these leveling and de-mocratizing forces, it was no longer possible for prominent gentlemen, in their speeches and writings, to make themselves felt in the way the founders had.[68]

In the new egalitarian society of the early nineteenth century, in which every man's opinion seemed as good as another's, either "men of genius" (they could no longer be simply educated gentlemen) became "a sort of outlaws," lacking "that getting-along faculty which is naturally enough the measure of a man's mind in a young country, where every one has his for-tune to make," or in trying to emulate the civic-consciousness of the founders, such would-be intellectual leaders ended up being "fettered by fear of popular offense or [of having] wasted their energies and debased their dignity in a mawkish and vulgar courting of popular favor."[69] It was not a world the founders wanted or expected; indeed, those who lived long enough into the nineteenth century to experience its full democratic force were deeply disillusioned by what they had wrought. Still, they had helped create this popular world, for it was rooted in the vital principle that none of them, Federalists included, ever could deny: the people. In the end nothing illustrates better the transforming power of the American Revolution than the way its intellectual and political leaders, that remarkable group of men, contributed to their own demise.

Notes

The following abbreviations are used throughout the notes section.

Abbreviation	Full Citation
Adams, ed., *Works*	Charles F. Adams, ed., *The Works of John Adams*, 10 vols. (Boston: Little, Brown, 1850–56).
Papers of Adams	Robert J. Taylor et al., eds. *The Papers of John Adams* (Cambridge, MA: Harvard University Press, 1977—).
BF, *Autobiography*	Leonard Labaree et al., eds. *The Autobiography of Benjamin Franklin* (New Haven: Yale University Press, 1964).
Papers of Franklin	Leonard W. Labaree et al., eds., *The Papers of Benjamin Franklin* (New Haven: Yale University Press, 1959—).
Franklin: Writings	J. A. Leo Lemay, ed., *Benjamin Franklin: Writings* (New York: Library of America, 1987).
Papers of Hamilton	Harold C. Syrett et al., eds., *The Papers of Alexander Hamilton*, 27 vols. (New York: Columbia University Press, 1962—).
Hamilton: Writings	Joanne B. Freeman, ed., *Alexander Hamilton: Writings* (New York: Library of America, 2001).
Papers of Jefferson	Julian P. Boyd et al., eds., *The Papers of Thomas Jefferson* (Princeton: Princeton University Press, 1950—).
Ford, ed., *Writings of Jefferson*	Paul L. Ford, ed., *The Writings of Thomas Jefferson*, 10 vols. (New York: G. P. Putnam's Sons, 1892–99).
L and B, ed., *Writings of Jefferson*	A. A. Lipscomb and Albert Ellery Bergh, eds., *The Writings of Thomas Jefferson*, 20 vols. (Washington, D.C.: Jefferson Memorial Association, 1903).
Jefferson: Writings	Merrill D. Peterson, ed., *Thomas Jefferson: Writings* (New York: Library of America, 1984).

Papers of Madison	William T. Hutchinson et al., eds., *The Papers of James Madison*, vols. 1–10 (Chicago: University of Chicago Press, 19—); vol. 11— (Charlottesville, VA: University Press of Virginia, 1977—).
Madison: Writings	Jack N. Rakove, ed., *James Madison: Writings* (New York: Library of America, 1999).
Papers of Washington: Presidential Ser.	W. W. Abbot et al., eds., *The Papers of George Washington: Presidential Series* (Charlottesville, VA: University Press of Virginia, 1987—).
Papers of Washington: Retirement Ser.	W. W. Abbot et al., eds., *The Papers of George Washington: Retirement Series,* 4 vols. (Charlottesville, VA: University Press of Virginia, 1998–99).
Fitzpatrick, ed., *Writings of Washington*	John C. Fitzpatrick, ed., *The Writings of George Washington*, 39 vols. (Washington, D.C.: U.S. Government, 1931–44).
Washington: Writings	John Rhodhamel, ed., *George Washington: Writings* (New York: Library of America, 1997).
JA	John Adams
AB	Aaron Burr
BF	Benjamin Franklin
AH	Alexander Hamilton
TJ	Thomas Jefferson
JM	James Madison
TP	Thoms Paine
GW	George Washington
WMQ	*William and Mary Quarterly*

PREFACE

1. TJ To William Stephens Smith, Oct 22, 1786, *Papers of Jefferson,* 479. Gaye Wilson, "Fashioning the American Diplomat: American Revolutionaries in European Courts." Unpublished paper in possession of the author and cited with permission.

INTRODUCTION: THE FOUNDERS AND THE ENLIGHTENMENT

1. Abraham Lincoln, "The Perpetuation of Our Political Institutions: Address Before the Young Men's Lyceum of Springfield, Illinois, January 27, 1838," in Roy P. Basler, ed., *Abraham Lincoln: His Speeches and Writings* (Cleveland: World Publishing Co., 1948), 84.

2. John Bach McMaster, *The Political Depravity of the Founding Fathers* (originally published as *With the Fathers* [1896], New York: Noonday Press, 1964), 71.

3. Wesley Frank Craven, *The Legend of the Founding Fathers* (Ithaca: Cornell University Press, 1956), 195.

4. Charles A. Beard, *An Economic Interpretation of the Constitution of the United States* (originally published in 1913; 1935 ed.; New York: Macmillan, 1986), xlvi, xliv.

5. Joseph J. Ellis, *Founding Brothers: The Revolutionary Generation* (New York: Knopf, 2000), 12.

6. Charles A. Beard, *The Supreme Court and the Constitution* (originally published in 1912; Englewood Cliffs, NJ: Prentice-Hall, 1962), 91.

7. David Eggers, *A Heartbreaking Work of Staggering Genius* (New York: Simon & Shuster, 2000), 265.

8. Peter C. Mancall, *Valley of Opportunity: Economic Culture Along the Upper Susquehanna* (Ithaca: Cornell University Press, 1991), 232.

9. Charles S. Sydnor, *Gentlemen Freeholders: Political Practices in Washington's Virginia* (Chapel Hill: University of North Carolina Press, 1952), 120–34.

10. Adam Smith, *An Inquiry into the Nature and Causes of the Wealth of Nations*, R. H. Campbell and A. S. Skinner, eds. (Oxford: Oxford University Press, 1976, 2), 688. The fullest account of the four-stage theory is Ronald L. Meek, *Social Science and the Ignoble Savage* (Cambridge, England: Cambridge University Press, 1976). For the eighteenth-century Americans application of the four-stage theory to their society see Drew R. McCoy, *The Elusive Republic: Political Economy in Jeffersonian America* (Chapel Hill: University of North Carolina Press, 1980), 13–47.

11. John Locke, *Two Treatises of Government*, Peter Laslett, ed. (Cambridge: Cambridge University Press, 2d ed., 1967), 301.

12. Henry Dwight Sedgwick, *In Praise of Gentlemen* (Boston: Little Brown, 1935), 130n.

13. Sheldon Rothblatt, *Tradition and Change in English Liberal Education: An Essay in History and Culture* (London: Faber and Faber, 1976), 23–31.

14. Noah Webster, "On the Education of Youth in America" (1790), in Frederick Rudolph, ed., *Essays on Education in the Early Republic* (Cambridge, MA: Harvard University Press, 1965), 56.

15. JA, *Defence of the Constitutions of the United States* (1787–88), Adams, ed., *Works*, 6: 185.

16. Aristotle, *Politics*, VII, ix, 1328b33, T. A. Sinclair, trans., rev. by Trevor J. Saunders (New York: Oxford University Press, 1981), 415.

17. Smith, *Wealth of Nations*, Campbell and Skinner, eds., II, 781–83.

18. Francis Hutcheson, *A System of Moral Philosophy in Three Books . . .* (London: A. Millar, 1755), 2: 113.

19. TJ to Richard Henry Lee, June 17, 1779, in *Papers of Jefferson*, 2: 298.

20. Jack N. Rakove, *The Beginnings of National Politics: An Interpretative History of the Continental Congress* (New York: Knopf, 1979), 216–39, quotation by William Fleming to TJ, May 10, 1779, at 237; George Athan Billias, *Elbridge Gerry: Founding Father and Republican Statesman* (New York: McGraw Hill, 1976), 138–39.

21. TJ, *Notes on the State of Virginia* William Peden, ed. (Chapel Hill: University of North Carolina Press), 165.

22. See William R. Taylor, *Cavalier and Yankee: The Old South and American Character* (New York: G. Braziller, 1961).

23. James Wilson, "On the History of Property," in Robert Green McCloskey, ed., *The Works of James Wilson* (Cambridge, MA: Harvard University Press, 1967), 2: 716; John Dickinson, "Letters of a Farmer in Pennsylvania" (1768), in Paul Leicester Ford, ed., *The Writings of John Dickinson, Vol. I, Political Writings, 1764–1774* (Pennsylvania Historical Society, *Memoirs*, XIV [Philadelphia, 1895]), 307.

24. Charles Chauncy to Richard Price, 1774, in Thomas and Bernard Peach, eds., *The Correspondence of Richard Price* (Durham, NC: Duke University Press, 1983), 170.

25. David Duncan Wallace, *The Life of Henry Laurens* (New York: G. P. Putnam and Sons, 1915), 69–70, 335.

26. David S. Shields, *Civil Tongues and Polite Letters* (Chapel Hill: University of North Carolina Press, 1997), 130.

27. Charles Royster, *A Revolutionary People at War: The Continental Army and American Character, 1775–1783* (Chapel Hill: University of North Carolina Press, 1979), 86–87.

28. William Livingston et al., *Independent Reflector* . . . Milton M. Klein, ed. (Cambridge, MA: Harvard University Press, 1963), 219.

29. Franco Venturi, *Utopia and Reform in the Enlightenment* (Cambridge, England: Cambridge University Press, 1971), 133.

30. *Boswell's London Journal, 1762–1763*, Frederick A. Pottle, ed. (New York: McGraw Hill, 1950), 47.

31. Steven J. Novak, *The Rights of Youth: American Colleges and Student Revolt, 1798–1815* (Cambridge, MA: Harvard University Press, 1977), 58.

32. Bernard Bailyn, *The Ideological Origins of the American Revolution* (Cambridge, MA: Harvard University Press, 1967), 89–92.

33. As Stephen Conway has pointed out, Halifax's opinion was extreme. Although Grenville himself seems to have regarded the colonists as separate from the British nation, apologists for the Stamp Act necessarily had to assume that the Americans were part of the same British community under Parliament; otherwise they would have no way of explaining why the

colonists should contribute taxes to the realm. Conway, "From Fellow-Nationals to Foreigners: British Perceptions of the Americans, circa 1739–1783," *WMQ*, 59 (2002), 83–84.

34. On the creative imagination stimulated by provincialism, see Bernard Bailyn, *To Begin the World Anew: The Genius and Ambiguities of the American Founders* (New York: Knopf, 2003), 3–36.

35. John Clive and Bernard Bailyn, "England's Cultural Provinces: Scotland and America," *WMQ*, 3d Ser., 11 (1954), 200–213; N. T. Phillipson, "Culture and Society in the 18th Century Province: The Case of Edinburgh and the Scottish Enlightenment," in Lawrence Stone, ed., *The University in Society: Europe, Scotland, and the United States from the 16th to the 20th Century* (Princeton: Princeton University Press, 1974), 2: 425; Stephan A. Conrad, "Polite Foundation: Citizenship and Common Sense in James Wilson's Republican Theory," *Supreme Court Review—1984*, Philip B. Kurland et al., eds. (Chicago: Chicago University Press, 1985), 362.

36. Livingston et al., *Independent Reflector*, Klein, ed., 220.

37. Robert F. Sayre, *The Examined Self: Benjamin Franklin, Henry Adams, Henry James* (Princeton: Princeton University Press, 1964), 12–43.

38. Joseph Addison, *The Spectator*, No. 10 (March 12, 1710–11), Alexander Chalmers, ed. (New York: D. Appleton, 1861), 129–30.

39. John Adams to Benjamin Rush, September 30, 1805, John A. Schutz and Douglass Adair, eds., *The Spur of Fame: Dialogues of John Adams and Benjamin Rush, 1805–1813* (San Marino, CA: Huntington Library, 1966), 42–43.

40. Benjamin Rush, "To———: Information to Europeans Who Are Disposed to Migrate to the United States," April 16, 1790, in Lyman H. Butterfield, ed., *The Letters of Benjamin Rush* (Princeton: Princeton University Press, 1951), 2: 554.

41. Duncan J. MacLeod, *Slavery, Race, and the American Revolution* (Cambridge, England: Cambridge University Press, 1974), 29.

42. Ellsworth, quoted in J. J. Spengler, "Malthusianism in Late Eighteenth-Century America," *American Economic Review*, 25 (1935), 705.

CHAPTER 1: THE GREATNESS OF GEORGE WASHINGTON

This chapter is a much revised and longer version of my article in the *Virginia Quarterly Review*, 68 (1992), 189–207, which is used with permission.

1. Hawthorne, Emerson, and Ward, quoted in James Morton Smith, ed., *George Washington: A Profile* (New York: Hill and Wang, 1969), xii.

2. Pauline Maier, *The Old Revolutionaries: Political Lives in the Age of Samuel Adams* (New York: Knopf, 1980), 47.

3. JA to Benjamin Rush, March 19, 1812, in Barry Schwartz, *George Washington: The Making of an American Symbol* (New York: Free Press, 1987), 5; TJ to Dr. Walter Jones, January 2, 1814, *Jefferson: Writing*, 1319.

4. Chateaubriand, in Gilbert Chinard, ed., *George Washington as the French Knew Him* (Princeton: Princeton University Press, 1940), 96.

5. GW to Lafayette, August 15, 1787, to Henry Knox, February 20, 1784, Fitzpatrick, ed., *Writings of Washington* 29: 259; 27: 341. See Paul Boller, Jr., *George Washington and Religion* (Dallas: Southern Methodist University Press, 1963), 94; Jay Fliegelman, *Prodigals and Pilgrims: The American Revolution Against Patriarchal Authority, 1750–1800* (Cambridge, England: Cambridge University Press, 1982), 212.

6. TJ, A Bill for Establishing Religious Freedom, 1779, *Jefferson: Writings*, 346.

7. GW to Reverend Jonathan Boucher, July 9, 1771, Fitzpatrick, ed., *Writings of Washington*, 3: 50.

8. Charles Moore, ed., *George Washington's Rules of Civility and Decent Behaviour in Company and Conversation* (Boston, 1926), 9, 5.

9. Frederic M. Litto, "Addison's *Cato* in the Colonies," *WMQ*, 3d Ser. (1966), 431–449.

10. GW to George Steptoe Washington, March 23, 1789, in *Papers of Washington: Presidential Ser.*, 1: 438.

11. Bernard Knollenberg, as noted by James Thomas Flexner, *George Washington: The Forge of Experience (1732–1775)* (Boston: Little, Brown, 1965), 254.

12. W. W. Abbot et al., eds., *The Papers of Washington: Colonial Series*, 10 vols. (Charlottesville: University Press of Virginia), 1: xvii.

13. Rush to JA, September 21, 1805, in John A. Schutz and Douglass Adair, eds., *The Spur of Fame: Dialogues of John Adams and Benjamin Rush, 1805–1813* (San Marino, CA: Huntington Library, 1980), 37.

14. GW to David Humphreys, July 25, 1785, Fitzpatrick, ed., *Writings of Washington*, 28: 203.

15. David S. Shields, *Civil Tongues and Polite Letters* (Chapel Hill: University of North Carolina Press, 1997), 116.

16. Brissot de Warville, in Chinard, ed., *Washington as the French Knew Him*, 87; JA to Rush, November 11, 1807, in Schutz and Adair, eds., *Spur of Fame*, 98.

17. GW to John Francis Mercer, September 9, 1786, *Washington: Writings*, 607.

18. GW to Tobias Lear, May 6, 1794, Fitzpatrick, ed., *Writings of Washington*, 33: 358.

19. GW's Last Will and Testament, July 9, 1799, *Papers of Washington: Retirement Ser.*, 4: 480. On Washington's attitudes toward slavery and his will, see Robert F. Dazell and Lee Baldwin Dalzell, *George Washington's Mount Vernon: At Home in Revolutionary America* (New York: Oxford University Press, 1998), and Henry Wiencek, *An Imperfect God: George Washington, His Slaves and the Creation of America* (New York: Farrar, Straus and Giroux, 2003).

20. Garry Wills, *Cincinnatus: George Washington and the Enlightenment* (New York, 1984), 3–16.

21. GW, Circular Letter to the States, June 8, 1783, in Fitzpatrick, ed., *Writings of Washington*, 26: 486; Wills, *Cincinnatus*, 13.

22. TJ to GW, April 16, 1784, *Washington: Writings*, 791.

23. James Thomas Flexner, *George Washington and the New Nation (1783–1793)* (Boston: Little, Brown, 1965), 3: 419.

24. See AH, *The Federalist*, No. 72, Jacob E. Cooke, ed. (Middletown, CT: Wesleyan University Press, 1961), 488.

25. TJ to Dr. Walter Jones, January 2, 1814, *Jefferson: Writings*, 1319.

26. GW to Benjamin Harrison, January 22, 1785, to William Grayson, January 22, 1785, to George William Fairfax, February 27, 1785, Fitzpatrick, ed., *Writings of Washington*, 28: 36, 85.

27. GW to Benjamin Harrison, January 22, 1785, to William Grayson, January 22, 1785, to Lafayette, February 15, 1785, to George William Fairfax, February 27, 1785, to Governor Patrick Henry, February 27, 1785, to Henry Knox, February 28, 1785, June 18, 1785, to Nathanael Greene, May 20, 1785, Fitzpatrick, ed., *Writings of Washington*, 28: 36, 37, 72, 80–81, 85, 89–91, 92–93, 167, 146.

28. GW to Henry Knox, March 8, 1787, to David Humphreys, March 8, 1787, Fitzpatrick, ed., *Writings of Washington*, 29: 172.

29. GW to Humphreys, December 26, 1786, Fitzpatrick, ed., *Writings of Washington*, 29, 128; Flexner, *Washington and the New Nation*, 3: 108.

30. Monroe to TJ, July 12, 1788, *Papers of Jefferson*, 13: 352.

31. GW to Henry Lee, September 22, 1788, in Fitzpatrick, ed., *Writings of Washington*, 30: 97, 98.

32. AH to GW, September 1788, *Papers of Hamilton*, 5: 221–222; GW to Lincoln, October 26, 1788, *Papers of Washington: Presidential Ser.*, 1: 71.

33. Douglas Southall Freeman, *George Washington: A Biography* (New York: Scribner's, 1954), 6: 86.

34. Abigail Adams, quoted in Flexner, *Washington and the New Nation*, 220; Garry Wills, *Cincinnatus: George Washington and the Enlightenment* (Garden City, NY: Doubleday, 1984), 23.

35. Rush, "To———: Information to Europeans Who Are Disposed to Migrate to the United States," April 16, 1790, Lyman H. Butterfield, ed., *Letters of Benjamin Rush* (Princeton: Princeton University Press, 1951), 2: 556.

36. JM, "Vices of the Political System of the United States," in *Papers of Madison*, 9: 352, 357.

37. Washington declared that "the Augustan age is proverbial for intellectual refinement and elegance," but he never suggested that it had any anti-republican political significance. GW to Lafayette, May 28, 1788, *Washington: Writings*, 681. On the Federalists and the Augustan age, see Linda Kerber, *Federalists in Dissent: Imagery and Ideology in Jeffersonian America* (Ithaca, NY: Cornell University Press, 1970).

38. Max Farrand, *The Records of the Federal Convention of 1787* (New Haven: Yale University Press, 1937), 1: 65, 119; 2: 513.

39. TJ to David Humphreys, March 18, 1789, in *Papers of Jefferson*, 14: 679.

40. Louise B. Dunbar, *A Study of "Monarchical" Tendencies in the United States from 1776 to 1801*, in *Illinois Studies in the Social Sciences*, 10(1922), 99–100.

41. James McHenry to GW, March 29, 1789, in *Papers of Washington: Presidential Ser.*, 1: 461.

42. Winifred E. A. Bernard, *Fisher Ames: Federalist and Statesman, 1758–1808* (Chapel Hill: University Press of North Carolina, 1965), 92.

43. David W. Robson, *Educating Republicans: The College in the Era of the American Revolution, 1758–1800* (Westport, CT., 1985), 149; Thomas E. V. Smith, *The City of New York in the Year of Washington's Inauguration, 1789* (New York, 1889, reprint ed., Riverside, CT: Chatham Press, 1972), 217–19.

44. GW, undelivered first inaugural address, January 1789, *Papers of Washington: Presidential Ser.*, 2: 162.

45. AH to GW, May 5, 1789, in *Papers of Hamilton*, 5: 335–37; JA to GW, May 17, 1789, *Papers of Washington*: Presidential Ser., 2: 314.

46. Flexner, *Washington and the New Nation*, 195.

47. Leonard D. White, *The Federalists: A Study in Administrative History* (New York: Macmillan, 1948), 108; S. W. Jackman, "A Young Englishman Reports on the New Nation: Edward Thornton to James Bland Burges, 1791–1793," *WMQ*, 18 (1961), 111.

48. David Waldstreicher, *In the Midst of Perpetual Fetes: The Making of American Nationalism, 1776–1820* (Chapel Hill: University of North Carolina Press, 1997), 120–22.

49. GW to JM, March 30, 1789, in *Papers of Washington: Presidential Ser.*, 1: 484; Don Higginbotham, *George Washington: Uniting a Nation* (Lanham, MD: Rowman and Littlefield, 2002), 10; JA to Benjamin Rush, Schutz and Adair, eds., *Spur of Fame*, 181.

50. Kenneth R. Bowling and Helen E. Veit, eds., *The Diary of William Maclay and Other Notes on Senate Debates: Documentary History of the First Federal Congress of the United States of America, 4 March 1789–3 March 1791* (Baltimore: Johns Hopkins University Press, 1988), 9: 21; Schwartz, *Washington*, 62.

51. Bowling and Veit, eds., *Diary of Maclay*, 21.

52. Page Smith, *John Adams* (New York: Doubleday, 1962), 2: 755.

53. TJ to JM, July 29, 1789, in *Papers of Jefferson*, 15: 316.

54. White, *Federalists*, 108.

55. Abraham Baldwin, November 30, 1806, in James H. Hutson, ed., *Supplement to Max Farrand's the Records of the Federal Convention of 1787* (New Haven: Yale University Press, 1987), 305.

56. S. W Jackman, "A Young Englishman Reports on the New Nation: Edward Thornton to James Bland Burges, 1791–1793," *WMQ*, 18 (1961), 104.

57. GW to John Augustine Washington, June 15, 1783, *Washington: Writings*, 527.

58. Bowling and Veit, eds., *Diary of Maclay*, 130; Glenn A. Phelps, *George Washington and American Constitutionalism* (Lawrence, KS: University Press of Kansas, 1993), 170.

59. GW to Philip Schuyler, December 24, 1775, in *Papers of Washington: Revolution Ser.*, 2: 599–600.

60. GW to the House of Representatives, March 30, 1796, in *Washington: Writings*, 931.

61. GW to JM, December 3, 1784, *Papers of Madison*, 12: 478; GW to John Hancock, September 24, 1776, in Fitzpatrick, ed., *Writings of Washington*, 6: 107–108.

62. Higginbotham, *Washington*, 53, 59–60, 55.

63. GW, Circular Letter to State Governments, June 8, 1783, *Washington: Writings*, 518.

64. TJ, notes of a conversation with Edmund Randolph [after 1795], *Papers of Jefferson*, 28: 568.

65. Higginbotham, *Washington*, 62, drawing on the work of David Shields and Fredrika Teute.

66. JM's conversations with GW, May 5–25, 1792, AH to GW, July 30–August 3, 1792, *Papers of Washington: Presidential Ser.*, 10: 351, 594; Elizabeth Willing Powel to GW, November 17, 1792, ibid., 11: 396.

67. TJ to JM, June 9, 1793, James Morton Smith, ed., *The Republic of Letters: The Correspondence Between Thomas Jefferson and James Madison 1776–1826* (New York: Norton, 1995), 781.

68. GW to Timothy Pickering, February 6, 1798, to Charles Carroll of Carrollton, August 2, 1798, *Papers of Washington: Retirement Ser.*, 2: 76; 483.

69. GW to the Marquis de Lafayette, December 25, 1798, *Papers of Washington: Retirement Ser.*, 3: 284.

70. GW to James McHenry, July 4, 1798, to JA, July 4, 1798, *Papers of Washington: Retirement Ser.*, 2: 378; 369.

71. GW to John Quincy Adams, January 20, 1799, *Papers of Washington: Retirement Ser.*, 3: 321.

72. Jonathan Trumbull, Jr., to GW, June 22, 1799, GW to Trumbull, July 21, 1799, *Papers of Washington: Retirement Ser.*, 4: 143–44, 202.

CHAPTER 2: THE INVENTION OF BENJAMIN FRANKLIN

This chapter is a much abbreviated summary of my book *The Americanization of Benjamin Franklin* (New York: Penguin, 2004).

1. *New York Times*, September 19, 1856, quoted in Nian-Sheng Huang, *Benjamin Franklin in American Thought and Culture, 1790–1990* (Philadelphia: American Philosophical Society, 1994), 31.

2. Richard D. Miles, "The American Image of Benjamin Franklin," *American Quarterly*, 9 (1957), 136.

3. See Douglass Adair, "Fame and the Founding Fathers," in Trevor Colbourn, ed., *Fame and the Founding Fathers: Essays by Douglass Adair* (New York: Norton, 1974), 3–26.

4. On Franklin's strategy of humility, see Paul W. Conner, *Poor Richard's Politicks: Benjamin Franklin and His New American Order* (New York: Oxford University Press, 1965), 149–69.

5. J. Philip Gleason, "A Scurrilous Colonial Election and Franklin's Reputation," *WMQ*, 3d Ser., 18 (1961), 76.

6. Jennifer T. Kennedy, "Death Effects: Revisiting the Conceit of Franklin's Memoir," *Early American Literature*, 36 (2001), 204.

7. BF, *Autobiography*, 75–76.

8. J. A. Leo Lemay, "The Theme of Vanity in Franklin's Autobiography," in Lemay, ed., *Reappraising Benjamin Franklin: A Bicentennial Perspective* (Newark, DE: 1993), 372–87.

9. Stanley Brodwin, "Strategies of Humor: The Case of Benjamin Franklin," *Prospects*, 4 (1779), 121–67.

10. Verner W. Crane, ed., *Benjamin Franklin's Letters to the Press, 1758–1775* (Chapel Hill: University of North Carolina Press, 1950), xxx.

11. J. A. Leo Lemay, *The Canon of Benjamin Franklin: New Attributions and Reconsiderations* (Newark, DE: University of Delaware Press, 1986), 135; Bruce Ingham Granger, *Benjamin Franklin: An American Man of Letters* (Ithaca, 1964).

12. BF, on censure and backbiting, 1732, *Franklin: Writings*, 192–95.

13. BF, on simplicity, 1732, *Franklin: Writings*, 183; BF, Poor Richard, 1743, *Papers of Franklin*, 2: 370.

14. Lionel Trilling, *Sincerity and Authenticity* (Cambridge, MA: Harvard University Press, 1972), 17–18.

15. BF, Poor Richard, 1735, *Papers of Franklin*, 2: 8.

16. AH to Edward Stevens, November 11, 1769, *Papers of Hamilton*, 1: 4.

17. BF, *Autobiography*, 80.

18. BF, Ibid., 113.

19. BF, Ibid., 121.

20. J. P. Brissot de Warville, *New Travels in the United States of America, 1788*, Mara Socianu Vamos and Durand Echeverria, trs. (Cambridge, MA: Harvard University Press, 1964), 188n; Carl Bridenbaugh, *The Colonial Craftsman* (Chicago: University of Chicago Press, 1950), 61–62.

21. In 1775, Franklin told his friends that "most of the little Property I have, consists of Houses in the Seaport Towns," which he assumed the British were going to burn. BF to John Sargent, June 27, 1775, BF to Jonathan Shipley, July 7, 1775, *Papers of Franklin*, 22: 72, 95.

22. Ronald W. Clark, *Benjamin Franklin: A Biography* (New York: Random House, 1983), 45.

23. BF, *Autobiography*, 196; BF to Cadwallader Colden, September 29, 1748, *Papers of Franklin*, 3: 318.

24. BF, *Autobiography*, 196.

25. BF to Whitefield, July 2, 1756, *Papers of Franklin*, 6: 468.

26. BF, *Proposals Relating to the Education of Youth in Pensilvania* (Philadelphia, 1749), *Papers of Franklin*, 3: 400.

27. BF to Peter Collinson, December 29, 1754, *Papers of Franklin*, 5: 454.

28. BF to William Parsons, February 22, 1757, *Papers of Franklin*, 7: 136.

29. BF to Mary Stevenson, March 25, 1763, *Papers of Franklin*, 10: 232.

30. BF to Richard Jackson, March 8, 1763, *Papers of Franklin*, 10: 210.

31. BF to Jared Ingersoll, December 11, 1762, *Papers of Franklin*, 10: 174–76.

32. BF, *Poor Richard Improved*, 1765, *Papers of Franklin*, 12: 64.

33. BF to John Hughes, August 9, 1765, *Papers of Franklin*, 12: 234–35.

34. BF to William Franklin, July 2, 1768, *Papers of Franklin*, 15: 161, 162, 164.

35. William Strahan to William Franklin, April 3, 1771, *Papers of Franklin*, 18: 65.

36. BF to David Hartley, October 3, 1775, *Papers of Franklin*, 22: 217.

37. *European Magazine* (London, March 3, 1783), quoted in P. M. Zall, ed., *Ben Franklin Laughing: Anecdotes from Original Sources by and About Benjamin Franklin* (Berkeley, 1980), 77.

38. BF to William Strahan, July 5, 1775, *Papers of Franklin*, 22: 85.

39. BF to William Franklin, August 19–22, 1772, *Papers of Franklin*, 19: 259.

40. BF to Sarah Bache, June 3, 1779, *Papers of Franklin*, 29: 613.

41. Alfred Owen Aldridge, *Franklin and His French Contemporaries* (New York: New York University Press, 1957), 50.

42. Vergennes to Layfayette, August 7, 1780, Stanley J. Idzerda et al., eds., *Lafayette in the Age of the American Revolution: Selected Letters and Papers, 1776–1790* (Ithaca, NY: Cornell University Press, 1977), 3: 130.

43. M. L. Weems, *The Life of Benjamin Franklin; with Many Choice Anecdotes and Admirable Sayings of This Great Man, Never Before Published by Any of His Biographers* (Philadelphia, 1829), 23.

CHAPTER 3: THE TRIALS AND TRIBULATIONS OF THOMAS JEFFERSON

This chapter is drawn from an essay with the same title in Peter S. Onuf, ed., *Jeffersonian Legacies* (Charlottesville, VA: University Press of Virginia, 1993), and is used with permission.

1. Lincoln to H. L. Pierce and others, April 6, 1859, in Roy P. Basler, ed., *Abraham Lincoln: His Speeches and Writings* (Cleveland: World Publishing Co., 1946), 489.

2. Merrill Peterson, *The Jeffersonian Image in the American Mind* (New York: Oxford University Press, 1960), 234.

3. Ibid., vii, 9.

4. Leonard W. Levy, *Jefferson and Civil Liberties: The Darker Side* (Cambridge, MA: Harvard University Press, 1963).

5. Bernard Bailyn, *Faces of Revolution: Personalities and Themes in the Struggle for American Independence* (New York: Knopf, 1990), 27.

6. R. R. Palmer, "The Dubious Democrat: Thomas Jefferson in Bourbon France," *Political Science Quarterly*, 72 (1957), 388–404.

7. TJ to Francis Hopkinson, March 13, 1789, *Papers of Jefferson*, 14: 650–51.

8. Robert McColley, *Slavery and Jeffersonian Virginia* (Urbana, IL: University of Illinois Press, 1964); William Cohen, "Thomas Jefferson and the Problem of Slavery," *Journal of American History*, 56 (1969), 503–26. To get some historical balance in these critiques it is important to remember that by the time of the American Revolution slavery had existed in Virginia and in America for more than a century without substantial criticism or moral censure. Therefore by condemning slavery and putting the institution morally on the defensive, Jefferson and many of his fellow revolutionaries did confront the slaveholding society in which they had been born and raised. It was an accomplishment of the Revolution that should never be minimized.

9. William W. Freehling, *The Road to Disunion: Secessionists at Bay, 1776–1854,* (New York: Oxford University Press, 1990), 1: 123, 127–28.

10. Jefferson, *Notes on the State of Virginia*, William Peden, ed. (Chapel Hill: University of North Carolina Press, 1954), 138–43.

11. See Jan Ellen Lewis and Peter S. Onuf, eds., *Sally Hemings and Thomas Jefferson: History, Memory, and Civic Culture* (Charlottesville, VA: University of Virginia Press, 1999).

12. Freehling, *Road to Disunion*, 1: 128–29.

13. Gary C. Bryner, "Constitutionalism and the Politics of Rights," in Gary C. Bryner and Noel B. Reynolds, eds., *Constitutionalism and Rights* (Provo, UT: Brigham Young University Press, 1987), 7–29.

14. Linda K. Kerber, *Federalists in Dissent: Imagery and Ideology in Jeffersonian America* (Ithaca: Cornell University Press, 1970), 20.

15. J.G.A. Pocock, "Virtue and Commerce in the Eighteenth Century," *Journal of Interdisciplinary History*, 3 (1972), 130–31, 134; Pocock, *The Machiavellian Moment: Florentine Political Thought and the Atlantic Republican Tradition* (Princeton: Princeton University Press, 1975), 532–33.

16. Garry Wills, *Inventing America: Jefferson's Declaration of Independence* (Garden City, NY: Doubleday, 1978); Ronald Hamowy, "Jefferson and the Scottish Enlightenment: A Critique of Garry Wills's *Inventing America: Jefferson's Declaration of Independence*," *WMQ*, 36 (1979), 503–523.

17. Kenneth S. Lynn, "Falsifying Jefferson," *Commentary*, 66 (October 1978), 66.

18. Joyce Appleby, *Liberalism and Republicanism in the Historical Imagination* (Cambridge, MA: Harvard University Press, 1992), 258, 300–1, 318.

19. Richard K. Matthews, *The Radical Politics of Thomas Jefferson* (Lawrence, KS: University of Kansas Press, 1984), 16.

20. Freehling, *Road to Disunion*, 1: 123.

21. TJ to Henry Lee, May 8, 1825, in *Jefferson: Writings*, 1501.

22. TJ, *Autobiography*, 1743–1790, *Jefferson: Writings*, 32, 3.

23. TJ to JA, October 28, 1813, Lester J. Cappon, ed., *The Adams-Jefferson Letters: The Complete Correspondence Between Thomas Jefferson and John Adams* (Chapel Hill: University of North Carolina Press, 1959), 2: 388.

24. Dumas Malone, *Jefferson the Virginian: Jefferson and His Time* (Boston: Little, Brown, 1948), 1: 8; TJ to John Page, May 25, 1766, *Papers of Jefferson*, 1: 19–20; Merrill D. Peterson, *Thomas Jefferson and the New Nation: A Biography* (New York: Oxford University Press, 1970), 14, 15; Eleanor D. Berman, *Thomas Jefferson Among the Arts: An Essay in Early American Esthetics* (New York: Philosophical Library, 1947), 1.

25. Seymour Howard, "Thomas Jefferson's Art Gallery for Monticello," *The Art Bulletin*, 59 (1977), 583–600; Marquis de Chastellux, *Travels in North America in the Years 1780, 1781 and 1782*, Howard C. Rice, ed. (Chapel Hill: University of North Carolina Press, 1963), 2: 391.

26. TJ to Giovanni Fabbroni, June 8, 1778, *Papers of Jefferson*, 2: 196.

27. TJ to Benjamin Harrison, January 12, 1785, *Papers of Jefferson*, 7: 600; GW to TJ, August 1, 1786, Fitzpatrick, ed., *Writings of Washington*, 28: 504; TJ to Nathaniel Macon, January 22, 1816, L&B, eds., *Writings of Jefferson*, 14: 408.

28. Berman, *Jefferson Among the Arts*, 84; TJ, *Notes on Virginia*, Peden, ed., 153; TJ to JM, September 20, 1785, *Papers of Jefferson*, 8: 535.

29. Stanley Grean, *Shaftesbury's Philosophy of Religion and Ethics: A Study in Enthusiasm* (Columbus, OH: Ohio University Press, 1967), 250; Lawrence Klein, "The Third Earl of Shaftesbury and the Progress of Politeness," *Eighteenth Century Studies*, 18 (1984–85), 186–214.

30. *New York Magazine*, II (1792), 406.

31. Conrad, "Polite Foundation," Philip Kurland, et al., eds., *Supreme Court Review–1984*, (Chicago: University of Chicago Press, 1985), 361, 363, 365.

32. Berman, *Jefferson Among the Arts*, 18.

33. TJ to Peter Carr, August 10, 1787, *Papers of Jefferson*, 12: 15; TJ to T. Law, June 13, 1814, L&B, eds., *Writings of Jefferson*, 14: 141–142.

34. For a fuller discussion of this radical celebration of politeness as a natural social adhesive see Gordon S. Wood, *The Radicalism of the American Revolution* (New York: Knopf, 1992), 215–25. See also Richard L. Bushman, *The Refinement of America: Persons, Houses, Cities* (New York: Knopf, 1992).

35. Drew R. McCoy, *The Last of the Fathers: James Madison and the Republican Legacy* (Cambridge, England: Cambridge University Press, 1989), 115.

36. TJ, Second Inaugural Address (1805), TJ to Dr. Joseph Priestley, January 29, 1804, *Jefferson: Writings*, 519, 1142.

37. Drew R. McCoy, *The Elusive Republic: Political Economy in Jeffersonian America*, (Chapel Hill: University of North Carolina Press, 1980).

38. For a critique of Jefferson's foreign policy see Robert W. Tucker and David C. Hendrickson, *Empire of Liberty: The Statecraft of Thomas Jefferson* (New York: Oxford University Press, 1990).

39. McCoy, *Last of the Fathers*, 144; TJ to Abigail Adams, February 22, 1787, Cappon, ed., *Adams-Jefferson Letters*, I, 173; TJ to William Stephens Smith, November 13, 1787; TJ to William Short, January 3, 1793, *Papers of Jefferson*, 12: 356; 25: 14.

40. TJ to Roger C. Weightman, June 24, 1826, *Jefferson: Writings*, 1517.

41. McCoy, *Last of the Fathers*, 29.

42. Wood, *Radicalism of the Revolution*, 318.

43. Dumas Malone, *The Sage of Monticello: Jefferson and His Time* (Boston: Little Brown, 1981), 331, 148–50.

44. TJ to John Holmes, April 22, 1820, *Jefferson: Writings*, 1434; Malone, *Sage of Monticello*, 336–37.

45. TJ to Albert Gallatin, December 26, 1820, Ford, ed., *The Writings of Jefferson*, 10: 177.

46. Malone, *Sage of Monticello*, 356.

47. TJ to JA, August 1, 1816, Cappon, ed., *Adams-Jefferson Letters*, 2: 485.

48. TJ to Edward Coles, August 25, 1814, *Jefferson: Writings*, 1348.

49. Malone, *Sage of Monticello*, 123.

50. TJ to Dr. Thomas Humphreys, February 8, 1817, Ford, ed., *Writings of Jefferson*, X: 77.

51. Robert E. Shalhope, "Thomas Jefferson's Republicanism and Antebellum Southern Thought," *Journal of Southern History*, 42 (1976), 542.

52. TJ to JM, February 17, 1826, *Jefferson: Writings*, 1514.

53. Malone, *Sage of Monticello*, 477.

54. TJ to Francis Adrian Van De Kamp, January 11, 1825, Ford, ed., *Writings of Jefferson*, X: 337.

CHAPTER 4: ALEXANDER HAMILTON AND THE MAKING OF A FISCAL-
MILITARY STATE

The chapter is largely taken from my review in *The New Republic*, October
15, 2001, and is used with permission.

1. John Morse, quoted in Stephen F. Knott, *Alexander Hamilton and the Persis-
   tence of Myth* (Lawrence, KS: University Press of Kansas, 2002), 71.

2. Herbert Croly, *The Promise of American Life* (New York: Macmillan), 29, 38.

3. Robert I. Warshow, *Alexander Hamilton: First American Business Man* (New
   York: Greenberg, 1931), ix, x.

4. AH to Theodore Sedgwick, July 10, 1804, to Gouverneur Morris, February
   29, 1802, in *Hamilton: Writings*, 1022, 986.

5. Robert Middlekauff, *The Glorious Cause: The American Revolution, 1763–1789*
   (New York: Oxford University Press, 1982), 568.

6. AH to James Duane, September 3, 1780, *Papers of Hamilton*, 2: 404.

7. Max Farrand, ed., *The Records of the Federal Convention of 1787* (New Haven:
   Yale University Press, 1937), 1: 282–93.

8. Robert Hendrickson, *Hamilton I (1757–1789)* (New York: Mason/Charter,
   1976), 246.

9. Leonard D. White, *The Federalists: A Study in Administrative History* (New
   York: Macmillan, 1948), 117; Jacob E. Cooke, *Alexander Hamilton* (New York:
   Scribner's, 1982), 73.

10. Freeman W. Meyer, "A Note on the Origins of the 'Hamiltonian' System,"
    WMQ, 3d. Ser., 21 (1964), 579–88.

11. TJ, The Anas, 1791–1806, *Jefferson: Writings*, 671.

12. David Hume, "Of the Independency of Parliament," *Essays and Treatises on
    Several Subjects* (London, 1793), 1: 51–52.

13. AH to Robert Troup, April 13, 1795, *Papers of Hamilton*, 18: 329; Sir James
    Steuart (1767), quoted in Stephen Copley, *Literature and the Social Order
    in Eighteenth-Century England* (London: Croom Helm, 1984), 120; AH,
    "The Defence of the Funding System," July 1795, *Papers of Hamilton*,
    13: 349.

14. AH, "The Continentalist No. VI," July 4, 1782, *Papers of Hamiltion*, 3: 105–6.

15. White, *Federalists*, 117; Cooke, *Hamilton*, 73.

16. Gouveneur Morris, quoted in *Hamilton Papers*, 26: 324n.

17. John Brewer, *The Sinews of Power: War, Money and the English State, 1688–1783*
    (New York: Knopf, 1989).

18. AH, "Opinion on the Constitutionality of a National Bank, February 23,
    1791, *Hamilton: Writings*, 613–46.

19. Bray Hammond, *Banks and Politics in America from the Revolution to the Civil
    War* (Princeton: Princeton University Press, 1957), 66.

20. TJ to Colonel Charles Yancey, January 6, 1816, Ford, ed., *Writings of Jefferson*, 10: 2; Hammond, *Banks and Politics*, 196.
21. AH, "Views on the French Revolution (1794)," *Papers of Hamilton*, 26: 739–40.
22. AH, "The Continentalist No. V," April 18, 1782, *Papers of Hamilton*, 3: 76.
23. Joanne B. Freeman, *Affairs of Honor: National Politics in the New Republic*, (New Haven: Yale University Press, 2001).
24. Ibid., xiv.
25. Adams, ed., *Works*, 9: 305–6.
26. AH to Theodore Sedgwick, February 2, 1799, *Hamilton: Writings*, 914.
27. AH to James McHenry, March 18, 1799, *Hamilton: Writings*, 915.
28. AH to Theodore Sedgwick, February 2, 1799, *Hamilton: Writings*, 914.
29. AH to Rufus King, August 22, 1798, *Papers of Hamilton*, 22: 154–55.

CHAPTER 5: IS THERE A "JAMES MADISON PROBLEM"?

This chapter is a revised version of a piece with the same title published in David Womersley, ed., *Liberty and the American Experience in the Eighteenth Century* (Indianapolis: Liberty Fund, 2006) and is used with permission.

1. For an excellent discussion of the differences between the two men see Drew R. McCoy, *The Last of the Fathers: James Madison and the Republican Legacy* (Cambridge, England: Cambridge University Press, 1989), 45–64.
2. TJ to Abigail Adams, February 22, 1787, Lester J. Cappon, ed., *The Adams-Jefferson Letters: The Complete Correspondence Between Thomas Jefferson and Abigail and John Adams* (Chapel Hill: University of North Carolina Press, 1959), 1: 173.
3. Jefferson quoted in Ralph Ketcham, *James Madison: A Biography* (New York: Macmillan, 1971), 162; Drew McCoy, "The Virginia Port Bill of 1784," *Virginia Magazine of History and Biography*, 83 (1975), 294; JM to Edmund Pendleton, January 9, 1787, to GW, December 24, 1786, in *Papers of Madison*, 9: 244, 225; A. G. Roeber, *Faithful Magistrates and Republican Lawyers: Creators of Virginia Legal Culture, 1680–1810* (Chapel Hill: University of North Carolina Press, 1981), 192–202.
4. McCoy, "Virginia Port Bill," *VMHB*, 83 (1975), 292; JM to GW, December 7, 1786, to Pendleton, January 9, 1787, to GW December 24, 1786, to TJ, December 4, 1786, *Papers of Madison*, 9: 200, 244, 225, 191; Ketcham, *Madison*, 172.
5. "Vices of the Political System of the United States" (April 1787), in *Papers of Madison*, 9: 354, 355–56.
6. GW to Henry Lee, April 5, 1786, Fitzpatrick, ed., *Writings of Washington*, 28: 402; Jerry Grundfest, *George Clymer: Philadelphia Revolutionary, 1739–1813* (New York: Arno Press, 1982), 165, 164; E. Wayne Carp, *To Starve the Army at Pleasure: Continental Army Administration and American Political Culture, 1775–1783* (Chapel Hill: University of North Carolina Press, 1984), 209; Knox,

quoted in William Winslow Crosskey and William Jeffrey, Jr., *Politics and the Constitution in the History of the United States* (Chicago: University of Chicago Press, 1980), 3: 420, 421.

7. TJ to JM, December 16, 1786, *Papers of Jefferson*, 10: 603.

8. Adam Smith, *The Theory of Moral Sentiments*, D. D. Raphael and A. L. Macfie, eds. (Oxford: Oxford University Press, 1776), 20–25.

9. Gordon S. Wood, *The Creation of the American Republic, 1776–1787* (Chapel Hill: University of North Carolina Press, 1969), 473.

10. JM to GW, April 16, 1787, *Madison: Writings*, 81.

11. Stuart Leibiger, *Founding Friendship: George Washington, James Madison, and the Creation of the American Republic* (Charlottesville: University Press of Virginia, 1999), 123.

12. Sailors confronted by a whale often threw a tub overboard, hoping to divert the whale's attention. See Kenneth R. Bowling, " 'A Tub to the Whale': The Founding Fathers and Adoption of the Federal Bill of Rights," *Journal of the Early Republic*, 8 (1988), 223–51.

13. AH to Edward Carrington, May 26, 1792, *Papers of Hamilton*, 11: 432.

14. Stanley Elkins and Eric McKitrick, *The Age of Federalism* (New York: Oxford University Press, 1993), 234; JM to TJ, May 1, 1791, in James Morton Smith, ed., *The Republic of Letters: The Correspondence Between Thomas Jefferson and James Madison, 1776–1826* (New York: Norton, 1995), 2: 685.

15. Smith, ed., *Republic of Letters*, 2: 881.

16. AH to Edward Carrington, May 26, 1792, *Papers of Hamilton*, 11: 429.

17. Smith, ed., *Republic of Letters*, 2: 747.

18. E. James Ferguson, *The Power of the Purse: A History of American Public Finance, 1776–1790* (Chapel Hill: University of North Carolina Press, 1961), 298.

19. Elkins and McKitrick, *Age of Federalism*, 136–45.

20. JM to TJ, October 5, 1794, in Smith, ed., *Republic of Letters*, 2: 857.

21. Marvin Myers, ed., *The Mind of the Founder: Sources of the Political Thought of James Madison* (Indianapolis: Bobbs-Merrill, 1973), xlv.

22. In a short article written over a half century ago, Neal Reimer emphasized Madison's consistency over time. Reimer, however, merely stressed Madison's lifelong commitment to republicanism, which is scarcely in doubt, and admitted that in the 1790s "Madison retreated somewhat from his earlier nationalism." Reimer, "The Republicanism of James Madison," *Political Science Quarterly*, 69 (1954), 45–64, quotation at 56. But it is Lance Banning, in his *The Sacred Fire of Liberty: James Madison and the Founding of the Federal Republic* (Ithaca: Cornell University Press, 1995), who argues most persistently that Madison was not a fervent nationalist in the 1780s. "He was," says Banning, "a nationalist . . . at certain times, on certain issues, and within the limits of his revolutionary hopes." In other words, says Banning, modern

scholarship has mistaken Madison's position in the 1780s. It "has generally misjudged the hopes and fears that he brought into the Constitutional Convention." It has "misinterpreted a major change of mind which started while the meeting was in process" and therefore it has come to "hold a poorly balanced view of what he said and what he was attempting in *The Federalist*." The opposition Jeffersonian Madison of the 1790s, concludes Banning, "was not as inconsistent with the 'father of the Constitution' as is usually believed." *Sacred Fire of Liberty*, 42, 9.

23. See JM to C. E. Haynes, February 25, 1831, in Gaillard Hunt, ed., *The Writings of James Madison* (New York: G. P. Putnam's Sons, 1910), 9: 442; and N. P. Trist, "Memoranda," September 27, 1834, in Max Farrand, ed., *The Records of the Federal Convention of 1787* (New Haven: Yale University Press, 1911, 1937), 3: 534.

24. Robert Dahl, *A Preface to Democratic Theory* (Chicago: University of Chicago Press, 1956); Richard K. Matthews, *If Men Were Angels: James Madison and the Heartless Empire of Reason* (Lawrence, Kansas: University Press of Kansas, 1995); Gary Rosen, *American Compact and the Problem of Founding* (Lawrence, KS: University Press of Kansas, 1999). For more recent uses of Madison by political theorists, see John Samples, ed., *James Madison and the Future of Limited Government* (Washington, DC: Cato Institute, 2002).

25. JM to William Cogswell, March 10, 1834, in Farrand, *Records of the Federal Convention*, 3: 533.

26. JM, "Vices of the Political System of the United States" (April 1787), *Madison: Writings*, 69–75.

27. JM to GW, April 16, 1787, *Madison: Writings*, 81.

28. Jack N. Rakove, *Original Meanings: Politics and Ideas in the Making of the Constitution* (New York: Knopf, 1996), 51.

29. JM to GW, April 16, 1787, *Madison: Writings*, 81. For Madison's downplaying of the executive in the state governments, see JM to Caleb Wallace, August 23 1785, *Madison: Writings*, 41–42.

30. Farrand, ed., *Records of the Federal Convention*, 1: 21, 140; 2: 28.

31. JM to TJ, September 6, 1787, in Smith, ed., *Republic of Letters*, 1: 491.

32. Farrand, ed., *Records of the Federal Convention*, 2: 73–75. On the role of the British Privy council in influencing Madison, see Mary Sarah Bilder, *The Transatlantic Constitution: Colonial Legal Culture and the Empire* (Cambridge, MA: Harvard University Press, 2004), 191–92.

33. JM, *The Federalist*, No. 10, *Madison: Writings*, 160–67.

34. On the colonial legislatures acting as courts see Wood, *Creation of the American Republic*, 154–55.

35. Note, for example, Samuel Adams's traditional use of judicial imagery in 1772 in describing what happens when a man leaves the state of nature and be-

comes a member of society. In the state of nature, wrote Adams, man by him-self was sole judge of his own rights and the injuries done him. By entering into society, however, "he agrees to an Arbiter or indifferent Judge between him and his neighbors." Samuel Adams, "The Rights of the Colonists," 1772, in Harry Alonzo Cushing, ed., *The Writings of Samuel Adams* (New York: G. P. Putnam's Sons, 1904–08), 2: 353.

36. JM to GW, April 16, 1787, in *Madison: Writings*, 81.

37. It was traditional to think that government, which for most states in the world meant a monarch, was supposed to be an impartial judge among the members of the state. A king was presumed to be more capable of this im-partiality than anyone else in the society precisely because his self-interest supposedly coincided with the general interest; this, in fact, had been the best justification of monarchy through the ages.

38. McCoy, *The Last of the Fathers*, 70–71, 102. Of course, as Oscar and Mary Handlin pointed out in *Commonwealth: A Study in the Role of Government in American Economy: Massachusetts, 1774–1861*, rev. ed. (Cambridge, MA: Har-vard University Press, 1969), Massachusetts and presumably other state gov-ernments in the first half of the nineteenth century, by doling out much of their sovereign power, especially in the creation of corporate charters that be-came private vested rights, did end up exercising just their police powers and acting to a large extent as merely impartial arbiters and umpires among the various competing interests in the society. Although these nineteenth-century liberal state governments did not very actively promote a positive public good in the way Madison and most other Revolutionaries had desired, they at least seem to have come to resemble the judicial-like government Madison had wanted for the United States.

39. JM, *Federalist*, No. 10, *Madison: Writings*, 160–67.

40. JM, "Vices of the Political System," *Madison: Writings*, 79.

41. JM, *Federalist*, No. 10, *Madison: Writings*, 166.

42. JM to TJ, March 29, 1789, Smith, ed., *Republic of Letters*, 1: 606.

43. There is a huge literature on early modern European state building. See es-pecially Charles Tilly, ed., *The Formation of National States in Western Eu-rope* (Princeton: Princeton University Press, 1975); John Brewer, *The Sinews of Power: War, Money, and the English State, 1688–1783* (New York: Knopf, 1989); Brian M. Downing, *The Military Revolution and Political Change: Ori-gins of Democracy and Autocracy in Early Modern Europe* (Princeton: Prince-ton University Press, 1992); Lawrence S. Stone, ed., *An Imperial State at War: Britain from 1689 to 1815* (London: Routledge, 1994); Thomas Ertman, *Birth of the Leviathan: Building States and Regimes in Medieval and Early Modern Europe* (Cambridge, England: Cambridge University Press, 1997). It was Brewer who originated the term "fiscal-military state," and I have been much

influenced by his book *Sinews of Power*. But the work that provoked my thinking about Madison anew was Max M. Edling, *A Revolution in Favor of Government: Origins of the U.S. Constitution and the Making of the American State* (New York: Oxford University Press, 2003), and I am much indebted to it.

44. For an important account of the different capacities of early modern states to extract money from their subjects or citizens without bankrupting them, see James Macdonald, *A Free Nation Deep in Debt: The Financial Roots of Democracy* (New York: Farrar, Straus and Giroux, 2002).

45. It is this opposition to modern state building that infuses Bernard Bailyn's *The Ideological Origins of the American Revolution* (Cambridge, MA: Harvard University Press, 1967).

46. JM, "Political Observations," April 20, 1795, *Papers of Madison*, 15: 518.

47. This is a much neglected topic. The only major account concerning America is Felix Gilbert's little book, *To the Farewell Address: Ideas of Early American Foreign Policy* (Princeton: Princeton University Press, 1961), which historians have much too casually dismissed. We have no major study of the Americans' model treaty of 1776, which attempted to embody these liberal ideas about war and commerce.

48. JM, "Universal Peace," February 2, 1792, *Madison: Writings*, 505.

49. Ibid., 507. Janus, the ancient Roman god, was noted not only for two-facedness. To commemorate Janus the Romans always left the temple of Janus open in time of war so that the god could come to their aid. The door was closed only when Rome was at peace.

50. JM, "Political Observations," *Papers of Madison*, 15: 518–19.

51. TJ to JM, March 24, 1793, to Tench Coxe, May 1, 1794, to Thomas Pinckney, May 29, 1797, to Robert R. Livingston, September 9, 1801, and Jefferson, Eighth Annual Message, November 8, 1808, *Jefferson: Writings*, 1006, 1014, 1045–46, 1093, 544.

52. J.C.A. Stagg, *Mr. Madison's War: Politics, Diplomacy, and Warfare in the Early American Republic 1783–1830* (Princeton: Princeton University Press, 1983), 22, 36.

53. Dumas Malone, *Jefferson the President: Second Term, 1805–1809* (Boston: Little, Brown: 1974), 76.

54. Albert Gallatin to TJ, March 10, 1812, in Henry Adams, *The Life of Henry Gallatin* (New York: J. B. Lippincott, 1879), 455–56.

55. Ralph Ketcham, *James Madison: A Biography*, (New York: Macmillan, 1971), 586, 604.

56. Irving Brant, *James Madison: Commander in Chief, 1812–1836* (Indianapolis: Bobbs-Merrill, 1961), 419, 407.

57. JA to TJ, February 2, 1817, Cappon, ed., *The Adams-Jefferson Letters*, 2: 508.

CHAPTER 6: THE RELEVANCE AND IRRELEVANCE OF JOHN ADAMS

This essay is derived from a chapter in my *The Creation of the American Republic, 1776–1787* (Chapel Hill: University Press of North Carolina, 1969) and is used with permission.

1. JA to Benjamin Rush, April 4, 1790, Lyman H. Butterfield, ed., *The Letters of Benjamin Rush* (Princeton: Princeton University Press, 1951), 1: 1207.

2. Gordon S. Wood, *The Creation of the American Republic, 1776–1787* (Chapel Hill: University Press of North Carolina, 1969), 132.

3. Actually Samuel Adams and some other Boston patriots were eager for Adams to take on the defense of the soldiers, perhaps in an effort to protect the reputation of Boston in the empire. Hiller B. Zobel, *The Boston Massacre* (New York: Norton, 1970), 220–21.

4. JA to James Warren, January 9, 1787, in Wood, *Creation of the American Republic*, 581; Peter Shaw, *The Character of John Adams* (Chapel Hill: University of North Carolina Press, 1976), 318.

5. TJ to JM, February 14, 1783, *Papers of Jefferson*, 6.

6. Wood, *Creation of the American Republic*, 195.

7. JA, entry, January 1759, Lyman H. Butterfield et al., eds., *Diary and Autobiography of John Adams* (Cambridge, MA: Harvard University Press, 1964), 1: 72–73. There have been many studies of Adams's political thought. See Correa M. Walsh, *The Political Science of John Adams . . .* (New York: G. P. Putnam's Sons, 1915); Joseph Dorfman, "The Regal Republic of John Adams," in his *Economic Mind in American Civilization* (New York: Viking, 1946–59), 1: 417–33; Zoltan Haraszti, *John Adams and the Prophets of Progress* (Cambridge, MA: Harvard University Press, 1952), esp. ch. 3; Edward Handler, *America and Europe in the Political Thought of John Adams* (Cambridge, MA: Harvard University Press, 1964); John R. Howe, Jr., *The Changing Political Thought of John Adams* (Princeton: Princeton University Press, 1966); and C. Bradley Thompson, *John Adams and The Spirit of Liberty* (Lawrence, KS: University Press of Kansas, 1998).

8. JA, unpublished newspaper communication, December 1765, Butterfield et al., eds., *Diary of Adams*, I: 282; JA to James Warren, March 31, 1777, Worthington C. Ford, ed., *Warren-Adams Letters . . .* (Massachusetts Historical Society, *Collections*, 72–73 [1917, 1925] 1: 308; JA to Abigail Adams, July 3, 1776, Lyman H. Butterfield et al., eds., *Adams Family Correspondence* (Cambridge, MA: Harvard University Press, 1963), 2: 28.

9. JA to Abigail Adams, July 3, 1776, Butterfield et al., ed., *Family Correspondence*, 2: 28.

10. JA to Mercy Warren, January 8, April 16, 1776, Ford, ed., *Warren-Adams Letters*, 1: 201–02, 222; JA to Abigail Adams, April 28, 1776, Butterfield et al., eds., *Family Correspondence*, I: 401.

11. [JA], "Dissertation on the Canon and Feudal Law" (1765), Adams, ed., *Works*, 3: 455–57; JA to Mercy Warren, January 8, April 16, 1776, Ford, ed., *Warren-Adams Letters*, I: 202, 201, 225; JA to Zabdiel Adams, June 21, 1776, Butterfield et al., eds., *Family Correspondence*, II: 21.

12. JA to James Warren, January 9, 1787, Ford, ed., *Warren-Adams Letters*, II: 280; JA, *Defence of the Constitutions of Government of the United States* (1787–1788), Adams, ed., *Works*, 4: 401; Mercy Warren to JA, July 28, 1807, recalling a comment Adams made in 1788, Massachusetts Historical Society, *Colls.*, 5th Ser., 4 (1878), 361.

13. JA, *Defence of the Constitutions*, Adams, ed., *Works*, 4: 392, 397.

14. Adams, ed., *Works*, 5: 488; 4: 406.

15. [JA], "Discourses on Davila" (1790), Adams, ed., *Works*, 6: 249–50.

16. JA, *Defence of the Constitutions*, Adams, ed., *Works*, 4: 390–400; [JA], "Discourses on Davila," Adams, ed., *Works*, 6: 257.

17. Ibid., 280; Adams, *Defence of the Constitutions*, Adams, ed., *Works*, 5: 488.

18. Ibid., 6: 95, 97, 95, 96; JA to Benjamin Rush, April 4, 1790, Alexander Biddle, ed., *Old Family Letters*, Ser. A (Philadelphia: J. B. Lippincott, 1892), 57. The Adams-Rush correspondence has been republished in John A. Schutz and Douglass Adair, eds., *The Spur of Fame: Dialogues of John Adams and Benjamin Rush, 1805–1813* (San Marino: The Huntington Library, 1966). For a discussion of the connection between Adams's personality and his political and social attitudes see Bernard Bailyn, "Butterfield's Adams," *WMQ*, 3d Ser., 19 (1962), 238–56.

19. [JA], "Discourses on Davila," Adams, ed., *Works*, 6: 247, 246; JA, *Defence of the Constitutions*, Adams, ed., *Works*, 4: 557, 5: 431; JA to TJ, October 9, 1787, *Papers of Jefferson*, 12: 221; JA, *Defence of the Constitutions*, Adams, ed., *Works*, 4: 557.

20. Ibid., 4: 358. De Lolme's *The Constitution of England* was published first in French in Amsterdam in 1771 followed by numerous London editions in English beginning in 1775. On De Lolme see R. R. Palmer, *Age of the Democratic Revolution* (Princeton: Princeton University Press, 1959, 1964), 1: 145–48. On Adams's "systematic reevaluation of American society and of the American political order" in the 1780s see Howe, *Changing Political Thought*, 133.

21. Boston *Independent Chronicle*, October 18, 1787.

22. On the *Essex Result* see Wood, *Creation of the American Republic*, 217–18.

23. The ten articles by "The Free Republican" in the *Independent Chronicle* ran from November 14, 1785, to February 9, 1786. The first six had been published earlier in the *Boston Magazine*, I (1784), 138–40, 192–95, 271–74, 375–78, 420–23, 546–49. Lincoln was identified as the author from James Freeman's copy of the *Boston Magazine* in the Massachusetts Historical Society, but it was Philip Mead who identified Lincoln as the son of the Revolutionary War general.

24. Boston *Independent Chronicle*, December 8, 1785; JA, "Defence of the Constitutions," Adams, ed., *Works*, 4: 557; 6: 128. What mattered for Adams was the equilibrium of the democratic, aristocratic, and monarchical elements of the classic mixed constitution, not the separation of the executive, legislative, and judicial functions of government. See Haraszti, *John Adams and the Prophets of Progress*, 27–28, 310.

25. JA, *Defence of the Constitutions*, Adams, ed., *Works*, 4: 290, 414.

26. Adams, ed., *Works*, 6: 10, 89, 10; 4: 289. See also Adams, ed., *Works*, 4: 290, 480; 6: 109–10.

27. Adams, ed., *Works*, 4: 285, 200, 585, 588.

28. Adams, ed., *Works*, 4: 379; JA to Abigail Adams, March quoted in Howe, *Changing Political Thought*, 166. [JA], "Discourses on Davila," Adams, ed., *Works*, 6: 272; Adams, *Defence of the Constitutions*, Adams, ed., *Works*, 4: 579. See also ibid., 4: 358–60, 462, 474; 5: 108; 6: 108.

29. JA, *Defence of the Constitutions*, Adams, ed., *Works*, 4: 293–94; JA to Philip Mazzei, June 12, 1787, quoted in Howe, *Changing Political Thought*, 67; JA, "Defence of the Constitutions," Adams, ed., *Works*, 4: 579–80.

30. JA to William Tudor, June 28, 1789, JA to James Lovett, June 4, 1789, in Adams Papers Microfilm, Reel 115.

31. JA to BF, January 27, 1787, John Bigelow, ed., *The Works of Benjamin Franklin* (New York: G. P. Putnam's Sons, 1887–88), 11: 298–99; JA to James Warren, January 9, 1787, Ford, ed., *Warren-Adams Letters*, II, 281.

32. *Providence Gazette*, June 23, 1787; TJ to JA, September 28, 1787, *Papers of Jefferson*, 12: 189; Joel Barlow, *An Oration Delivered . . . at the Meeting of the . . . Cincinnati, 4 July 1787* (Hartford, CT: 1787), 15; Benjamin Rush to Richard Price, June 2, 1787, Farrand, ed., *Records of the Federal Convention*, 3: 33.

33. William Davie to James Iredell, August 6, 1787, Griffith J. McRee, *Life and Correspondence of James Iredell* (New York: D. Appleton, 1857–58), 2: 168; JM to TJ, June 6, 1787, *Papers of Jefferson*, 11: 401–02; Reverend James Madison to JM, June 1787, James McClurg to JM, August 22, 1787, and the Richmond Virginia *Independent Chronicle*, August 15, 1787, all quoted in Charles Warren, *The Making of the Constitution* (New York: Barnes and Noble, 1928, 1937), 816–18.

34. Baltimore *Maryland Journal*, July 6, 1787; [Samuel Bryan], "Centinel, No. I," October 5, 1787, John Bach McMaster and Frederick D. Stone, eds., *Pennsylvania and the Federal Constitution, 1787–1788* (Philadelphia: Historical Society of Pennsylvania), 568–69.

35. [John Stevens], *Observations on Government, Including Some Animadeversioins on Mr. Adams' Defence of the Constitutions* (Boston, 1791), 46–47, 4–7.

36. Ibid., 39–40, 30–32, 14.

37. JA to Samuel Adams, October 18, 1790, Samuel Adams to JA, November 20, 1790, Adams, ed., *Works*, 6: 415, 420–21.

38. JA, *Defence of the Constitutions*, Adams, ed., *Works*, 5: 453; JA to Roger Sherman, July 17, 1789, Roger Sherman to JA, July 20, 1789, ibid. 6: 428, 457.

39. JA, *Defence of the Constitutions*, ibid., 5: 454; JA to Benjamin Lincoln, June 19, 1789, Adams Papers Microfilm, Reel 115; JA to Roger Sherman, July 17, 18, 1789, Adams, ed., *Works*, 6: 430, 428–29.

40. Roger Sherman to JA, July 20, 1789, Adams, ed., *Works*, 6: 438, 441.

41. JA to Benjamin Rush, February 8, June 9, 19 and July 5, 24, 1789, Biddle, ed., *Old Family Letters*, 31, 37, 39, 40, 44, 46.

42. John Taylor, *An Inquiry into the Principles and Policy of the United States* (New Haven: Yale University Press, 1950, first published 1814), 32, 37, 118, 158–59.

43. Ibid., 364, 171, 33, 150, 422, 200, 356, 393, 374.

44. Ibid., 373, 461, 469, 355, 356, 355.

45. JA to John Taylor, no dates, Adams, ed., *Works*, 6: 464, 463, 482–83, 514; JA to Benjamin Rush, January 8, 1812, Biddle, ed., *Old Family Letters*, 369.

CHAPTER 7: THOMAS PAINE, AMERICA'S FIRST PUBLIC INTELLECTUAL

A somewhat different version appeared as "Disturbing the Peace," in *The New York Review of Books*, June 8, 1995, and is used with permission.

1. David Freeman Hawke, *Paine* (New York: Harper and Row, 1974), 7.

2. Thomas Paine, *Rights of Man* (1791), in Eric Foner, ed., *Thomas Paine: Collected Writings* (New York: Library of America, 1995), 605.

3. TJ to Thomas Paine, March 18, 1801, quoted in John Keane, *Tom Paine: A Political Life* (Boston: Little, Brown, 1995), 456.

4. Keane, *Paine*, xiv, x, xiii.

5. Ibid., 84.

6. Paine, *Common Sense* (1776) in Philip S. Foner, ed., *The Complete Writings of Thomas Paine* (New York: Citadel Press, 1969), 1: 45.

7. George W. Corner, ed., *The Autobiography of Benjamin Rush* (Princeton: Princeton University Press, 1948), 114–15.

8. Sarah Bache to BF, January 14, 1781, *Papers of Franklin*, 34: 272.

9. Paine, *Common Sense*, Philip S. Foner, ed., *Complete Writings of Paine*, I: 4.

10. Paine, *Rights of Man*, Eric Foner, ed., *Paine: Collected Writings*, 538–59.

11. Paine, *Common Sense*, Philip Foner, ed., *Complete Writings of Paine*, 1: 20.

12. Ibid., 22–21.

13. Paine, "American Crisis, I," December 23, 1776, in ibid., 1: 50.

14. Paine, "American Crisis, VII," November 21, 1778, in ibid., 1: 144.

15. Hawke, *Paine*, 256.

16. Keane, *Paine*, 371.

17. Hawke, *Paine*, 53; Keane, *Paine*, 105.

18. Paine, "American Crisis, VII," November 11, 1778, in Philip Foner, ed., *Complete Writings of Paine*, 1: 146.

19. TP, "A Serious Address to the People of Pennsylvania," December 1778, in Philip Foner, ed., *Complete Writings of Paine*, 2: 279; Hawke, *Paine*, 108.

20. Hawke, *Paine*, 110.

21. TP to Henry Laurens, September 14, 1779, in Philip Foner, ed., *Complete Writings of Paine*, 2: 1178; TP to Robert Livingston, May 19, 1783, in Keane, *Paine*, 242.

22. TP to GW, October 16, 1789, *Papers of Washington: Presidential Ser.*, 4: 197.

23. TP to Benjamin Rush, in Eric Foner, ed., *Paine: Collected Writings*, 372.

24. Hawke, *Paine*, 201.

25. Paine, *Rights of Man* in Philip Foner, ed., *Complete Writings of Paine*, 1: 348.

26. TP, "To the Citizens of the United States," November 15, 1802, in Philip Foner, ed., *Complete Writings of Paine*, 2: 911.

27. TP to Henry Laurens, September 14, 1779, in Philip Foner, ed., *Complete Writings of Paine*, 2: 1178.

28. Bernard Bailyn, *The Ideological Origins of the American Revolution* (Cambridge: Harvard University Press, 1967), 23.

29. TP, *Common Sense*, in Philip Foner, ed., *Complete Writings of Paine*, 1: 13.

30. TP, "On Mr. Deane's Affair," December 1778, in Philip Foner, ed., *Complete Writings of Paine*, 2: 111; Eric Foner, *Tom Paine and Revolutionary America* (New York: Oxford University Press, 1976), 82–86; Bernard Bailyn, "Common Sense," in Library of Congress Symposia on the American Revolution, 2d, 1973, *Fundamental Testaments of the American Revolution* (Washington, DC: Library of Congress, 1973), 7–22; Keane, *Paine*, x; TP, *Common Sense*, in Philip Foner, ed., *Complete Writings of Paine*, 1: 8; James T. Boulton, *The Language of Politics in the Age of Wilkes and Burke* (London: Routledge and Kegan Paul, 1963), ch. 7.

31. Joyce Appleby, *Capitalism and a New Social Order: The Republican Vision of the 1790s* (New York: New York University Press, 1984), 60.

32. TP, *The Age of Reason*, Eric Foner, ed., *Paine, Collected Writings*, 825.

33. Keane, *Paine*, 393, 457, 475.

CHAPTER 8: THE REAL TREASON OF AARON BURR

An earlier and somewhat different version of this essay appeared in "The Revenge of Aaron Burr," *The New York Review of Books*, February 2, 1984, and is published with permission.

1. Milton Lomask, *Aaron Burr: The Conspiracy and Years of Exile, 1805–1836* (New York: Farrar, Straus, Giroux, 1982), 398.

2. Charles J. Nolan, Jr., *Aaron Burr and the American Literary Imagination* (Westport, CT: Greenwood Press, 1980).

3. Samuel H. Wandell, *Aaron Burr in Literature* (Port Washington, NY: 1972, originally published 1936), 265.

4. Matthew L. Davis, *Memoirs of Aaron Burr*, 2 vols. (New York: 1836); James Parton, *The Life and Times of Aaron Burr* (New York: 1858).

5. Lomask, *Aaron Burr*, 2 vols. (New York, Farrar, Straus, Giroux, 1979, 1982).

6. Matthew L. Davis, ed., *The Private Journal of Aaron Burr*, 2 vols. (New York: Harper Bros., 1838).

7. Davis, *Memoirs of Burr*, I: 375–76, v–vi.

8. *The Papers of Aaron Burr, 1756–1836*, microfilm edition in 27 reels (Glen Rock, NJ: 1978); Mary-Jo Kline et al., eds., *Political Correspondence and Public Papers of Aaron Burr*, 2 vols. (Princeton: Princeton University Press, 1983).

9. AB to Timothy Green, June 25, 1795, in Kline et al., eds., *Burr Papers*, 1: 221.

10. AH to James A. Bayard, January 16, 1801, *Papers of Hamilton*, 25: 323.

11. W. W. Abbot, "An Uncommon Awareness of Self: The Papers of George Washington," in Don Higginbotham, ed., *George Washington Rediscovered* (Charlottesville: Unversity Press of Virginia, 2001), 280.

12. AB to Samuel Smith, May 19, 1801, in Kline et al., eds., *Burr Papers*, 1: 583.

13. AB to TJ, June 21, 1797, in Kline et al., eds., *Burr Papers*, 1: 301.

14. Lomask, *Burr*, I, 87.

15. AB to William Eustis, October 20, 1797, to Charles Biddle, November 14, 1804, to John Taylor, May 22, 1791, to Peter Van Gaasbeek, May 8, 1795, to James Monroe, May 30, 1794, to Jonathan Russell, June 1, 1801, to Théophile Cazenove, June 8, 1798, in Kline et al., eds., *Burr Papers*, 1: 316; 2: 897; 1: 82, 211, 180; 2: 601; 1: 344.

16. AB to Theodore Sedgwick, February 3, 1791, in Kline et al., eds., *Burr Papers*, 1: 68.

17. Theodore Sedgwick to AH, January 10, 1801, AH to James Bayard, January 16, 1801, in *Papers of Hamilton*, 25: 311, 321, 320.

18. James Parton, *The Life and Times of Aaron Burr* (New York: Mason Bros., 1858), 1: 235.

19. Lomask, *Burr*, 1: 37, 44.

20. Davis, *Memoirs of Burr*, 1: 297.

21. Editorial note, Kline et al., *Burr Papers*, 1: 882; AB to Joseph Alston, November 15, 1815, in Kline et al., eds., *Burr Papers*, 1: 1166.

22. Gordon S. Wood, *The Radicalism of the American Revolution* (New York: Knopfs 1992), 198–212.

23. Editorial note, Kline et al., eds., *Burr Papers*, 1: 267; Nolan, *Burr and the American Literary Imagination*, 50.

24. AB to Aaron Ward, January 14, 1832, in Kline et al., eds., *Burr Papers*, 2: 1211.

25. TJ, *Anas* (1804), in *Jefferson: Writings*, 693.

26. Mary-Jo Kline, "Aaron Burr as a Symbol of Corruption in the New Republic," in Abraham S. Eisenstadt et al., eds., *Before Watergate: Problems of Corruption in American Society* (Brooklyn: 1978), 71–72.

27. AB to Victor Du Pont de Nemours, August 11, 1802, in Kline et al., eds., *Burr Papers*, 2: 736.
28. Davis, *Memoirs of Burr*, 1: 297.
29. Beatrice G. Reubens, "Burr, Hamilton, and the Manhattan Company," *Political Science Quarterly*, 72 (1957), 578–607; 73 (1958), 100–125.
30. AB to William Eustis, March 29, 1801, in Kline et al., eds., *Burr Papers*, 1: 549.
31. On this proper role for gentlemanly leaders see Gordon S. Wood, "Interests and Disinterestedness in the Making of the Constitution," Richard Beeman et al., eds., *Beyond Confederation: Origins of the Constitution and American National Identity* (Chapel Hill: University of North Carolina Press, 1987), 69–109.
32. On Smith and this kind of leadership see Gordon Wood, *The Radicalism of the American Revolution* (New York: Knopf, 1992), 68–69.
33. AH, *The Federalist*, No. 35.
34. Robert Troup to AH, March 31, 1795, *Papers of Hamilton*, 18:310.
35. AH to Troup, April 13, 1795, *Papers of Hamilton*, 18: 329.
36. Kline, "Burr as Symbol of Corruption," Eisenstadt et al., eds., *Before Watergate*, 75.
37. Theodore Sedgwick to AH, January 10, 1801, *Papers of Hamilton*, 25: 311–12.
38. AH to Oliver Wolcott, Jr., December 16, 1800, to Gouverneur Morris, December 24, 1800, in *Papers of Hamilton*, 25: 257, 272.
39. AH to Theodore Sedgwick, December 22, 1800, to Harrison Gray Otis, December 23, 1800, to Gouverneur Morris, December 24, 1800, in *Papers of Hamilton*, 25: 270, 271, 272.
40. AH to Gouverneur Morris, December 26, 1800, in *Papers of Hamilton*, 25: 275.
41. Henry Adams, *History of the United States of America During the Administrations of Thomas Jefferson* (New York: Library of America, 1986), 1: 226.

EPILOGUE: THE FOUNDERS AND THE CREATION OF
MODERN PUBLIC OPINION

This is a revised and expanded version of my article "The Democratization of Mind in the American Revolution," in Library of Congress Symposia on the American Revolution, 3d, 1974, *Leadership in the American Revolution* (Washington: Library of Congress, 1974), 63–89.

1. Samuel Eliot Morison, ed., "William Manning's 'The Key of Libberty,'" *WMQ*, 3d Ser., 13 (1956), 208.
2. BF to Caldwallader Colden, October 11, 1750, *Papers of Franklin*, 4: 68.
3. TJ to JM, May 20, 1782, *Papers of Jefferson*, 6: 186.
4. David D. Hall has contended that eighteenth-century evangelical religious writing was already popular and designed to reach a wide readership. No doubt he is correct about the early transformation of evangelical writing, but

most of the political literature remained part of the cosmopolitan "system" that "presumed hierarchy and privilege." David D. Hall, *Cultures of Print: Essays in the History of the Book* (Amherst, MA: University of Massachusetts Press, 1996), 152.

5. For the intimate nature of the networks of communication in the eighteenth century see Richard D. Brown, *Knowledge Is Power: The Diffusion of Information in Early America, 1700–1865* (New York: Oxford University Press, 1989), 89–90, 271, 278. This public sphere is essentially the polite and clubby world David S. Shields has reconstructed so brilliantly in his *Civil Tongues & Polite Letters in British America* (Chapel Hill: University of North Carolina Press, 1997). Although Shields emphasizes the ways the "discursive manners" of this world crossed social ranks and spread throughout American society, it seems evident that in comparison to what followed in the nineteenth century the eighteenth-century world he describes was still at heart an aristocratic one.

6. Joanna B. Freeman, "Dueling as Politics: Reinterpreting the Burr-Hamilton Duel," *WMQ*, 3d Ser., 53 (1996), 289–318; Freeman, *Affairs of Honor: National Politics in the New Republic* (New Haven: Yale University Press, 2001).

7. [John Randolph], *Considerations on the Present State of Virginia* (n.p., 1774), quoted in Merrill Jensen, "The Articles of Confederation," in Library of Congress Symposia on the American Revolution, 2d, 1973, *Fundamental Testaments of the American Revolution* (Washington, D.C.: Library of Congress, 1973), 56.

8. On the refined and restricted nature of classical rhetoric in the eighteenth century see Kenneth Cmiel, *Democratic Eloquence: The Fight over Popular Speech in Nineteenth-Century America* (Berkeley: University of California Press, 1990), ch. 1.

9. Kenneth R. Bowling and Helen E. Viet, eds., *The Diary of William Maclay and Other Notes of Senate Debates, March 4, 1789–March 3, 1791*, in the *Documentary History of the First Federal Congress of the United States of America*, 9 (Baltimore: The Johns Hopkins University Press, 1988), 76.

10. Homer L. Calkin, "Pamphlets and Public Opinion During the American Revolution," *Pennsylvania Magazine of History and Biography*, 64 (1940), 30, 35.

11. Frank Luther Mott, *American Journalism: A History, 1690–1960*, 3d ed. (New York: Macmillan, 1962), 3–64; Mott, *A History of American Magazines, 1741–1850* (New York: D. Appleton, 1930), 13–67; Arthur M. Schlesinger, *Prelude to Independence: The Newspaper War on Britain, 1764–1776* (New York: Vintage, 1965), 51–66, 303–4; Philip Davidson, *Propaganda and the American Revolution, 1763–1783* (Chapel Hill: University of North Carolina Press, 1941). Charles Evans's great bibliography of American publications between 1639 and 1799 numbers twelve volumes. Three volumes are all that are needed for

the publications of the first 125 years of American history up to 1764; the remaining nine volumes contain the publications of the last 35 years of the century—a graphic measure of the explosion of reading material in the revolutionary era.

12. By assuming that a large and impersonal public sphere existed well before the Revolution and that the participants in this sphere were unknown and unknowable, Michael Warner seems to be anticipating the future too quickly. Although a public sphere was certainly growing quite rapidly in the eighteenth century, many authors continued to write as if they and their readers were known to one another. See Warner, *The Letters of the Republic: Publication and the Public Sphere in Eighteenth-Century America* (Cambridge: Harvard University Press, 1990), chs. 1–2. That different scholars emphasize different public spheres seems to stem from the fact that the boundaries of cultural change can never be sharply demarcated: The future is always present in the past and the past is always present even after the future arrives.

13. References to the "republic of letters" are common in the revolutionaries' writings. See, for example, Brooke Hindle, *The Pursuit of Science in Revolutionary America, 1733–1789* (Chapel Hill: University of North Carolina Press, 1956), 384.

14. Calkin, "Pamphlets and Public Opinion," *Pennsylvania Magazine of History and Biography*, 64 (1940), 28, 35.

15. John Adams, *Diary and Autobiography*, L. H. Butterfield et al., eds., 4 vols. (Cambridge: Harvard University Press, 1961), 3: 331–32.

16. Bernard Bailyn, *The Ideological Origins of the American Revolution* (Cambridge: Harvard University Press, 1967), 4–5, 17.

17. John J. Teunissen, "Blockheadism and the Propaganda Plays of the American Revolution," *Early American Literature*, 7 (1972), 148–162. It was no easy matter for women to participate in the public sphere. They were prohibited from speaking in public, and only a few, like Mercy Otis Warren, were able to get their writings published, and then only anonymously. On Warren see Rosemarie Zagarri, *A Women's Dilemma: Mercy Otis Warren and the American Revolution* (Wheeling, IL: Harlan Davidson, 1995).

18. Maynard Mack, "The Muse of Satire," in Richard C. Boys, ed., *Studies in the Literature of the Augustan Age: Essays Collected in Honor of Arthur Ellicott Case* (New York: Gordian Press, 1966).

19. On eighteenth-century rhetoric see Wilbur Samuel Howell, *Eighteenth-Century British Logic and Rhetoric* (Princeton: Princeton University Press, 1971); Peter France, *Rhetoric and Truth in France: Descartes to Diderot* (Oxford: Clarendon Press, 1972); Warren Guthrie, "The Development of Rhetorical Theory in America, 1635–1850," *Speech Monographs*, 13 (1946), 14–22, 14 (1947), 38–54, 15 (1948), 61–71.

20. Gary B. Nash, "The Transformation of Urban Politics, 1700–1765," *Journal of American History*, 60 (1973), 605–32.

21. J. R. Pole, *Political Representation in England and the Origins of the American Republic* (London: St. Martin's, 1966), 9–70, 277–78.

22. Alexander Martin to Governor Caswell, July 27, 1787, in Max Farrand, ed., *The Records of the Federal Convention of 1787*, 4 vols. (New Haven: Yale University Press, 1911–37), 3: 64.

23. Jared Sparks, Journal, April 19, 1830, in ibid., 3: 479.

24. John Dickinson, ibid., 2: 278.

25. John Marshall (Va.), in Jonathan Elliot, ed., *The Debates in the Several State Conventions on the Adoption of the Federal Constitution*, 2d ed., 5 vols. (Washington, D.C., 1836–45), 3: 222; Gordon S. Wood, *The Creation of the American Republic, 1776–1787* (Chapel Hill: University of North Carolina Press, 1969), 524, 526–64.

26. Gordon S. Wood, "Conspiracy and the Paranoid Style: Causality and Deceit in the Eighteenth Century," *WMQ*, 39 (1982), 403–441.

27. Gordon S. Wood, *The Radicalism of the American Revolution* (New York: Knopf, 1992), 237–38.

28. JA to Patrick Henry, June 3, 1776, in Adams, ed., *Works*, 9: 387–88; TJ to BF, August 13, 1777, in *Papers of Jefferson*, 2: 26; Roger Atkinson to Samuel Pleasants, November 23, 1776, quoted in James Kirby Martin, *Men in Rebellion: Higher Governmental Leaders and the Coming of the American Revolution* (New Brunswick, NJ: Rutgers University Press, 1973), 190.

29. Jay Fliegelman refers to these changes as "the elocutionary revolution." See his *Declaring Independence: Jefferson, Natural Language, and the Culture of Performance* (Stanford: Stanford University Press, 1993), 20–35.

30. Rhys Isaac, *The Transformation of Virginia, 1740–1790* (Chapel Hill: University of North Carolina Press, 1982), 267–69; Arthur H. Shaffer, ed., *Edmund Randolph: History of Virginia* (Charlottesville: University Press of Virginia, 1970), 179–181.

31. On Paine, see above, "Thomas Paine, America's First Public Intellectual." Shaffer, ed., *Randolph: History of Virginia*, 1970, 179–81.

32. Meyer Reinhold, "Opponents of Classical Learning in America During the Revolutionary Period," *Proceedings of the American Philosophical Society*, 112 (1968), 221–34; Linda K. Kerber, *Federalists in Dissent: Imagery and Ideology in Jeffersonian America* (Ithaca: Cornell University Press, 1970), 95–134.

33. George L. Roth, "American Theory of Satire, 1790–1820," *American Literature*, 29 (1958), 399–407; Roth, "Verse Satire on 'Faction,' 1790–1815," *WMQ*, 3d Ser., 17 (1960), 473–85; Bruce I. Granger, *Political Satire in the American Revolution, 1763–1783* (Ithaca: Cornell University Press, 1960), 2.

34. Virginia Ratifying Convention, in John P. Kaminski and Gaspare J. Sal-

adino, eds., *The Documentary History of the Constitution* (Madison: University of Wisconsin Press, 1999), 9: 1044–45.

35. Robert E. Spiller et al., *Literary History of the United States*, 3d ed. (New York: Macmillan, 1963), 175; Benjamin Spencer, *The Quest for Nationality: An American Literary Campaign* (Syracuse: Syracuse University Press, 1957), 65.

36. Fisher Ames, "American Literature," Seth Ames, ed., *Works of Fisher Ames*, 2 vols. (Boston: Little, Brown, 1854), 2: 439–40.

37. Richard Buel, Jr., *Securing the Revolution: Ideology in American Politics, 1789–1815* (Ithaca: Cornell University Press, 1972), 113; Gerald Stourzh, *Alexander Hamilton and the Idea of Republican Government* (Stanford: Stanford University Press, 1970), 95–106.

38. John Rutledge, Jr., to Harrison Gray Otis, April 3, 1803, quoted in David Hackett Fischer, *The Revolution of American Conservatism: The Federalist Party in the Era of Jeffersonian Democracy* (New York: Harper & Row, 1969), 140; AH to Theodore Sedgwick, February 2, 1799, in *Papers of Hamilton*, 22: 452; [Fisher Ames], "Laocoon. No. 1," in his *Works*, 2: 113.

39. Thomas Truxtun to JA, December 5, 1804, quoted in Fischer, *American Conservatism*, 133–34.

40. Donald H. Stewart, *The Opposition Press of the Federalist Period* (Albany: State University of New York Press, 1969), 634, 638, 640.

41. Sidney I. Pomerantz, *New York: An American City, 1783–1803* (Port Washington, NY: Ira J. Friedman, 1965), 440.

42. Mott, *American Journalism*, 167; Merle Curti, *The Growth of American Thought*, 3d ed. (New York: Harper & Row, 1964), 209; Stewart, *Opposition Press*, 15, 624.

43. Fischer, *American Conservatism*, 129–49; Stewart, *Opposition Press*, 19; Jere R. Daniell, *Experiment in Republicanism: New Hampshire Politics and the American Revolution, 1741–1794* (Cambridge: Harvard University Press, 1970), 235–36.

44. Buel, *Securing the Revolution*, 75–90.

45. TJ to JA, August 30, 1787, in Farrand, ed., *Records of the Federal Convention*, 3: 6; Madison, "Public Opinion," *National Gazette*, December 19, 1791, in Gaillard Hunt, ed., *The Writings of James Madison*, 9 vols. (New York: G. P. Putnam's, 1900–1910), 6: 70.

46. TJ to James Callender, October 6, 1799, *Papers of Jefferson*, 31: 201.

47. Samuel Miller, *A Brief Retrospect of the Eighteenth Century . . .* , 2 vols. (New York: T. and J. Swords, 1803), II: 254–55.

48. Alfred Young, *The Democratic Republicans of New York: The Origins, 1763–1797* (Chapel Hill: University of North Carolina Press, 1967), 509–10.

49. Alan Taylor, *William Cooper's Town: Power and Persuasion on the Frontier of the Early Republic* (New York: Knopf, 1995), 244–46.

50. Amos Singletary (Mass.), in Elliot, ed., *Debates*, 2: 102.

51. Young, *Democratic Republicans of New York*, 511–12; Taylor, *William Cooper's Town*, 245–46.

52. Wood, *Radicalism*, 237–38.

53. Fisher Ames to Jeremiah Smith, December 14, 1802, quoted in Fischer, *American Conservatism*, 135.

54. James Thomas Flexner, *George Washington: Anguish and Farewell (1793–1799)* (Boston: Little, Brown, 1969, 1972), 277; John C. Miller, *The Federalist Era, 1789–1801* (New York: Harper & Row, 1960), 233; Paine, "Letter to Washington, July 30, 1796," in Philip S. Foner, ed., *The Complete Writing of Thomas Paine* (New York: Citadel Press, 1969), 2: 695, 710, 704.

55. See especially Joanne B. Freeman, "Explaining the Unexplainable: The Cultural Context of the Sedition Act," in Meg Jacobs et al., eds., *The Democratic Experiment: New Directions in American Political History* (Princeton: Princeton University Press, 2003), 20–49.

56. Norman L. Rosenberg, *Protecting the Best Men: An Interpretative History of the Law of Libel* (Chapel Hill: University of North Carolina Press, 1986), 77.

57. Wood, *Radicalism*, 86

58. Buel, *Securing the Revolution*, 156.

59. James Morton Smith, *Freedom's Fetters: The Alien and Sedition Laws and American Civil Liberties* (Ithaca: Cornell University Press, 1956), 116; Miller, *Federalist Era*, 233; Charles Warren, *Jacobins and Junto or Early American Politics as Viewed in the Diary of Dr. Nathaniel Ames, 1758–1822* (New York: Benjamin Blom, 1931, 1968), 96.

60. [George Hay], *An Essay on the Liberty of the Press . . .* (Philadelphia: Printed at the Aurora office, 1799), 40; TJ, Inaugural Address, March 4, 1801, *Jefferson: Writings*, 493.

61. Samuel Dana, debates in Congress, January 1801, quoted in Buel, *Securing the Revolution*, 252.

62. Jefferson, Inaugural Address, March 4, 1801, *Jefferson: Writings*, 493; Benjamin Rush to TJ, March 12, 1801, Lyman H. Butterfield, ed., 2 vols., in *Letters of Benjamin Rush* (Princeton: Princeton University Press, 1951), 2: 831.

63. Tunis Wortman, *A Treatise Concerning Political Enquiry, and the Liberty of the Press* (New York: Printed by G. Forman for the author, 1800), 118–23, 155–57.

64. William Crafts, Jr., *An Oration on the Influence of Moral Causes on National Character, Delivered Before the Phi Beta Kappa Society, on Their Anniversary, 28 August, 1817* (Cambridge: Hilliard and Metcalf, 1817), 5–6; Wortman, *Treatise*, 180.

65. JM, "Public Opinion," *National Gazette*, December 19, 1791, *Madison: Writings*, 500–01.

66. Wortman, *Treatise*, 118–19, 122–23.

67. TJ to JA, January 11, 1816, in Lester J. Cappon, ed., *The Adams-Jefferson Letters*, 2 vols. (Chapel Hill: University of North Carolina Press, 1959), 2: 458.

68. Samuel Williams, *The Natural and Civil History of Vermont*, 2d ed., 2 vols. (Burlington, VT: Printed by Samuel Mills, 1809), II: 394; Joseph Hopkinson, *Annual Discourse, Delivered Before the Pennsylvania Academy of the Fine Arts . . .* (Philadelphia: Bradford and Inskeep, 1810), 29; Theodore Sedgwick to Rufus King, May 11, 1800, quoted in Richard E. Welch, Jr., *Theodore Sedgwick, Federalist: A Political Portrait* (Middletown, CT: Wesleyan University Press, 1965), 211.

69. [Richard Henry Dana, Sr.], "Review of the Sketch Book of Geoffrey Crayon, Gent.," *North American Review*, 9 (1819), 327; Theron Metcalf, *An Address to the Phi Beta Kappa Society of Brown University, Delivered 5th September, 1832* (Boston: n.p., 1833), 6.

Index

ideas and politics combined by, 9–10
Jefferson collects portraits of, ix
as means of assessing contemporary
    America, 3, 7
on public office, 17
special significance for Americans, 3–4,
    9–10
wealth and position desired by, 11
as writing for people like themselves,
    247–50
France
    Federalists concerned about, 61–62, 153–54
    Franklin as American agent in, 85–88
    French Revolution, 110, 153–54, 217–18
    Hamilton on war with, 139
    Louis XVI, 86, 87, 218
    relations of orders as issue in, 192–93
Franklin, Benjamin, 65–90
    eulogies for, 88–89
    and other founders
        and Adams, 54, 175, 177
        Jefferson acquires bust of, ix
        meets Paine, 208–9, 215
        as older than others, 69–70
        and Washington, 32, 35, 42, 43, 68, 69,
            90
    personal characteristics of
        becomes a gentleman, 77, 214
        bourgeois values associated with, 74,
            89–90
        as bundle of contradictions, 67–68
        as classic American success story, 67–68,
            74–75
        Continental reputation of, 85
        as entrepreneur, 76, 285n21
        origins of, 71, 89, 214
        patronage in rise of, 75–76, 89
        personas and role playing by, 67, 72, 73,
            214
        public character of, 23–24
        retires from business, 20, 76–77, 214
        as scientist, 68, 70
        as self-educated, 25
        as self-made, 68, 76, 89
        slaves acquired by, 77
    political career of
        and Albany Plan of Union, 69, 78
        attempts to resolve crisis between Britain
            and America, 81–84
        British government position sought by,
            81–83
        as deputy postmaster of North America,
            78, 84

in England, 1757–62, 78–80
in England, 1764–75, 80–84
in France during Revolution, 85–88
as having everything to lose by
    Revolution, 70
and Hutchinson letters, 83
participation in Revolution as not
    assured, 68–71
in public office, 77–78
revolutionary fervor of, 84–85
and Stamp Act, 80–81
political and social views of
    Americanness begins to be felt by, 81
    as Anglophile, 79–80
    expansion of British Empire supported
        by, 78–79
    as loyalist in early 1760s, 80
    on ordinary people trying to be
        gentlemen, 265
    on presidency and monarchy, 49
    on public service as duty, 247
symbolic importance of, 74, 90
as writer
    Autobiography, 71–72, 82, 88, 89
    journalism of, 72
    Poor Richard, 72, 85, 87, 89, 214
    Proposals Relating to the Education of
        Youth in Pennsylvania, 78
Franklin, William, 80, 82, 85, 86
freedom of the press, 269–70
Freeman, Douglas Southall, 47
Freeman, Joanne B., 137
French Revolution, 110, 153–54, 217–18

Gallatin, Albert, 170–71
gentlemen
    blurring of distinction between common
        people and, 252–53
    Burr as, 232–33, 237
    classical languages known by, 258
    commoners contrasted with, 15–16
    Constitution designed to elect, 239
    as disinterested, 16, 237
    eighteenth-century conception of, 14–20
    founders aspiring to be, 22–23
    founders as first-generation, 25–26, 214,
        233
    Franklin becomes, 77, 214
    Franklin on ordinary people trying to be,
        265
    Paine as not, 214, 215
    politics ceases to be exclusive business of,
        254